INCORPORATE & GET RICH!

SAGE INTERNATIONAL, INC.

**We Show You
How to Cut Your Taxes by 70%
and Protect Your Assets Forever!**

Authors:
C. W. "Al" Allen
Cheri S. Hill

Dedication:

To the most influential people (so far) in our lives:

Robert Kiyosaki for including us in his book Rich Dad Poor Dad. He rocked our business!

Napolean Hill who taught us to Think and Grow Rich.

Jay Abraham who taught us the ultimate marketing systems.

John R. Burley who taught us the Money Secrets of the Rich.

Keith Cunningham who taught us that negotiating can be more than just win-win!

Robert Forman who taught us that perseverance will ultimately produce a product.

Michael Gerber who taught us why you must work "on" your business instead of "in" your business.

Bob Proctor for his gift of "You Were Born Rich."

Tim Taylor who totally expanded our tool box and taught us everything it takes to become a Certified Estate Planner.

Lisa Tom, CPA who taught us that accounting by someone who is brilliant, professional, and a totally out of the box thinker will create awesome bottom line results!

Meggin McIntosh, Ph.D. who taught us how to optimize our productivity and keep chaos at bay!

Ronald R. Mueller who taught us it's how much you keep that counts, not how much you make!

Neal Inscoe for his insight to build professional alliances with Advisors around the country.

The Estate Plan chairman Henry Abts III for his diligence to educate America about the pitfalls of probate and estate taxes.

Larry Whitesides who continues to teach us through his vast insight and unique wisdom that we need to be clear on life's priorities first and foremost and to recognize within ourselves exactly why we want to create wealth and more important, what are we going to do with it once we have it?

Our Sage Family (treasured and successful clients) who continually push, motivate and inspire us to keep moving forward to keep answering the question, "Now that I'm Incorporated what do I do next?" We are extremely blessed to be in touch with so many like-minded, proactive individuals who have a purpose and a mission to change their own circumstances, take charge of their own destiny and through their unlimited imagination improve the world in which we live.

The Sage Team: Our fundamental belief is that our most valuable and important resource is our staff. Our tools are our minds. Consistent with this belief, we encourage their obsession with ongoing and consistent training so that they harness the results of personal empowerment and enrichment, expand their ability to master the fundamentals and without hesitation are willing to share their knowledge with the clients we serve. Great companies surround themselves with great people. We have a truly awesome team excited about changing the world one life at a time!

Our Mission:

Sage International, Inc. fosters the entrepreneurial spirit by first educating our clients. We are motivated to provide affordable business and personal financial solutions that create a solid foundation to grow, protect, and leverage our clients' hard-earned wealth, promoting

Financial Simplicity…Service…Empowerment!

"The Master Mind Principle: Two or more people actively engaged in pursuit of a definite purpose with a positive mental attitude, constitute an unbeatable force."
– Napoleon Hill

Praise for Incorporate & Get Rich!

"I picked up your book and I've learned more about corporations in the first three chapters than in all the other books I've read on the subject, and I've understood it! Thank you for publishing this book and I look forward to learning more as I continue past chapter 3." ~ *David Hill, Davis CA.*

"I just finished reading Incorporate & Get Rich! What a great book. Thank you for writing it!" ~ *Patrick Egan, Allen TX*

"I have purchased your book Incorporate & Get Rich! and would like to thank you. This book was very insightful and worth more than the purchase price. It will be in our family and business library for generations. Thanks for all you do!"
~ *Evet Johnson, Shreveport LA*

"It is with great pleasure that I write this testimonial. When I first met with Al and Cheri in 1999 to discuss the possibilities of forming a corporation, I was overwhelmed with the information they offered. Their enthusiasm and confidence was unlike that of any other company I had ever worked with. Al and Cheri were totally approachable and spent hours educating me on the advantages and benefits of a corporation. They told me that there are lots of people who will show you how to make a million dollars, but very few who show you hot to keep it. I was convinced that I was in great hands and took the necessary steps to follow their advice. It has taken me five years to totally get it. The light went on and the flood gates opened. I then remembered Al and Cheri informing me that this would happen. And did it ever!

My company has finally broken the million dollar mark and we are growing comfortably each year. It was that great advice and years of nurturing from Sage International that I accredit my foundation for freedom today. Additionally, Al and Cheri turned me on to many of their associates and I have seen incredible growth from those referrals also. My personal assets have also continued to grow thanks to their consistent advice.

I cannot say enough to show my gratitude fro the time they have invested in my business and me personally. If you are seeking ways to grow your business and your bottom line, I strongly recommend the team of professionals at Sage International, Inc. Enjoy the journey." ~ *Mike Kitson, President OCG Creative, Inc., Reno NV*

This book is available at a special discount when ordered in bulk quantities.
For information, call 1-800-254-5779.

Seventh Edition February 2009

Publisher:
Sage International, Inc.
1135 Terminal Way, #209
Reno, Nevada 89502
(800) 254-5779
www. sageintl.com
E-mail: corpinfo@sageintl.com

Editor: Cheri S. Hill
Cover Design: OCG Creative, Inc.
Book Layout: Mike Kitson, OCG Creative, Inc.

www.OCGcreative.com

Reprint. Originally published: Inc. & Grow Rich! and Incorporate & Grow Rich!
ISBN 0-967-1871-0-9

Disclaimer
The authors, by writing this book, do not engage in offering legal, accounting, professional or investment advice. A client's financial or legal situation may be unique in terms of its facts and in the application of the law to the facts. Any action taken with regard to the information contained in this book should be undertaken only upon the advice and counsel of a trained legal and/or accounting professional.

ISBN 9781439226605
Printed in the USA

Table of Contents

Section Four: Your Corporate Operation
Starting Smart by Running Your Corporation
to Maximize All the Benefits

Section Five:
Protecting Your Assets
Everyone Shows You How to Make a Million...
We Show You How to Keep It!

Section Six:
The Buck Stops Here!

Section Seven:
Building Your Wealth
Securing Financial Freedom the Easy and Simple Way by Letting Your Corporate Tax Savings Work for You — Automatically

Introduction

What is most fundamental in your life? I believe it should be what America was founded upon. It's what we have fought wars for as our God-given right. Yes, it's FREEDOM.

When you think about it, it all boils down to freedom to make our own decisions, to call our own shots and to do what we want, when we want, the way we want, justly, freely and peacefully. That's what it really means to be your own person.

This book is written to help you achieve freedom.

This book is for people who not only want to survive this era of the new millennium, but prosper and have peace of mind about life, income, assets and the future. It is written for people who are already in business for themselves, which includes:

- the sole proprietors
- the 50/50 partners, and
- the owners of corporations

It is also written for entrepreneurs at heart who are:

Struggling from a downsizing and/or have moved from a salary to an hourly wage; the middle manager and former executive who can't find a job; the college graduate who has little opportunity to make it to the top in today's business structure, today or tomorrow; the professionals — the doctors and nurses, the lawyers, the accountants, the engineers and the teachers who don't fit or soon won't fit into the evolving systems of the new world economy. This book is also written for the millions of employed people who inside themselves wonder if "I, too, will be out the door and on the road to unemployment soon."

Reading the writing on the wall

… Job security, as we once knew it, is no more. Now or in the near future, you will have to make your own job security by going into business for yourself either part-time or full-time. When you do this, you will start making your own job security day by day. You will then start to experience the ultimate value of running your own business — FREEDOM! Being in business for yourself creates financial freedom for you and your family, now and in the future. This book will show you how.

Wake up call, Mister or Madame President!

I know this morning, when you woke up, before you had even opened your eyes, before you pushed back the covers, before you had your first cup of coffee, the very first thought on your mind was: "I've got to have a corporation. I've got to be the president of my own company!"

In reality, this business strategy was probably the very last thing you thought about. This is because you may have never been taught to be a president, to think like a president or how to create the opportunity to be a president. Did you ever take "President Making 101" in college? Did you ever take "Stockholder 404" or "CEO-Builder 511?"

No? That doesn't surprise me since I've never seen such classes offered.

So waking up and thinking, "I've got to be the president of my own corporation," was probably the farthest thing from your mind this or any other morning.

A Corporation — A Conversation Piece?

Can you imagine a corporate minute book sitting on your coffee table and somebody coming into your house and asking, "What is that?"

"Oh, that's a corporation. Isn't it beautiful? See the colorful stock certificates. Feel the weight of the corporate seal."

Can you hear them call you — Mister or Madame President?

It's not the corporate minute book that is important. It's what the corporation can do for you. As you absorb the information in this book and keep in mind everything we are sharing with you, you will discover how you can get what you want more than anything else — freedom. Yes, you will get freedom to live the life and lifestyle you want. You will get the peace of mind and lifelong security that you long for and which no one can take away from you.

Every technique you encounter within this book, every idea, every thought, every word on every page will show you how to get what you want. As you read on, you find yourself compelled…

… to take advantage of incorporating your business as well as forming another corporation to benefit from dual corporate strategies; or to structure your business activities to maximize the rewards to you while running your business properly, legally and profitably.

Let's imagine the benefits that would be available to you if you were incorporated and running your corporation properly.

Tax Benefits:

Can you imagine slashing your taxes by 70 percent? Imagine how you could spend all that money. Imagine tax-deductible cars and tax-deductible educational expenses. Imagine tax-deductible life, health and automobile insurance. Imagine tax-deductible trips, tax-deductible food, tax-deductible housing and much more.

"When nothing seems to help, I go and look at a stonecutter, hammering away at his rock, perhaps a hundred times without as much as a crack showing in it. Yet at the hundred and first blow it will split in two, and I know it was not that blow that did it-but all that had gone before."

– Jacob Riis

Being Lawsuit Proof:

Can you imagine never being sued personally? Imagine how free you would feel. Let's review the Chappaquiddick tragedy. Ted Kennedy drove the car into the river, and Mary Kopechne drowned. Kennedy never had to worry about a lawsuit. He didn't own the car. The car was owned by a trust or other entity separate and apart from him. Kopechne's family received $125,000 from the insurance company. There was never a lawsuit. There was nothing to sue. Kennedy didn't own the car, nor did he have any other possessions for anyone to take. All his possessions were, and I'm sure still are, controlled at arm's length through various legal entities.

No Probate Costs:

Imagine never having to pay probate costs. Imagine never having to pay inheritance taxes. Just imagine being rich or financially independent. Wouldn't you agree this would be truly exhilarating?

J. Paul Getty understood these principles very well. He was able to transfer $1.3 billion in his estate to his heirs without ever going through probate, which costs alone could have been as much as $650 million in estate taxes.

Concrete Reality:

You see, there is nothing overly theoretical or abstract about this entire process of planning and doing as the rich do. It's how you put your imagination to work and apply these principles of the rich to your life. You simply need to learn how the rich get rich and do the same thing. What works for the rich will work for you, too.

The Rich People's System:

Are you ready to discover the key secrets the rich use to get rich? Now, let's just take one principle — slashing your taxes up to 70 percent. You're probably saying, "What does slashing your taxes have to do with helping you get rich?" We promise you, when you finish reading this book, you will know exactly what that means.

Life-Changing Strategies:

What you need is life-changing strategies that will transform:
- the way you think,
- the way you work,
- the way you conduct your business and
- how much you pay in taxes

You need to understand the get-rich system. This is not a "get-rich-quick" system, but a strategy of doing business that, over time, will bring you tremendous and satisfying results.

"Freedom comes from human beings, rather than from laws and institutions."
~ Clarence Darrow

The Flaming Arrows of Challenge:

This is not all there is to it. This get-rich system will be challenged. There are challenges lurking at every turn of success. These challenges are like flaming arrows ready to strike us at any time — arrows such as lawsuits, taxes and probate.

Civil Lawsuits:

There are some unbelievable lawsuits these days. With more than 90 million civil lawsuits filed annually, it's an epidemic of massive proportions in this country. Everyone is familiar with the McDonald's hot-coffee spill case, but there are millions of lesser-known cases. What about the school burglar who tried to enter a Los Angeles school by walking along its rooftop on a very dark night? He tripped, fell through an unlit skylight and injured himself permanently. He received more than $250,000 up-front and $1,200 a month disability compensation for the rest of his life with a three percent annual cost of living increase. There are thousands and thousands of other such cases.

Divorce and Liability:

What do you think the foremost civil lawsuit filed in this country is? You're right. It's divorce. Divorce is always lurking out there. Nationwide, the divorce rate is higher than 50 percent. The repercussions in regard to settlements can be long reaching and unexpected. Have you ever heard of vicarious liability? According to the law, vicarious liability means you are responsible for another's actions.

Anyone who has filed a joint tax return with a spouse is vicariously liable for the spouse. If you file a joint tax return, you are equally liable for that return. Even long after you have received a divorce, you are still liable for 100 percent of the taxes on your joint tax returns.

A Joint Tax Return Disaster:

A woman had been divorced for more than four years. One day there was a knock on her door. Two men greeted her by asking, "Are you Mrs. John Smith."

"Yes," she replied.

The men identified themselves as agents for the Internal Revenue Service. In short, they said, "You owe the IRS $212,000." She was horrified.

"Why?" she asked.

When she was married, each year she had faithfully and loyally signed a joint tax return with her husband. He was quite liberal with his deductions. Because he now had no assets, the IRS returned to her. She, therefore, owed $212,000. To pay the IRS, she lost her home and everything she owned.

Joint Ownership:

Another IRS story: An elderly couple wanted to make sure their son, Johnny, got everything they had when they passed away. The couple went to a financial planner who advised them to put Johnny's name on all their accounts, and so they did. They put him on their home, bank accounts, savings accounts, stocks and bonds and everything else they had. Guess with whom Johnny got in trouble? Yep, the IRS! He owed a gift tax on all the assets he received. To collect it, the IRS took all of Johnny's assets. It didn't matter that his parents' names were on the assets as well. The parents were really indignant, as

"What lies behind us and what lies before us are tiny matters compared to what lies within us."
–Oliver Wendell Holmes

you can imagine. They took on the IRS and sued them. The case went all the way up through the appellate channels and the court upheld the IRS. The parents, who had worked hard all their lives, and their son, lost everything they had. It was a far-reaching, landmark case.

Another loss due to joint ownership:

A couple of childhood friends started a little business in junior high school. It was a simple business — buying and selling baseball cards. They became experts, and in high school they expanded the business to include many other collectibles, such as comic books, posters, magazines and the like. After high school they set up a little storefront and prospered. They each married their high school sweethearts and had children.

Each of the families worked in the business. They were such good friends that they often co-signed for one another's loans — homes, motor homes, boats — and even jointly bought an airplane.

Well, one of the partners suddenly took off with a woman — a gambler of some reputation.

You can guess what took place next, can't you? The partner got the gambling bug, too. Gambling debts soon arrived, and all the assets of both families and their business were lost.

Only IF … they had had some type of protection: corporations, limited partnerships and trusts. No, they just had a handshake that ended in disaster.

There are thousands more such cases. You never need be another one.

Probate:

Let's look at probate costs and estate taxes. They are extremely time-consuming. The average probate runs between 18 and 24 months. They are very costly. Probate and estate taxes can consume more than 50 percent of the inherited estate. Through probate, everything becomes public information. Some companies and individuals prey upon people who must sell within a short time frame to satisfy probate and estate taxes. These scavengers buy for pennies on the dollar.

Most people do not call for protection strategies until they are in a disaster-prone situation. Don't let it be too late to do something about your financial structure to protect your assets for you and your heirs.

Double Lines of Defense:

The flaming arrows of lawsuits, probate costs and excess taxation are always pointed at personal and business assets today. People have to form a double line of defense to survive these flaming arrows in our society. The first line of defense is the corporation. If there is an attack on the corporation, then you need a second line of defense to protect all your assets. You can form additional corporations, limited partnerships, various types of trusts, foundations and limited liability companies, for example, to protect specific assets. These help prevent the flaming arrows from igniting your assets.

Protection Despite Loss:

A major developer and builder from Los Angeles had to file bankruptcy when the real estate market plummeted. This multimillion-dollar corporation lost everything it had. Fortunately, the owners had established a children's trust, which was worth more than a million dollars. The corporation had been leasing equipment over a long period of time from the children's trust. The money kept growing. The company was able to start all over again with a loan from the children's trust. Because it was a totally separate entity from the corporation, the trust was protected. The owners had a pretty good place from which to start, didn't they?

With smart business planning, you can too.

The principles you will learn in this book include:

1. How to position yourself in today's society so that you can take advantage of change and not be downtrodden by it
2. The most effective ways of running your business and how to take advantage of the tax codes so you can slash your taxes by as much as 70 percent
3. How to create a corporate strategy that will take advantage of the Nevada corporate structure
4. How to be the CEO and president of your corporation and run it effectively and legally
5. How to set up a simple accounting system and keep financial records correctly
6. How to protect your assets now and for a secure future
7. How to create financial freedom for yourself and your family

Yes, these seven how-tos give you the freedom you want, need and deserve. When implemented, they give you freedom immediately in your life and business.

You may never have considered being the president of your own company, or you may already be the president and wondering what else you can do to get ahead. The answers lie within the pages of this book. It has taken us over two years to write this book as well as the combined wisdom of the authors, totaling more than 23 years of higher education in their respective fields and 120 years of real-world experience and application. But most importantly, this book gives you the simple facts of how you can do what you need to, simply and easily.

Our Promise to You: Once you've implemented the changes revealed in this book you will have control over your business because it will reflect your personal wishes. Before you close this book, you will be forced to come to certain conclusions:

- about your ongoing relationship with money
- about your success and your own personal power
- about your own ability to make changes in your life
- about how you can produce the kinds of results you want to have

These conclusions will create within you an overwhelming desire to:

- learn more and continue these successes
- continue to set goals
- continue to aim for higher outcomes
- produce power in your life that enables you to take giant leaps forward with confidence and conviction

By allowing this book to move you this way, you will have control over your business and your life, which will enhance and develop all your personal wishes.

You will experience personal freedom for you and for your family.

It is our pleasure to present this vitally important information to you and share in helping you express your freedom to be successful, to live at peace, to prosper and to protect your assets now and for future generations to come.

If you have questions, call 1-800-254-5779 or
E-mail us at corpinfo@sageintl.com
www.sageintl.com

Much Success.

8

NOTES

Section One:
Surviving the Millennium
As Entrepreneurs:
Why You Must and How
You Can Come of Age

Chapter 1:
Why Is It Such a Struggle to Get Ahead in Today's Society?

We have:
- No lifelong job security for today
- An explosion of entrepreneurs entering business
- Worldwide competition
- Not just change, but rapid change
- High technology replacing jobs
- A higher number of skilled youth entering the workforce
- High taxation
- High debt

We are:
- Taught to dream
- Taught to want (from constant advertising)

We live with:
- High crime
- High litigation
- High probate costs

Chapter 2:
Is It Still Our Right to Live the American Dream?
- The federal government and the IRS actually make it possible to slash your taxes by 70 percent and prosper as the rich do
- You can also protect your assets during your lifetime and for generations to come

"The basic fact of today is the tremendous pace of change in human life."

Chapter 1:
Why Is It Such a Struggle to Get Ahead in Today's Society?

We have:
- No lifelong job security for today
- An explosion of entrepreneurs entering business
- Worldwide competition
- Not just change, but rapid change
- High technology replacing jobs
- A higher number of skilled youth entering the workforce
- High taxation
- High debt

We are:
- Taught to dream
- Taught to want (from constant advertising)

We live with:
- High crime
- High litigation
- High probate costs

Is there a way to freedom?

Case Study 1 (Selma) — Part I

Selma had not intended to fight for her rights, but all at once, she experienced the landslide of four financial threats. Unfortunately, each ended in disaster despite her determined efforts. Selma's turmoil began when her employer of twenty years downsized, leaving her jobless. She couldn't find another job, so she turned her hobby into a small business. It didn't make her a lot of money, but she loved it. She was a doll collector and prided herself on her ability to make old dolls look new again. She had about $100,000 invested in her own doll collection and earned about $20,000 a year in doll appraisals and repairs for others.

Selma's second blow began one day in her studio/showroom. A mother entered with her child, believing the studio was a second hand doll store. Before the possibility of an introduction, the child managed to lay hold of and severely damage a most expensive doll. This was not Selma's doll, nor was it any ordinary doll. Previous to the unfortunate beheading, it was a perfectly preserved, highly prized Shirley Temple doll. Of course, the owner of the doll was outraged.

Little could anyone imagine that the court would award the owner of the headless Shirley Temple doll $50,000. And who paid? Not the mother, nor the child, as they had nothing with which to pay. Selma was directed to pay, and she did so by giving up half of her doll collection. Although the Shirley Temple doll was only valued at $900 with its head in place, the rest of the damages were for personal trauma as the doll had meant a great deal to the owner.

As if the two previous challenges were not enough in Selma's life, her mother passed away unexpectedly. Although Selma inherited the family home, valued at $150,000, there were back taxes to be paid. When all was settled, Selma had to pay $25,000 in court costs and attorney's fees. She got nothing from the inheritance, as she had to sell the house in a slow market for less than the amount of taxes owed.

Selma's final challenge of that year was the most devastating. Her former husband had never been a good businessman and was even worse in paying his taxes. Selma had filed joint tax returns with him until five years ago when they were divorced. One day the IRS came to her door and demanded payment for his back taxes. Her former husband had nothing, so the IRS took possession of what Selma had left, including her home. This succession of tragic events left Selma without her dolls, no job, no home and no money. Although this happened to Selma, it doesn't have to happen to you!

Key Points
- We have to face the reality of today's rapidly changing workplace.
- Entrepreneurs are joining the Quiet Revolution.
- To survive we have to overcome many challenges.

What Can I Do to Get Ahead in Today's Society?

Unfortunately, we have no lifelong job security today, nor will we have any in the future. We have to recognize the facts about today's society. No matter if you're an executive or a day laborer, a college graduate or a high school dropout, an unemployed or employed man, woman or child, there is no lifelong security in any job situation today. You cannot rely on a big, medium-sized or small company to employ you indefinitely. You need to be self-employed for your primary or supplemental source of income. If not an immediate income source, consider self-employment as one source within the next few years.

Change is scary to most of us. And excessive job losses have caused a revolution. And revolutions are scary. No one knows the outcome.

The Quiet Revolution

We are in what *Entrepreneur Magazine* calls the "Quiet Revolution of the Entrepreneur." Forty million people have already joined. That's 8,000 per day and one every eleven seconds.

"Who will succeed?" is today's up-front and personal question.

That's a lot of competition for people in business for themselves. That's more competition than at any other time in the history of man. And the competition is growing.

It is estimated that 60 million people will be entrepreneurs in a $600 billion a year industry in this country alone. That's a lot of competition within this country and it's

"Anyone may arrange his affairs so that his taxes shall be as low as possible. He is not bound to choose that pattern which best pays the treasury. There is not even a patriotic duty to increase one's taxes."
– Federal Court Judge,
Learned Hand

even bigger worldwide. Globally the competition compounds. Can you compete with wages of two dollars a day? Much of the world offers such labor pools.

Why is Change Today so Different?

It's not just change — but rapid change. Yes, rapid change has impacted our society more drastically than any other revolution known to man. It took us a hundred years to change from an agricultural to an industrial age, but only five years to feel the drastic impact of the technological/global age upon the work force including blue-collar workers and executives, young college graduates and seasoned professionals. This impact of the technological/global age clearly spans all professions and work classes.

Conservatively, over 2 million people in the last half of the 1990s have lost their jobs due to downsizing by major U.S. corporations. What about the government job downsizing, the overseas downsizing and the professional downsizing? They add to these great numbers as well.

Politicians always say that new jobs have increased. However, according to Steve Forbes, 95 percent of those new jobs are part-time and temporary jobs.

We are not just experiencing job cuts but lowered wages, too. This is due to supply and demand. When job seekers outnumber the available jobs, employers take advantage of the situation. They pay less and expect more. They call all this activity right-sizing, but nothing seems very right about it.

Will Downsizing Go Away and Job Security Come Back?

Not likely. There are other factors. It used to take 100 people to do a job that five people can do in a factory today. This trend is entering all areas of the work force — be it manufacturing, scientific exploration, medicine or education. Technology has become so advanced that it is hard to compete in the marketplace without it.

Secondly, today's child of 12 already has eight years of computer know-how. Children today grow up with computer toys and games. They are on the Internet communicating worldwide in the first grade. By the time they enter the work world, they will be able to outperform any 30, 40 or 50-year-old who has much less computer experience.

And there is more … It isn't just the huge gray cloud of uncertain job security that hangs over us — it is taxation as well. Taxes consume about 70 percent to 80 percent of our income.

Facts About Taxes
- Federal taxes range, on average, between 28 percent and 39 percent.
- State income taxes reach up to 12 percent.
- Social Security and Medicare taxes or self-employment taxes are 15.3 percent. (That's already from 43 percent to 66.3 percent of our income gone in income taxes.)
- Add (in some states) sales taxes up to 7.5 percent or more.
- Add county and city sales taxes and business license fees in some areas.
- Add hidden taxes on gasoline, phone service, utilities, entertainment, hotel accommodations, luxury items and on and on. You can see that it can add up to 70 percent or more.

I am not saying we don't need to pay our fair share of taxes, but I am saying we need to really find out what our fair share is and pay that and no more.

What is Our Fair Share of Taxes?

Federal Court Judge Learned Hand states, "Anyone may arrange his affairs so that his taxes shall be as low as possible. He is not bound to choose that pattern which best pays the treasury. There is not even a patriotic duty to increase one's taxes."

Let me cite just two United States Supreme Court cases:

Raymond Pearson Motor Company v. Commissioner, 246. F. 2d 509 states, "Taxpayers are not required to continue that form of organization which results in the maximum tax."

Moline Properties, Inc. v Commissioner 319 U.S. 436 states, "… Whether the purpose (of incorporating) be to gain an advantage under the law of the state of incorporation or to avoid or comply with the demands of creditors … so long as the purpose is the equivalent of a business activity or is followed by the carrying on of business by the corporation, the corporation remains a separate taxable entity…"

That separate entity (your corporation) can allow you to pay less in taxes.

I have to ask this question: When 70 percent of our income is spent in taxes, how are we ever expected to become prosperous?

No One can be Expected to Live and Succeed on 30 Percent of a Downsized Income.

That's the problem. You just can't live and succeed, when you live in a world of debt. House payments, car payments, student loans and worst of all — credit card payments.

When another 20 percent goes to pay the banks on money spent with plastic before it is earned, what can we do to get ahead? Yet advertising demands that we buy and buy and buy.

It is now very easy to buy, but it's very hard to earn, to pay back, to save, to become FREE from financial concerns.

Think of the youth today graduating from college with:

1. no job prospects in their field of study
2. $10,000 to $100,000 in student loans and
3. thousands upon thousands of dollars in credit card debts

Charging with plastic comes easily. Payback is hard. The more "savvy" adult is often in the same boat. That's our dilemma.

What Do We Do?

We are taught from very early childhood to imagine the "good life" and that it is good to live the "good life."

- Imagine living in the home you want.
- Imagine driving the car you want.

14

- Imagine taking vacations, real vacations, to places you have always wanted to visit.
- Imagine giving your children the opportunities they deserve in education and training.
- Imagine retiring and not having to worry if your money is going to run out before you die.
- Imagine being able to help your less fortunate neighbor, help an endangered species survive, help an orchestra or an art museum meet its financial obligations, help a child grow up and prosper and on and on.

This imagining is painful today because the dreams seem unattainable.

Your Assets

Everyone has assets. We have personal assets such as our homes, cars, stock, bonds, jewelry and the like, and those in business also have business assets such as equipment, office furniture, real estate, buildings and accounts receivable. Together these form our financial base. Take a brief moment and list your assets that build your financial base.

What are your personal assets?

_____

_____

_____

What are your business assets?

_____

_____

_____

What can attack them?

_____

_____

_____

Now let's look at the flaming arrows that come in the form of lawsuits and judgments, income taxes, probate costs and estate taxes. They are constantly pointed at us.

Your assets, no matter how meager, are all subject to lawsuits. There are more than 750,000 lawyers in this country alone and more than 90 million civil lawsuits annually. That's one-in-four of our adult population. If a woman can spill coffee on herself and take McDonald's to the cleaners — literally (the jury awarded her $2.7 million), who is safe?

Does real justice have anything to do with it?

It doesn't seem so. There are probate costs and estate taxes that grab your possessions away from your heirs and even from the not-for-profit organizations to which you have chosen to donate your wealth after you have gone. Every family has its experiences with this type of situation.

I know a woman who inherited her mother's home after taking care of her for 20 years. This woman not only lost her mother, but her mother's home. She had to sell it for pennies on the dollar to pay taxes and attorney's fees. She ended up with nothing, instead of the $200,000 at which the home was valued. On and on...

Frightening, isn't it? It seems impossible in today's society to beat the "jungle" system. The jungle reaches out with an unexpected trap at every turn.

Conclusion

- Know the facts concerning today's society.
- Know what you can do to prosper.
- Know how to protect your assets.
- Know how to pass your assets on to the ones you love.

"There are two things to aim at in life: first to get what you want; and, after that, to enjoy it."
– *Logal Pearsall Smith*

Chapter 2:
Is It Still Our Right to Live the American Dream?

- The federal government and the IRS actually make it possible to slash your taxes by 70 percent and prosper as the rich do
- You can also protect your assets during your lifetime and for generations to come

Case Study 1 (Selma) — Part II

Selma wanted to give up. But her internal drive would not let her. She acquired a small-business loan, based on her past performance, and started over. A friend advised her to do what the rich people do — plan ahead and protect herself and her business properly. She did. Selma found with her new business structure she not only cut her taxes in half but also she had acquired the protection she should have had earlier. She not only survived, she succeeded.

Key Points
- Dare to dream.
- Let the IRS and federal government help you slash your taxes by 70 percent.
- Protect your assets: you can and should.

Some People do Make It, so Why Can't Most of Us?

Some people do have beautiful homes. Some people have great cars, own boats and airplanes. Some people can travel at will. Some people work and love their work. Some let their money work for them. It hurts to see others around you with all these great benefits when you work just as hard and don't have them.

It becomes the age-old struggle between the haves and have-nots. We have been taught that we can have (and it is our right to have); therefore, we want more deeply than we have ever wanted before. Legal crimes (taking something that does not belong to you through legal manipulation by using unethical business practices or through frivolous lawsuits) escalate. More and more legal crime, just as with its illegal counterpart, runs like wildfire for seemingly unimportant wants - such as name-brand tennis shoes, designer jackets, gold chains. Tragic.

It should not be this way.

Shouldn't Everyone Have the Right to be Rich or at least Have Enough to Live with Dignity?

We should have the right to be rich. We should have the right to earn a good living. We should have the right to feed and educate our children. We should have the right to

18

live a good life and not live in fear of loss. We should have the right to make the world a better place.

We should have the right of freedom to do at will what we want, the way we want, to help ourselves, our families and the world around us. Freedom is behind every person's dream, every person's desire, every person's goals. That freedom is our birthright. That's the freedom of the rich.

When we study how the rich have obtained their freedom to do what they want, we achieve this same freedom.

Yes, in fact, it is very simple. It begins with the understanding that if you prepare yourself, you are more likely to emerge not just a survivor - but a winner. At present very few people are winners.

The ones that are winners do the following:

1. They work for themselves. Our present economic system does not allow you to become financially free as an employee of anyone but yourself. Think of all the wealthy people. Do they work for someone else? No. Do they work for their own company? Yes. Has that company, with all its assets, been properly structured? Yes, of course.

2. The tax codes set up by the United States government are the same tax codes that the IRS follows. They are designed to help entrepreneurs, just like you, slash taxes.

If you slashed your taxes by 70 percent would this impact your life? Of course. This would give you the freedom the government and the IRS actually offer you — the freedom to be your own person and to structure your business to make a profit.

You've got to use those tax codes as they are supposed to be used, just like the rich do. As a result, you too can have the freedom of the rich. I'll show you how.

The following charts illustrate the "Rich System." This system begins with all business being conducted through a corporation, which creates the first line of defense against lawsuits and excessive taxation.

If the corporation is challenged, your personal assets are protected with a second line of defense. By using additional corporations, trusts, limited partnerships, foundations and the like, you will place yourself under an umbrella of protection. A bombardment of attacks can come your way, but will not penetrate your umbrella. That's freedom. Without that protection, you are at high risk of being burned. With the proper business structure you can survive and succeed in reaching your goals.

Internal Revenue Code Section 162 (a): There shall be allowed as a deduction all the ordinary and necessary expenses paid or incurred during the taxable year in carry on on any trade or business…

Internal Revenue Code Section 212: In the case of an individual, there shall be allowed as a deduction all the ordinary and necessary expenses paid or incurred during the taxable year for the production or collection of income…

"The great tragedy in America today is not the waste of our natural resources. The real tragedy is the waste of human resources."
~ Oliver Wendell Holmes

19

Section 1 • Chapter 2: Is It Still Our Right to Live the American Dream?

That's it. Sixty words. Our goal is to help you understand these two basic principles and how you can use the power of these sixty words to get rich.

Double Levels of Defense
Lawsuits and Taxes Strike from Many Different Directions

> *The corporation is the first line of defense. A second corporation plus other entities form a second line of defense to protect you from attackers of your personal and business assets.*

Corporation
- Insurance Trusts
- Children's Trusts
- Irrevocable Trusts
- Limited Liability Companies
- Limited Partnerships
- Foundations
- Family Living Trust

What Can Happen?
- You can collapse and burn or you can survive and succeed.
- Your business structure makes the difference.

Conclusion
The economic climate of today demands the following:
- You have to go into business for yourself.
- You have to use the financial structures that the rich use.
- You have to know how the IRS and the United States government actually help you, as an entrepreneur, become prosperous and enjoy your freedom.

This brings us to the second most frequently asked question:

- What business structures will work best for me?

Section Two holds the answers.

NOTES

_____

_____

_____

_____

_____

_____

_____

_____

_____

_____

_____

_____

_____

_____

_____

_____

_____

Success is not just the end result, but the process of achieving it as well. In fact, the degree of success in the product of our lives is in direct proportion to the degree of success we have in the process.

Section Two:
Your Business Structure
Structuring Your Business for the Best Profit-Centered, Tax-Reduced, Asset Protection Possible

Chapter 1:
Structure Your Business for the Greatest Advantages to You
Three ways to do business
- Sole proprietorship
- General partnership
- Corporation

Eight Legal Business Structures
- Sole proprietorship
- General partnership
- Limited partnership
- Corporation
- C vs. S corporation
- The professional corporation
- Not-for-profit corporation
- Limited liability company

Chapter 2:
Dollars in Your Pockets from Corporate Tax Savings
- Your corporate tax advantage
- The Golden Tax Secrets
- Tax advantage of incorporating your home-based business
- Case studies

Chapter 3:
Simple Steps to Tax Savings
- How you can use the Golden Tax Secrets to your advantage
- Application of Golden Tax Secrets to specific business situations
- Advantages of fiscal year end planning

Chapter 1:
Structure Your Business for the Greatest Advantages to You

Three ways to do business
- Sole proprietorship
- General partnership
- Corporation

Eight Legal Business Structures
- Sole proprietorship
- General partnership
- Limited partnership
- Corporation
- C vs. S corporation
- The professional corporation
- Not-for-profit corporation
- Limited liability company

What is a corporation?
- What are the types of corporations?
- What are the advantages of incorporating?

Case Study 1 (Alexander)
The Trials of a Sole Proprietorship - The Way Not to Run a Business

Alexander was an enthusiastic, brilliant young man with a tremendous desire for making and selling things. At 15, his involvement with Junior Achievement brought him recognition when he won the most promising young entrepreneur award. He had the spirit; he had the support of his parents, and everything he touched turned a profit. He was often tempted to quit school and go into business full-time. But Alexander did the smart thing: He persisted with his education and graduated with the highest honors, not just from high school, but also from Harvard with a master's degree in Business Administration. Alexander continued making and selling things throughout high school, college and graduate school, which brought him excellent survival skills and success. The year was 1968. At age 25, Alexander had saved $50,000 and, as a sole proprietor, plunged it all into a promising business. After thriving three years, he sold the business for $400,000. By the time he was 30, with a string of wise investments, Alexander was a millionaire. By the time he was 31, Alexander was flat broke after being sued for creating an unsafe product. Although it was safe when used properly, the jury opposed his pleas and awarded the plaintiff millions.

The Trials of a 50/50 Partnership
- The Way Not to Run a Business

Alexander was still young and ambitious. Soon he recovered by selling everything and starting over. He started out small and became impatient as the cash flowed in more slowly than he wanted it to. If only he had enough capital to expand, he could achieve beyond his cash flow problems. His father's friend offered him some advice: "Get a partner with money because two can succeed faster than one."

Alexander took that advice and joined with a friend who had just the right amount of money. They had known each other for years. It was a natural, as Alexander handled the manufacturing and his friend Willis handled the advertising and sales. They were a perfect match. A handshake and a smile sealed their agreement - 50/50. It worked out perfectly, and the business flourished. Soon they were both drawing a six-figure salary.

All through the eighties the business boomed. Alexander and Willis had a few differences, but for the most part, it was a good match. On January 1, 1992, Willis was suddenly killed in an accident. There was no will and no provisions for the business. Alexander had grown very dependent on Willis. He was devastated as he realized what the full impact of losing Willis would mean to the business.

Willis was survived by his wife, five children, seven brothers, his mother and father. They all claimed his 50 percent of the partnership. Some wanted to sell, some wanted to work, some just wanted whatever they could get. Willis' wife, Wilma, had her own plan to be the sole 50 percent partner. Her plan worked. She went wild with authority and money, buying a new house and investing in real estate with money from the business. Within a year, Wilma went bankrupt, causing Alexander to be wiped out again. As Wilma's business partner, Alexander was jointly responsible for all her actions.

The Success and Protection of a Corporation -
The Way to Run a Business

Alexander, at age 52, was forced to start over again. With less ambition and a disastrous business climate, the struggle was tough, and he realized he wanted to give up. There had to be a lesson here. He was a genius and a great businessman, yet twice he had lost it all. Alexander had not protected his business against lawsuits, against death, against unwanted ownership. He failed to understand the one essential cornerstone of building a business structure - incorporate first to build your business on a solid foundation. Look at some of the corporate advantages:

- Bring in investors as stockholders, not partners. (If the president dies, the business does not have to.)
- Keep control over your business.
- Structure your business so no one can take anything.
- Don't pay more taxes than necessary.

Alexander incorporated his business and offered stock. This created sufficient capital to allow his business to take off instantly. Within a year he was back on top. Only this time he protected his every move. He prepared himself for any event and enjoyed the ability to pass his assets to his children and spouse without fear of loss, taxation, court or legal costs.

Key Points
- Learn how the rich structure their businesses.
- Learn how you can structure your business as the rich do.
- Incorporate your business to get maximum benefits.

Understand the Corporate Benefits Available to You
- Slash your taxes by 70 percent
- Tax-deductible cars
- Tax-deductible educational expenses
- Tax-deductible life, health and automobile insurance
- Tax-deductible trips
- Tax-deductible food
- Tax-deductible housing
- Protect your personal and business assets
- Don't pay probate costs
- Don't pay inheritance taxes
- Structure your financial affairs for wealth, not poverty

> *You simply need to learn how the rich get rich and do the same thing!*
> *What works for the rich will work for you, too.*

Eight Legal Business Structures
- ### I - The Sole Proprietorship:
  When you run your business as a sole proprietorship, you are the business. In essence, you (as the owner of that business) and your business are one and the same. Your assets are the business' assets, and the business' assets are your assets. The same applies for liabilities. Your debts and the business debts are one and the same. If your business is sued, it is the same as if you are sued. Conversely, if you are sued personally, your business is sued. Everything you own and everything your business owns are up for grabs in a lawsuit. The same applies regarding the IRS. You file one tax return because all the income is yours. You pay self-employment taxes (15.3 percent at the bottom of Schedule C) before any deductions. This is true whether you use your name or a business name. When you use a DBA (Doing Business As), you and your business are still one.

- ### II - The General Partnership:
  When you enter into an agreement (verbal or written with another party to do business together), you are acting in partnership with one another. All is operated as if it were one person. This is like a sole proprietorship, except with twice the exposure. Each is responsible for everything each of you own, owe, do and have done. You have joint and several liability with your partners. This means you are completely liable for everything, whether you are involved or not.

"Transformation is the ability and willingness to live beyond your form."
– Wayne Dyer

- ### *III - Limited Partnerships (LPs):*

  LPs are pass-through entities that have the same basic characteristics as a general partnership except that the LP has limited partners who typically have neither liability for business activities nor management responsibilities. These limited partners are liable (or at risk) for only the amount they have invested in the LP. The general partner, having responsibility and full liability for the activities of the partnership, provides full direction and management of the LP.

  The Limited Liability Partnership (LLP) is designed to offer an existing professional partnership, such as an engineering firm, the ability to be transformed to an LLP without the need to dissolve an existing partnership.

- ### *IV - The Corporation:*

  A corporation is a separate legal entity governed by state law. It operates through its bylaws as well as through resolutions written and adopted by the shareholders and directors. It must not function as the alter ego of its stockholders. In other words, you must remain separate from your corporation. The chart on page 28 graphically illustrates the separation between you, as founder and stockholder/owner of the corporation, and the corporation itself. Corporate formalities (the flow of activity and paperwork) must be followed to maintain a corporation as a separate legal entity. The state of incorporation has its own statutes, rules and regulations from which a corporation must operate.

- ### *V - C vs. S Corporation:*

  What corporation structure should you consider for your wealth-building advantage?

  Although both C and S corporations offer ease of ownership transfer and tremendous liability protection to shareholders, directors and officers, the S corporation is considerably different in its accounting structure and deduction capability. The S corporation, like the LP and the LLC is a flow-through entity, meaning the net income (or loss) flows through to the shareholders and is taxed (or deducted) on the individual returns.

  The S Corporation is organized by creating a C corporation and applying for the S election with the IRS. This election occurs by shareholders signing and submitting IRS Form 2553 in the year preceding the target year or within 2 1/2 months after the start of the target year.

  Most of the advantages of the S Corporation were deleted in the 1986 tax revision act. Since that time, change has been slow for professionals to acknowledge that the S corporation no longer can serve as the overall ideal business entity.

  While the C corporation is essentially the premier wealth-building entity in the United States for the vast majority of business enterprise, the S corporation does prove to be superior in three primary ways:

1. The S corporation offers advantages and an alternative to the professional service corporation (PSC). As outlined below, the PSC has a rather high flat tax, and by using the S election, individuals can disperse income to a lower personal rate.
2. As business activity expands for individuals, the need for multiple corporation strategy is often considered. In some circumstances, this strategy may need to avoid a controlled group ruling by the IRS and therefore create an S corporation as an alternative.
3. The third way offers relief to the tax burden of the W-2 wage earners. The S corporation can incur losses from business start-up and/or ordinary business operations. These losses can be applied toward the earnings of the shareholders. As described later in this chapter under the Home-Based Business topic, the personal tax savings involved will cause anyone to sit up and take note.

Because situations vary, consult your strategy advisor to determine your best interest.

- ### VI - The Professional Corporation:
  Although most of us consider ourselves professionals in our fields, there is a select group that the IRS considers "professional." These professionals in the fields of health, veterinary services, law, engineering, architecture, accounting, actuarial science, performing arts or certain consulting services are admired so much that when incorporating, they are required to file as a professional service corporation. This PSC category is also "admired" with its own flat tax category of 35 percent.

  Your options for relief as a "professional" are few, but can be effective. As mentioned above, the S corporation is a viable alternative. Another route to take is forming a C corporation that can contract with the PSC for services such as advertising, marketing, purchasing, bookkeeping, office retail and maintenance to name a few that could spin off income and lower PSC taxes.

- ### VII - Nonprofit or Not-For-Profit Corporations:
  All nonprofit corporations have three characteristics in common:
  1. They are designated as "nonprofit" when organized.
  2. Profits or assets cannot be divided among corporate members, officers or directors as corporate share dividends.
  3. They may lawfully pursue only such purposes as are permitted for such organizations by statute.

There are three categories:
1. Public benefit (such as museums, schools and hospitals)
2. Mutual benefit (such as cooperatives, trade or professional associations and clubs)
3. Private benefit (such as tax-exemption-benefit-seeking organizations — low-cost housing developments and the like.)

- **VIII - *The Limited Liability Company:***
  The LLC is a relatively new form of business organization that offers advantages and benefits not otherwise obtainable when operating an S corporation or partnership. The LLC combines the corporation characteristics of limited liability for all investors with the income flow-through attributes of a partnership. The LLC is attractive when the limited liability of all members is important, such as in real estate or oil and gas investments. See Section Five for more detailed information.

At a Glance - The Positives and Negatives of Business Structures

The sole proprietorship and the general (or 50/50) partnership have many negatives. The corporation offers many advantages as seen in the last column.

Sole Proprietorship

Liability
- Business assets exposed to business creditors
- Personal assets exposed to business creditors and lawsuits

Life
- Person becomes ill/dies and business depreciates in value or closes

Sale
- Value is based upon the owner, not the business

The General or 50/50 Partnership

Liability
- Personal assets of both parties can be attacked regardless of fault

Life
- Partnership ends when one partner pulls out, dies or becomes bankrupt
- Business is uncertain and can end at the whim of either partner
- Death of one partner can cause the family to claim partial ownership or sale of business

Sale
- Partners may not agree upon price or desire to sell, and prospective buyer(s) may not want to risk being in partnership with owners

"The first problem for all of us, men and women, is not to learn, but to unlearn."

~ Gloria Steinem

The Corporation

Liability
- Corporation shields its investor(s) from personal liability (exception: fraud + or penalties under environmental laws)
- The shareholder is not liable for the debts of the business +
- Only risk to shareholder is money invested in the corporation +
- Directors / officers / employees Indemnified against corporate acts +
- Corporation allows selective investment, not all assets +

Life
- Corporation has perpetual life despite shareholder's illness, death or desire + to sell out
- Shares are transferable without ending the business +

Sale
- Corporation can sell stock to generate capital +
- Corporation can attract passive investors +
- Corporation is the easiest type of business to sell +

Note: This chart is a simplification and is not meant to be definitive.

What is the Structure of a Corporation?

The chart on the following page illustrates graphically the separation between you, as the founder and stockholder/owner of the corporation, and the corporation itself. Corporate formalities (the flow of activity and paperwork) must be followed to maintain a corporation as a separate legal entity. The state of incorporation sets up the statutes from which a corporation in its jurisdiction must operate. The following chart depicts the legal flow. Line one shows that you (through the corporation) can be one or all of the stockholders, directors, officers and employees. Line 2 shows the benefit flow that you (as a corporate employee, officer, director and stockholder) can receive. You, as the founder and stockholder of the corporation, are placed outside the boundary of the corporation for protection from direct attack.

Who has C Corporations?
- Most corporations operate as C corporations
- International companies are C corporations
- The wealthy use C corporations

Conclusion
- The rich have corporations and use their benefits and advantages for maximum gains and security.
- There are more advantages to running your business as a corporation than as a sole proprietorship or 50/50 partnership.
- Incorporate, so you gain the corporate advantage, too.

WHAT IS A CORPORATION?

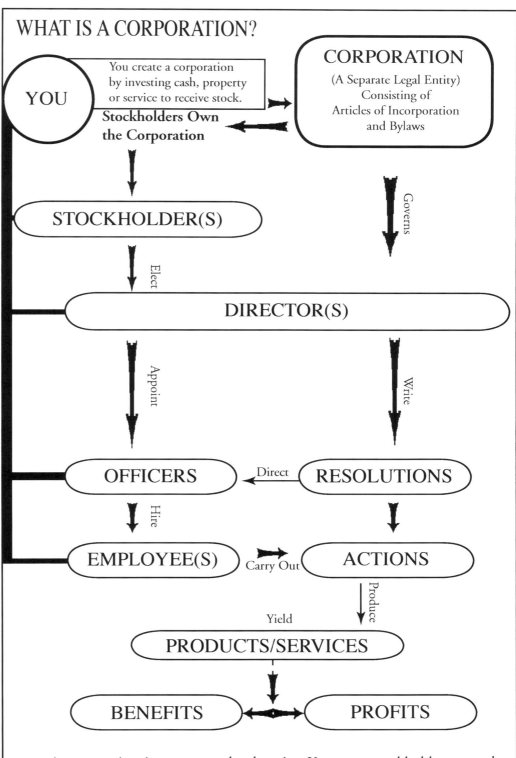

YOU

You create a corporation by investing cash, property or service to receive stock.

Stockholders Own the Corporation

CORPORATION

(A Separate Legal Entity)
Consisting of
Articles of Incorporation
and Bylaws

Governs

STOCKHOLDER(S)

Elect

DIRECTOR(S)

Appoint

Write

OFFICERS ← Direct ← RESOLUTIONS

Hire

EMPLOYEE(S) → Carry Out → ACTIONS

Produce

Yield

PRODUCTS/SERVICES

BENEFITS ←→ PROFITS

A corporation is a separate legal entity. You, as a stockholder, own the corporation and elect directors who appoint officers. You can be all the members of the corporation, perform all the activities and receive all the benefits and profits if you follow the corporate rules.

Chapter 2:
Dollars in Your Pockets from Corporate Tax Savings

- Your corporate tax advantage
- The Golden Tax Secrets
- Tax advantage of incorporating your home-based business
- Case studies

Case Study 2 (You)

You are to write this case study. Write the first part of it now. Just get out your tax returns for the past three years. Write down how much you paid in taxes - all your federal taxes, self-employment taxes and state income taxes. Do this for your personal income as well as your business income. Then read this chapter, study the case studies and write what you could have paid as an individual and as a corporation. How much would you have saved if you utilized multiple corporations? The facts and figures tell the story.

Key Points

- Compare taxes as a sole proprietor to those of a corporation.
- Choose the structure best for you.
- Apply the Golden Tax Secrets to your business.

Why a Corporation Helps You Save Taxes

Let's look at the tax advantages of the corporation. The difference between how much or how little you pay in taxes is determined by when you pay your taxes as an individual or as a corporation and what your tax rate is.

Your Tax Base and Tax Rate Make a Big Difference to Your Savings!

Individual
Your Income (Your Tax Base)
Tax at 28 percent (average)
Expenditures
Savings

Corporation
Income
Expenditures
Tax Base
Tax at 15 percent (under $50,000 net income)
Savings

Look at Section 119 of the Internal Revenue Code

Not one in a thousand Americans realizes the fortune that could be saved. You can deduct the "obvious" items, but you can also deduct much more, such as:

- Home repair under certain conditions
- Home insurance under certain conditions
- Some or all meals/clothes under certain conditions
- Your heat, phone and other utilities under certain conditions

You can also deduct many other expenses including:

- Health insurance
- Travel expenses
- Retirement plans
- Dependent care plans
- Auto insurance
- College funds

Your Home is Your Financial Command Post

You can live a much richer life when you make your home your "Financial Command Post." There are literally hundreds of ways you can save on taxes by incorporating your home-based business. By actively running a small or home-based business with the intent for profit, you have both created a second source of income – *and begun to qualify for the huge tax breaks discussed in this chapter*. The write-offs are many and substantial. By operating your business, as a corporation, out of your home, you can completely reverse the old way of looking at it. You can stop viewing your house as an endless money pit and start seeing it as your financial command post – the center of your wealth-making dreams.

How do you do this? First, you need to understand the tax codes. But reviewing the tax code and trying to understand its content will be an overwhelming task. After all, in book form, they weigh over 18 pounds and contain over 13 million words on some 12,000 pages. However, after extensive research, I have found a few tax codes hidden within all those pages that I call the "Golden Tax Secrets".

The next few pages are dedicated to giving you a clear understanding of a few of these secrets.

The Corporate Tax Advantage

IRC #	Golden Tax Secrets	Amount	Your $s
79	1. **Group Term Life Insurance.** You can receive up to $50,000 in coverage and the premium is not included in your gross income, and it is 100 percent deductible to your corporation.	$50,000	
74	2. **Achievement and Awards for Safety and Longevity.** These awards have to be in writing and can be up to $1,600 each. In a family corporation, both the husband and wife can receive these awards annually. The wife might receive the longevity award because she has been with the company since its inception. The husband might receive the safety award because he maintains a safe work environment. These awards are tax-free deductions for the company.	$1,600	
105	3. **Health Insurance.** If you already have a health insurance program, the corporation can reimburse you for any expenses paid.	No Limit	
106	4. **Insured Medical Plans.** Your corporation can pay 100 percent of your medical plan. The amount is not included in your gross pay.	100 percent	
125	5. **Cafeteria Plan.** Your corporation can provide a cafeteria plan, which may include a combination of the above sections. This does not affect your gross income.	100 percent	
129	6. **Dependent Care.** Your corporation can provide you up to $5,000 a year for dependent care, and it is not considered part of your gross income.	$5,000	
127	7. **Educational Assistance.** Your allotment is up to $5,250, not part of your gross income.	$5,250	

IRC #	Golden Tax Secret	Amount	Your $s
162	8. **Seminar Expenses.** This includes business and lodging for business-related seminars. Not included as part of your income, these costs are 100 percent deductible to the corporation.	100 percent	
132 (e)	9. **"De-minimis fringes."** This includes any property or service the value of which is so small that accounting is unreasonable, such as coffee, company barbecues at the office and other miscellaneous expenses. Frequency must be considered according to the code.	Open	
217	10. Moving Expenses. All reasonable moving expenses, except meals, can be paid for and are not included in your gross pay.	100 percent	
132 (h) (s)	11. Physical Fitness. You can have a physical fitness facility on your premises totally paid for by the corporation.	100 percent	
179	12. Depreciation. You can deduct or depreciate $133,000 of your office equipment in a single year. Vehicles	$133,000 $25,000	
243	13. Dividends. If your corporation is receiving dividends from another corporation, such as stocks, mutual funds, etc., you can eliminate 79 percent to 100 percent of the gain. You are only taxed on 20 percent. If your company receives $1,000 in capital gains, $800 is forgiven.	80/20	
2501	14. Stock freezing.		
331	15. Inter-Corporate Transfers of Assets.		
221	16. Production of Income.		

Other corporate tax advantages include split dollar life insurance, key person life insurance, non-qualified profit sharing, non-qualified deferred compensation, qualified retirement (defined benefit) plan, buy/sell agreement and 210 others. Note: "You" and "your" in the above chart refer to the officers, directors and key employees of the corporation.

Email: Corpinfosageintl.com for a Special Report that lists over 300 Tax Deductions you can use.

Let's Examine Some of These Advantages More Closely

Section 74 covers achievement awards for safety and longevity. It remains one of my favorites. Tip O'Neil, in his great wisdom, when he was Speaker of the House, took out the ability to receive awards for outstanding and meritorious service.

The achievement awards are now for safety and longevity. So if you don't electrocute yourself when you turn on the computer or you've been there from the beginning, you can receive up to $1,600 a year in awards.

The smart way to take this award is through gifts. I'm sure nobody would mind having a $1,600 watch or a $1,600 home entertainment center. That way there's no FICA. All of the expense is deductible to the corporation.

Section 79 covers group term life insurance. You can receive up to $50,000 in coverage, and the premiums are not included in your gross income. The premium is totally deductible, and it's tax-free to you.

Section 105 covers health insurance. If you already have a health insurance program, the corporation can reimburse you with no limit, and it's not included in your income and is totally deductible to the corporation.

Section 106 deals with insured medical plans except as otherwise provided in this section. The corporation can have a medical plan and can pay up to 100 percent of the medical plan for you. And this benefit is not included in your income, and it's deductible to the corporation.

Section 199 can be for those of you who operate a home-based business. If you qualify under this section, and if your home is your business or corporate headquarters, meals and lodging may be a requirement of your employer to stay there on the premises. These can be deductible to the corporation and not included as part of your income.

Section 120 covers a group legal plan.

Section 125 cafeteria plan includes a variety of employee benefits. This could include Section 105 where you receive unlimited reimbursement for health insurance premiums or you could use Section 106 and have a health care plan paid by the company. Or take advantage of Section 127 educational assistance.

You can allot up to $5,250 per employee for continuing education and seminars, which would not be included in the employee's income. Seminars relating to your business can be considered continuing education.

You can be reimbursed for those expenses under the education category, or you can be reimbursed under Section 162 or 212, which cover seminars. There are several different ways to take advantage of these tax-free benefits.

Section 243 is the one savings that is a real key for me concerning dividends. If your corporation owns stock in other corporations or stocks, bonds or mutual funds and it receives dividends from those investments, there could be as much as 100 percent (but let's say at least 80 percent) forgiveness on capital gains on those dividends received by the corporation. For instance, if you receive $1,000 in dividends, $800 of it disappears as revenue as though it didn't exist.

The other thing that's really great about the corporation is that it has so many different retirement plans available. You, as an individual, cannot take advantage of these. You can put much more money away in your retirement program through the corporation. There are qualified plans and unqualified plans depending on where you are and what you are trying to do. The list of what you can save with the corporation is virtually endless.

But the key is doing it right! It's not about operating in the gray area. You know there are some people that try to scam everything. Don't be one of them.

Some people can get very creative about figuring: "Well, we'll try it this year to see if we can get away with it." But when the government and the IRS want to help you save on taxes, why not do it in the white area of the law so that you can take full advantage of legitimate tax savings and be able to sleep at night?

$$$$ — Put Yours to Work

Use the "Your $s" column from the Golden Tax Secrets chart beginning on page 31 and on the chart below to record your legal tax deductions. This will help you see the savings incorporating would make on your current tax return. Federal corporate tax is 15 percent on year-end earnings of $50,000 or less.

Incredible Corporate Benefits

Your Home-Based Business

Incorporate & Get Rich! C.W. "Al" Allen & Cheri S. Hill

	Individual		Corporation	
	Sample	Your $s	Sample	Your $s
Your Income	$50,000.00	_____	$50,000.00	_____
Individual Tax at 28% $50,000 x 28% =	-$14,000.00	_____		
Spendable Base	$36,000.00	_____	$50,000.00	_____
Expenditures	-$35,000.00	_____	-$35,000.00	_____
Remainder	$ 1,000.00	_____	$15,000.00	_____
Corporation Tax at 15% $15,000 x 15%=$2,250			-$ 2,250.00	_____
Savings	$ 1,000.00	_____	$12,750.00	_____
Taxes per Day	$ 38.36	_____	$ 6.16	_____
Savings per Month	$ 83.33	_____	$ 1062.80	_____

In many scenarios, there are tremendous tax advantages in incorporating your home-based business. In the past, the IRS did its best to disallow deductions claimed by home-based businesses. However, Congress got fed up with the IRS's viewpoint and enacted Section 932 (a) of the Taxpayer Relief Act of 1997, which dramatically expanded the definition of a home office. In the past the IRS would have considered your place of work where the work was performed and where you actually got paid. However, under the expanded definition, the IRS is now required by law to recognize your home-based business if there is no other fixed location where the business owner conducts the management or administrative functions of the business.

A good example would be a plumber operating out of his home. If Mr. Plumber gets a call from a guy with a stopped sink, Mr. Plumber obviously can't tell the guy to bring his sink over to his place. He has to go out to perform the work and get paid. Under the old rules this would not be considered a home-based operation, however, under the new rules, so long as there was no other location where Mr. Plumber conducted the management of his business, this would be considered a home-based business.

"The Home has been dubbed 'The New American Workplace,' and that's probably not far from the truth. If the industry's unprecedented growth continues-and experts predict it will-the majority of Americans will work at home in the 21st century. Who was it that called homebased business a 'fad' in the 1980s, anyway? None other than Megatrends guru John Naisbitt. He now works at home."

~ Stephanie Barlow, Senior Writer, Entrepreneur magazine

This rule applies whether you are operating as a sole proprietor or as a corporation. However, let's consider a moment the impact of operating your home-based business as a sole proprietor as opposed to a corporation. Unfortunately, there is a great deal of incomplete information being solicited and advocating the home-based business to be run as a sole proprietorship. I ask you, why pay a 15.3 percent self-employment tax if you don't have to? Well, friend, if you operated your home-based business under the title of corporation, you not only avoid the self-employment tax, but you will enjoy a far-superior range of deductions and benefits which are paid for with pre-tax dollars.

As you should recall from the previous pages, corporations earn, deduct and are taxed only on what is left. However, if your home-based business is run as a sole proprietorship, your federal tax is determined before the self-employment tax and without a self-employment tax credit.

Not only are the self-employed faced with this 15.3 percent tax after federal tax, this tax is calculated at the bottom of the Schedule C before personal deductions!

You can let the facts determine your most profitable and safe alternative. Believe me, by using a corporation to represent your home-based business you demonstrate to the IRS and the world that you are a legitimate business.

The most common misconception when considering a corporation for a home-based business is not making enough income to justify setting one up. Not making enough home-based business income is a valid concern, especially operating as a sole proprietor, as the IRS will consider the Hobby Rule. However, if you are either just starting out with a home-based business or have been at it for some time and are making a small but reasonable income, you can certainly justify incorporating by what you are about to learn.

If you are making a small home-based business income, say $1,000 a year or about $83 per month, you can incorporate and take the S corporation election to create windfall losses that can be applied toward your W-2 income. That's right, against your W-2 income! Certainly your home-based business will incur $10,000 to $15,000 or beyond in start-up and operating expenses. With the S corporation, you can apply these losses against your family's W-2 income.

Imagine knowing today that you are going to have a $15,000 deduction at year-end. Wouldn't you want to charge to work tomorrow morning and change your W-4 to provide more weekly income to you now? Why not give yourself an instant raise of $100, $200 or more per week?

Once your home-based business corporation begins to make a profit, we will logically change the S election back to a C in order to take advantage of the full scope of deductions and benefits that C corporations offer.

Now, if your home-based business were profitable, it would most likely be more beneficial to incorporate and stay as a C corporation, unless of course your W-2 income far exceeds this home-based business income. In such a case, you should seek a credible advisor and strategist.

The questions you have to ask yourself are, are you creating a red flag by operating your home-based business (or other operations) the way you are, or are you going to create a vehicle that allows you to prosper while letting the government and the IRS help you do it?

38

Perhaps you don't have a home-based business. Well, my friend, if you suffer from losing too much of your income to taxes, and don't have a home-based business, the time to look into one is now!

Now let's apply what we have learned so far and look at some real case studies.

Case Study 3 (George and Laurie) — Bottom Line Comparisons

George and Laurie were an enthusiastic young couple dedicated to growing a trucking business. Although George only owned one truck at the time, he had visions of owning several and making a substantial presence in the local earth moving industry. George was on the road all day, and Laurie worked as a part-time bookkeeper for the business while being a dedicated mother to their children.

They owned their own home and paid $6,000 per year in mortgage interest, $2,000 per year in real estate taxes. The couple contributed $5,000 to their church. The medical insurance required an annual $2,600 per year and the oldest child received braces that cost $3,500.

In today's fast-paced economy, this family of four can benefit greatly with a few extra thousand dollars a year. By incorporating your business, the bottom line can offer some startling results. (See comparison chart on page 38).

With $100,000 as net income (income after normal business expenses) reported on their Schedule C, they were first attacked by a 15.3 percent self-employment tax of $11,139 and a personal income tax of $15,516 for a total of $26,655 in taxes.

George and Laurie were justified in their anger and dismay of having such a large tax burden. They agreed they needed to change the way they were handling their financial affairs and began asking questions of everyone they knew. They were determined to find a legal solution. A friend recognized their quest and suggested that they read "Rich Dad Poor Dad," a number one best seller by Robert Kiyosaki. They did, and they haven't been the same since.

Robert Kiyosaki's book suggested contacting Sage International, Inc. for business structure and tax slashing strategies. Contacting Sage International, Inc. and requesting information lead them to activate a client questionnaire. The comparison chart on page 38 is a result of that questionnaire and contrasts using a C corporation as opposed to operating as the above sole proprietorship.

The C corporation was showing taxable income of $9,057. If you look closely you will notice that the dividend income took advantage of the 70 percent forgiveness on the $7,000 gain. Also, George and the two children were receiving salaries, which were subject to payroll taxes. Note the $7,200 a year home office rent, which was calculated at $2 per square foot. Laurie set up a lease agreement between herself and the corporation. Although this sum became personal income, it was passive income, not subject to FICA and FUTA, and also could be offset by home deductions.

Church contributions were paid through the corporation and a maximum 25% of salary was contributed to a pension plan. There is a children's education plan, medical reimbursement and medical insurance all being provided with pretax dollars.

This illustration resulted in personal income taxes of $4,474, payroll taxes of

$8,185 and corporate income taxes of $1,358 for a total of $14,017 and tax savings of $12,471.

After receiving these results by fax, George and Laurie were elated and enthusiastically expressed their thanks during the phone consultation a few moments later. They faxed in their incorporation order documents, which were processed and filed within a few short days. This couple soon had their Corporate Minute Book and a host of ongoing support material that insured operations and corporate formalities began smoothly.

Although, on an average, this is a conservative example of an aggressive strategy. This couple does, however, offer a great illustration and a prime success story of using a C corporation to turn their financial affairs around. Through Sage's unlimited ongoing support and educational programs, this enthusiastic couple decided to grow in financial intelligence and wisely invested their savings. Two years later, they were able to realize several new profit centers that opened up to them as a result, and the rest is profit-building history.

The following comparison is based on the difference between doing business as a sole proprietor versus a corporation.

Knowledge = Money

Individual (Schedule C)	
Income	$100,000
Office in the home.........-800	99,200
Dividend Income.............7,000	106,200
Less:	
1/2 Self-employment Tax....-5,943	
60% Insurance Premium.......-810	
IRA Contribution..............-2,000	
8,753 97,447	
Itemized Deductions:	
Interest & Taxes	
(8,000-800)........................-7,200	
Medical Expenses......................0	
Contributions....................-5,000	
.....................-12,200......85,247	
Exemptions:	
(2,900 x 4).....................-11,600......73,647	
Taxable Income 73,647	
Income Tax 14,603	
Self-employment Tax.......................11,885	
Total Tax Due **$26,488**	
Tax Bracket: 28%	

Corporation	
Income	$100,000
Dividend Income	
(7,000 less 70%).......2,100 ..102,100	
Wages...................-45,000	
Wages — Children..-8,500	
Payroll Taxes............ -4,093	
Rent for Office use	
($600/month) ..... -7,200	
Contributions .... -5,000	
Pension Plan	
25% .... -11,250	
Education	
Reimbursement* ..... -9,500	
Medical Costs.......... -3,500	
Medical Insurance	
Premiums................ -2,600	
Taxable Income 9,057	
Income Tax 1,358	
Payroll Tax..............................8,185	
Income Tax (Personal) 4,474	
Total Tax Due **$14,017**	
Tax Bracket: 15%	

Total Tax Savings $12,471!

* Special rules may apply. Speak to your advisor regarding attribution rules.

Compare the Tax Savings as an Individual and as a Corporation.

Which way would you rather do business? As an individual or as a corporation? The rich take advantage of corporations. Isn't this how the rich get rich? Think about it. You too can grow rich by using the corporate advantage. Incorporate, invest your tax savings and grow rich!

---

*If corporate year-end earnings are over $50,000, consult with your accountant to see if forming an additional corporation is necessary to reduce earnings in each company.

Isn't That Exciting?

So when I say, "Incorporate & Get Rich!" do it. Incorporate your business, take some of the tax savings and apply them to investments and a retirement program. You can become rich and have much more money in your pockets right now.

When asked to name the Seven Wonders of the World, Baron De Rothchild once said, "I cannot. But I know that the Eighth Wonder of the World is Compound Interest." Refer to Section Seven to discover how that Eighth Wonder of the World can work for you.

Conclusion

- Use the corporate tax codes to your advantage for building wealth.
- If you don't have a home-based business, start one.
- Let Sage International, Inc. help you strategize for maximum results.

"Why does a slight tax increase cost you $200 and a substantial tax cut saves you thirty cents?"

– Peg Bracken

NOTES

Chapter 3:
Simple Steps to Tax Savings

- How you can use the Golden Tax Secrets to your advantage
- Application of Golden Tax Secrets to specific business situations
- Advantages of fiscal year-end planning

Case Study 4 (Diane Kennedy, CPA) — Lost and Found (Deductions, that is...)

I had a tough decision to make when I started my own CPA firm. On one hand, I was well positioned to take a risk and a great opportunity had emerged to buy a small practice. But on the other hand, I would have to give up a very well paying job as Chief Financial Officer of a large development company. No matter how I ran the numbers, I calculated it would take at least five years before I could hope to make the amount of money that I was currently making. Plus, I currently had the security of someone else paying the bills and didn't worry whether there would be enough money to pay myself.

After much soul-searching, I took the plunge anyway. The first year my tax return showed (totally legitimately) an income of less than half of what I had earned working for others. Yet my lifestyle had not significantly changed! That was because many of the "lifestyle" expenditures I had — travel, magazines, better computers — could now be written off! Incidentally, by the end of the third year, I had reached taxable income equal to what I had previously made. My disposable income was double the taxable amount! Now I invest much of that extra income and tax savings. I want to help you do the same.

Key Points

- Remain mindful and use the Seven Secrets of Success.
- Become familiar with tax codes that can reduce your taxes.
- Apply the Golden Tax Secrets to your advantage and tax situation.
- Apply the tax codes to your advantage from your home-based business.
- Apply the tax codes to your advantage from your storefront business. Consider multiple corporate strategies.
- Avoid "Tax Traps," including those related to a personal holding company and a personal service company.

"Nearly all men can stand adversity, but if you want to test a man's character, give him power."
~ Abraham Lincoln

Seven Secrets of Success: Use Your Corporate Advantage!

The most often-asked question by a new business owner is, "What's deductible?" This question is probably the hardest question for a CPA to answer completely. The answer is actually that it depends entirely on you and the way you run your business. Basically, anything that promotes your business is a deduction. It is necessary for the new business owner to shift his or her entire way of thinking, so that you look for ways to create deductions.

Study the Following Secrets of Success

#1 Secret of Success:
Find items that provide benefits for you, without tax, and still are deductible for the corporation.

This will minimize your overall taxes! The following information will walk you through typical expenses that a business may have. Many of these can be provided to you, as an employee of the corporation, without tax to you and yet still provide a deduction for the company.

#2 Secret of Success:
Look for ways to make your normal expenses deductible.

What do you usually spend your money on? Do you invest a lot on computers and programs? Or do you like to entertain? Maybe you like to travel? First, identify where your income goes now, and then find a way to make it deductible for your business. For example, the computers and software are an easy-to-prove deduction for more businesses these days. When you travel, find a business purpose for the travel. If you entertain, invite prospective clients, employees or vendors with whom you deal — then write it off!

#3 Secret of Success:
Use the fiscal year-end option that is special for corporations.

You can easily defer taxes for over 11 months — perfectly legally. We will discuss later in this chapter how this unique benefit of corporations can help you. For now, realize that you can choose any year-end you wish for the corporation and that the standard default of December 31 is generally the worst possible choice.

#4 Secret of Success
Establish a good accounting system to make sure you get all of the deductions that should be coming to you.

Section Six discusses setting up an accounting system and what you should know before purchasing software.

#5 Secret of Success
Document!

Make sure you can keep all your corporate advantages by having good corporate records. Section Six will help you set up a filing system and alert you to potential pitfalls if the IRS comes looking for receipts.

#6 Secret of Success
Make use of the lowest tax rates at both the individual and corporate levels.

"That which we persist in doing becomes easier—not that the nature of the task has changed, but our ability to do so has increased."
– Ralph Waldo Emerson

As part of your annual "business physical" you will look at the projected income both for you and for your corporation. The information I give you will help you maximize the lowest rates for both taxpaying units — you, as an individual, and your corporation.

#7 Secret of Success
Become familiar with the character of income — portfolio, passive and ordinary.

Learn the ways to change the character of income to your benefit. The characterization of income is an advanced topic that many CPAs don't even fully comprehend. Yet it is important for a truly comprehensive tax planning strategy to take into account your individual circumstances and take advantage of the corporation to change the character of income that you receive. This can free up otherwise lost deductions or accelerate "suspended" or "limited" losses.

How You Can Use the Golden Tax Secrets to Your Advantage

The following information gives you a brief but accurate idea of some of the tax codes that can be used to reduce the taxes you pay. Each of these needs to be applied to your specific situation correctly. Your very awareness of them will help you in this process. Consult with your accountant. If your accountant does not know how to apply them to your situation, ask another accountant. You need to allow the tax codes to work for you.

Cost of Goods

General Business Deductions
Question:

I have a business making and selling jewelry. How do I deduct expenses for products that I manufacture?

Discussion:

First, you need to understand the concept of "inventory." As you buy products or parts for an item that you are going to resell, these become part of the assets of the company. They are not an expense (and not a deduction) until you sell the product. This is a fundamental fact.

Tax Trap:

Items bought for resale purposes or for the manufacture of an item for resale are inventory. It is not a deduction until you sell the product.

You could spend a lot of money in your early business years building an inventory and not be able to deduct any of the expenses in those years!

These expenses, called cost of goods, are generally any expenses that are directly involved in the product. Ask yourself, if I didn't make this particular product, would I have this expense? If the answer is yes, then it is a direct cost. If the answer is no, for example with office expenses, then it is not a direct cost. The goal is to minimize the direct costs so that you are not in danger of having to spend money you can't deduct.

Examples:

Examples of cost of goods would be all merchandise purchased for resale, cartons and other shipping expenses and parts and labor needed for assembly.

How do I get this deduction?

These are common deductions for any business. Keep track of your expenses with either a good accounting software package or manual system. Save your canceled checks and invoices. Because these are common expenses, you do not need to do anything extraordinary, such as adopting a corporate plan.

Exception:

Writers, photographers and artists. There is a special advantage to being a writer, photographer or artist. You are exempt from uniform capitalization requirements. What does this mean? This means if you are a writer and you want to write a book about travel in Europe, you deduct the expenses of traveling to Europe to research it. Or if you want to paint a picture you can travel to Europe to look at the architecture or art. However, expenses for producing jewelry, silverware, pottery, furniture and similar household items are not exempt.

Tax Code:

See Code 263(A).

Office Expense

Question:

What expenses can I deduct for my office? What qualifies as my office?

Discussion:

There are really two aspects to this question. The first part refers to the general expenses of running an office and the second part to the aspects of having a home office. This second point will be discussed in more detail under Special Business Deductions. Always keep in mind the basic premise of business deductions. If an expense is necessary or otherwise enhances your business, then it's deductible. Examples of office expenses are: letterhead, telephones, paper, pens, calculators and computers — anything that you must have to make your business work!

How do I get this deduction?

These are common deductions for any business. Keep track of your expenses with a good manual or computerized accounting system and save your canceled checks and invoices. In the case of the telephone expense, check out the special section on Home Office deductions to make sure you correctly allocate personal and business usage.

Tax Code:

See the general points of business deductions under Reg 1.162-1.

Advertising

Question:

Can I deduct the cost of printing mailers about my business? What about shirts with my logo?

Discussion:

Advertising costs can be from anything that promotes your business — yellow page ads, mailers, a logo on the side of your car or your shirt, and the cost of items given away for advertising purposes (pencils, pens, calendars, golf putters). Promotional expenses can be very similar to advertising expenses. However, advertising targets a specific market and promotional expenses could range from putting on a community show to giving a gift to an organization. Don't spend too much time worrying if a deduction should be an advertising or a promotional expense. Just make sure you get the deduction.

How do I get this deduction?

Advertising costs are, in general, very common. However, the subject of uniforms (also in this section) can be more difficult to prove and subject to question. For this reason, I recommend taking a picture of the logo on the shirt, or keep a copy of the artwork, just in case you need to prove the deduction. Also, as with all deductions, keep track of your expenses and save your canceled checks and invoices.

Tax Code:

See Reg 1.162-1

Charitable Contributions and Promotions

Question:

Can I donate used office equipment to the local shelter and get a deduction? What if I donate my time to help them print a brochure?

Discussion:

Note that charitable contributions are limited to 10 percent of your corporation's net income. However, if you can change the character of the contribution to promotion (say you get free advertising in a newsletter in exchange for the gift), then it is fully deductible and is not subject to the net income rule.

There can be a fine line between advertising and promotional expenses. As we discussed previously in this chapter, advertising expenses are generally used for targeting specific persons.

An example would be printing your logo on pens that go to your customers. Whereas promotional expenses are for larger, organized activities. Don't worry too much about this distinction.

Since we are discussing charitable donations, let's clarify a commonly misunderstood point. You can take a deduction for the cost of items that you contribute or you can take a deduction for the fair market value (get an appraisal first) of an appreciated asset. But you cannot take a deduction for your time.

You must first have an expense before you can take a deduction. In other words, if you donate paper to your church, you have incurred an expense — you bought the paper. But if you are an accountant, you cannot take a deduction for your volunteered time balancing their checkbook. You had no actual expense (other than your time). You can bill and be paid for your time, and make an equivalent contribution that is deductible.

How do I get this deduction?

As always, track expenses with a good accounting system and save canceled checks and invoices. If you contribute an appreciated asset — such as artwork — get an independent appraisal of value. I also recommend keeping proof or deductions that you want to prove are promotional, not charitable. For example, a client of mine donated some used office equipment from her business in exchange for a promotion in the non-profit organizations' newsletter. She kept a copy of the newsletter. This proves she donated the items for promotional reasons and can then take a full deduction. The alternative would have been to get a charitable contribution deduction, which could have been limited, depending on her company's income level.

Tax Code:

See Code 170(b)(2) and Reg 1.170A-11.

Uniforms
Question:

Can I deduct my work clothes?

Discussion:

There is an old accountant's joke that the answer to every client's question should be: "It depends." In this case, it depends! The cost and upkeep of a uniform (including dry cleaning and laundry) is deductible only if the uniform is required as a condition of employment and is not adaptable to general wear. This means that, for most of us, our work clothes are not deductible because most are adaptable to general wear. However, if you have a business that would lend itself to a logo (and most would) then you have created a unique uniform that is deductible.

How do I get this deduction?

Be sure that the uniform you have is a condition of employment by having a written policy that requires wearing the uniform and make sure it is not adaptable to general wear by putting a logo on the shirt. If you have a profession in which you do wear uniforms that get simply too stained or dirty to wear for general wear (such as a painter or drywaller) then this deduction is an easy one for you. And, as for all deductions, keep track of your expenses and save canceled checks and invoices.

Tax Code:

See Reg 1.62-2 © P 2-28 (4).

Dues/Subscriptions/Education

Question:

Can I deduct my magazine subscriptions?

Discussion:

I have included dues, subscriptions and education together in this category, because these deductions are similar. They include dues to educational organizations, magazine subscriptions and continuing education. There are a few key points to consider.

First, education expenses are deductible (even if they lead to a degree) if the education that is undertaken 1) maintains or improves a skill required by the individual in the individual's employment or other trade or business or 2) meets the requirements of the individual's employer or the requirements of law or regulations.

Club dues are no longer deductible. The rule applies to any club organized for business, pleasure, recreation or other social purposes. However, this disallowance provision does not extend to professional organizations (such as legal and accounting associations) or public service organizations (Rotary, for example) as long as the organization's principal purpose is not to conduct entertainment activities for their guests.

How do I get this deduction?

Subscriptions are fairly easy to prove for deductibility — just make sure the magazine subscription can somehow be justified for your business. Dues are deductible as long as they are not "club" dues, and the professional or public service organizations are organized for business purposes. Investigate the purpose of the organization before you join. Document, in writing, the business purpose of every class or seminar you take. Also, where appropriate, adopt an education assistance plan.

Tax Code:

See Reg 1.162-1, Reg 1.162-5 and Code 274(a)(3)

Traveling Expenses Away from Home — Within the United States

Question:

How much can I claim for deductions when I'm working away from home?

Discussion:

A deduction is allowed for ordinary and necessary traveling expenses incurred by a taxpayer while away from home in the conduct of a trade or business. That seems like a simple statement, but there are many parts of that statement that need further definition.

First, there are special rules for foreign travel. "Foreign" refers to places other than the United States, its possessions and the Trust Territory of the Pacific Islands. No deduction is allowed, however, in a country (such as Iran) found to discriminate in its tax laws against conventions held in the United States.

"The reward for work well done is the opportunity to do more."

– Jonas Salk

Where is home?

A taxpayer's home is one's regular place of business. When there are multiple areas of business activity or places of regular employment, the principal place of business is treated as the tax home. In determining the principal place, the following factors are considered:

- the time spent on business activity in each area
- the amount of business activity in each area
- the amount of the resulting financial return in each area

For most of us, the regular place of business is our office — whether an outside facility or a home office. Business travel expenses incurred while away from the principal place of business are deductible.

How long can I stay?

If the assignment is temporary in nature, the taxpayer is considered "away from home," and a traveling expense deduction is allowed. However, if the assignment is for an indefinite period of time, the location of the assignment becomes the individual's new tax home, and the taxpayer may not deduct travel expenses.

What is deductible?

You can deduct a whole range of items: travel, meals, lodging, transportation, hotel rooms, sample showrooms, telephone and fax services and others.

How do I get this deduction?

First, make sure the location of your taxpayer "home" qualifies you for this deduction. As you remember from all of the previous deductions, you must document your deductions in order to keep them. But I have found that many people lose receipts as they travel. In this case, I recommend having a credit card that is either in the corporation's name or in your name personally and use it exclusively for business. Charge all of your business expenses when you travel. You will then have a full listing of the expenses when you receive your credit card bill!

Tax Code:

See Code 162(a)(2), Reg 1.162-2 and Rev. Rul. 93-86.

Foreign Travel

Question:

How can I write off a trip to Australia? What does foreign travel mean?
There are different aspects to this category. Let's go through them sequentially:

Discussion:

Foreign travel expenses are deductible without limitation if all three of the following conditions are met:

> "We need to learn to set our course by the stars, not by the lights of every passing ship."
> ~ Omar Bradley

- There is a business purpose to the travel
- You spend one week or less (not counting the day spent traveling to the country)
- You spend 75 percent or more of the time during the travel involved in business

If you spend part of a day on business activities, the entire day counts as a business day. In addition, if you have business activities before a weekend or holiday and business activities directly following, then the days off count as business days also.

If you do not meet all three of the above qualifications, then you must allocate the costs on a day-to-day basis.

- **Luxury Water Travel (Cruise Ship)**

A deduction of up to $2,000 per individual per year is allowed in the case of travel via cruise ships taken for seminars, meetings, etc. only if the vessel is registered in the United States and all ports of call are located in the United States or territories of the United States. There is no deduction allowed for foreign cruises regardless of business purpose.

A deduction for travel other than taken for seminars, meetings, conventions and the like is limited to twice the highest per diem travel amount allowable to employees of the federal government.

- **Travel for Education**

A deduction for travel is deductible only if there is a purpose to it that is other than the educational value of travel. In other words, it is deductible if the travel is to attend a conference or to go somewhere or see something that is specifically applicable to your business.

How do I get this deduction?

In addition to the normal actions of keeping track of the expenses, also keep literature or a narrative documentary that proves the business purpose of the travel. This could be in the form of a diary that lists what you did each day, notations in your personal calendar and/or brochures from places you visited. Remember that you are trying to prove that the travel was necessary for business purposes.

Tax Code:

See Code 274(c)(2), Reg 1.162-2(b), Code 274(m), Code 274(h)(2) and Reg 1.274-4.

Question:

Can I write off a convention on a cruise ship?

Discussion:

- **Convention Expenses**

Deductible travel expenses include those incurred in attending a convention related to the taxpayer's business. Note that expenses or a convention or meeting in connection with investments, financial planning or other income-producing property are not deductible.

- **United States Cruise Ships**

A limited deduction is available for expenses incurred for conventions on U.S. cruise ships. This deduction is limited to $2,000 and applies only if: 1) all ports of such cruise ships are located in the United States or in United States possessions, 2) the taxpayer establishes that the convention is directly related to the active conduct of his or her trade or business, and 3) the taxpayer includes certain specified information in the return on which the deduction is claimed.

- **Foreign Conventions**

You must establish that a foreign convention is directly related to the active conduct of your trade of business, and that, after taking all factors into account, it is "as reasonable" for the meeting to be held outside the North American area as within it. The factors to be taken into account are: 1) purposes and activities of the sponsoring organization or group, 2) the places of residence of the active members of the sponsoring organization or group and the places at which other meetings of the organization or group have been held or will be held and 3) such other relevant factors as the taxpayer may present. Expenses for foreign conventions on cruise ships are not deductible.

How do I get this deduction?

In addition to the normal actions (keep track of the expenses, etc.), keep literature or a narrative documentary that proves the business purpose of the travel. The necessary elements to be proven are:

- amount
- time
- place
- description
- business purpose

This could be in the form of a diary that lists what you did each day or notations in your personal calendar supplemented by brochures from places you visited. Remember you are trying to prove that the travel was necessary for business purposes.

Tax Code:

See Code 274(h)(7) and Reg 1.162-2(d).

Equipment Purchases and Contributions

Question:

Can I write off my computer? Do I get a deduction for the desk I owned before I started the business?

Discussion:

Large purchases, generally more than $500, are depreciated. This means that you do not immediately get a full deduction for the entire purchase price of these large purchases. Instead, a percentage of the amount is allowed for each of a specified number of years. For example, a computer is depreciated for five years. For each of five years, you will get a portion of the amount as a deduction. To make things even more complicated, there is an accelerated depreciation rate available. In the first years following the purchase of an asset, you are allowed more of a deduction and in subsequent years the amount decreases.

There are a few twists to the basic rules stated above. First, a one-time deduction (check with your CPA for current amount) is allowed each year for new purchases which means you do not have to wait five or more years to get the deduction. That's good.

The second twist is not good. There are specific limitations to the amount you can deduct for a luxury auto. And the definition of a luxury auto is very broad! Any vehicle that costs more than $15,300 qualifies as a luxury auto and that severely limits the amount you can deduct. But there is a trick to this. Vehicles over 6,000 GVW (gross vehicle weight) are exempt from the luxury auto requirements. And you can take the $25,000 deduction on these items.

The second part of the above question is how to treat assets that you donate to your company. It is very common for new business owners to have much of the needed start-up equipment — file cabinet, desk, adding machine, computer and the like.

Make sure you keep track of contributed assets and their fair market value. Don't neglect this step! You are the only one who can provide this information, and you can greatly shortchange yourself if you don't do it!

How do I get this deduction?

As always, track expenses with a good accounting system, and save canceled checks and invoices. Be aware of the potential limitations of depreciation when you do your tax planning. And, for contributed assets, get a fair market value for each asset. You can do this by checking the newspaper or visiting a local used office furniture outlet. Document (make a note in writing) the values of similar equipment.

Tax Code:

See Code Sections 1245 and 1250 and Revenue Ruling 87-56.

Auto Allowance, Purchase or Lease?

Question:

Should my company buy a vehicle or should I? When should I get an auto allowance?

Discussion:

First, I'll quote my favorite answer: "It depends." There are many options to car ownership. First, your company can buy or lease the vehicle. The company will be subject to the luxury auto rules if the vehicle is under 6,000 GVW and costs more than

54

$15,300. If this is the case, you are probably better off purchasing the car yourself and receiving an auto allowance. By the way, remember that even if your company leases a vehicle, it still can be subject to the luxury auto rules. If your company does buy or lease the vehicle, then the company should pay for all gas, oil, repairs, tires, etc. You should calculate the amount of your personal use of the vehicle and report it on your year-end W-2 or 1099. If your vehicle exceeds 6,000 GVW, your company will be able to take the Section 179, deduction plus a straight line depreciation over five years. In this case, it may be better to take the deduction.

It may be more advantageous for you to purchase the vehicle yourself and have the company reimburse you for mileage. The current mileage rate (at the time of this writing) is $0.49 per mile. You may either request reimbursement periodically or have the company reimburse you on a monthly basis at a fixed rate based on your estimated use (an auto allowance). And you can have the company reimburse you under either an accountable or non-accountable plan.

At any rate, keep track of your mileage. I carry an electronic scheduler to note all of my appointments and "to do" items. From this listing, I can easily reconstruct the mileage for each appointment or errand. I reconstruct this mileage at the end of the year, in case it is ever questioned.

Now for my opinion: I have never seen a lease that makes economic or tax sense. If you are considering that option, weigh your alternatives carefully. Read everything thoroughly and then have a professional read it thoroughly, too. If you still think it makes sense, send me a copy, and I'll read it thoroughly.

A few more points: commuting expenses between a taxpayer's residence and business location are generally not deductible. If you have more than one regular place of business, then daily transportation expenses commuting between your residence and a temporary location can be deducted.

Tax Code:
See Reg 1.162-1(a).

Special Tax Deductions

The preceding pages dealt with general business expenses. They are common to most business-owners, and tax advisors are generally very familiar with these deductions. Many of these are limited to corporations and so are added bonuses to having a corporation. However, some of them are available to any business owner. With very few exceptions most business owners and their advisors are not aware of these deductions.

I once did a quick case study for a taxpayer and showed him what benefits would be available if he incorporated. I included most of the deductions you see on the following pages. He was understandably upset to discover that he had been paying three times the amount of tax that he should have been for years. He took the case study to his CPA, whose only comment was that the figures were "… somehow misleading because some of the deductions would have been available to him without incorporating." In other words, he should have been taking them all along! And there were even more tax savings available through incorporation. That was my entire point!

However, you can have a leg up on your advisors! Study the following deductions to see which can be applied to you and learn how to make use of them.

Accountable and Non-Accountable Plans

Question:

How can I get reimbursement from my company for travel expenses? Or, how do I set up an auto allowance?

Discussion:

A business can provide for either accountable or non-accountable plans for the employees. An accountable plan is a reimbursement or expense allowance arrangement under which employees must substantiate the covered expenses to employers and return any excess amounts received. There are three criteria to meet to satisfy the accountable plan requirements:

- business connections
- substantiation
- return of amounts exceeding expenses

If your plan does not have all three of the above criteria, then it is a non-accountable plan. Amounts paid to an employee under a non-accountable plan are reported on the employee's year-end W-2 form. Amounts paid under an accountable plan are not reported anywhere.

An accountable plan may provide for an allowance for meals, incidental expenses and mileage allowances. One important point: a greater than 10 percent owner in a corporation is not allowed to take a per diem rate for meals. You may receive an expense allowance, but you must substantiate all expenditures and return any excess.

In practical terms, you would first estimate approximately how much incidental expenses, mileage allowance and meal allowance would be reasonable for a given period, such as a month. This amount is paid to you each month. Then on a periodic basis, at least annually, you would substantiate the total amount paid with a mileage log, expense reports and receipts.

Following is a summary of requirements for a non-accountable and accountable plan:

How do I get this deduction?

Determine if you are going to use a non-accountable or accountable plan. Although it is more work, you get more deductions with an accountable plan. Adopt a formal plan. Keep track of your expenses and periodically turn in your expense report to the company.

"If you think education is expensive, try ignorance."
– Derek Bok

Type of Reimbursement	Employer Reports on Form W-2
Accountable Expenses and Reimbursements are Equal	Not Shown
Reimbursements Exceed Expenses	Excess Shown
Expenses Exceed Reimbursements	Not Shown
Non-accountable	Entire Amount on W-2

Tax Code:

See Section 62(c) and Rev Proc 95-50.

Achievement Awards

Question:

How can I create a deduction for the corporation that is not taxable to me (deduction with no resulting income)?

Discussion:

One of the many items available for your business is an achievement award. In general, an employee achievement award is an item of personal property that is awarded to an employee as a presentation for length of service or safety achievement. There are two different kinds of awards that a company can make which are deductible for the corporation and tax-free to the individual. These two are the non-qualified plan and the qualified plan:

- **Non-qualified Plan Award**

An award valued up to $400 per year can be made. There are no specific guidelines, just give yourself an award for doing a good job!

- **Qualified Plan Award**

A qualified plan does require additional work, but offers a larger deduction. First, it must have a written plan that does not discriminate in favor of highly compensated employees as to eligibility or benefit. A length of service award will not qualify if it is received during the employee's first five years of service or if the employee has received a length of service award during the year or within the last four years. An award will not be considered a safety achievement award if made to a manager, administrator, clerical employee or other professional employee or if, during the tax year, awards of safety achievements previously have been made to more than 10 percent of the employees, excluding managers, administrators, clerical employees or other professional employees.

Up to $1,600 can be given under a qualified plan. Tax Tip: If you are the president and manager of your company, consider awarding your employed family members under a qualified plan. You can receive the non-qualified plan award.

How do I get this deduction?

You will need to draw up a written plan in order to use the qualified plan deduction. Regardless of which plan you use, always document the award in your minutes with the reason why the award was given (in honor of going one year with only one paper cut, the corporation awards you a set of $400 golf clubs). As always, track your expenses with a good accounting system and save your receipts!

Tax Code:

See Code 274(j)(2), Code Sec. 274(j)(3)(A), Code Sec. 274(j)(3)(B), and Code Sec. 274(j)(4).

Business Gifts

Question:

What kind of gifts can I deduct? Does the recipient have to declare it as income?

Discussion:

You are allowed to give "business gifts," up to a value of $75 per recipient per year. What is a business gift? As with most deductions, first, find a business purpose. Maybe you want to foster some goodwill with your employees, your vendors, or your next-door neighbor. These could all qualify as business gifts. Items that are clearly of advertising nature, such as an embossed coffee mug or pen and pencil, aren't counted in the total. You can exclude signs, display racks or other promotional materials given for use on business premises.

How do I get this deduction?

As always, keep track of the expenditure with a good accounting system. Additionally, make a notation (maybe on the invoice) as to whom the recipient was and maybe a few words as to why there is a business purpose. For example, let's say you give turkeys away for Thanksgiving. On the receipt from the grocery store, make a notation that you gave a turkey to each of your employees and your neighbor who collects UPS packages for you when you are gone. Also, since the cost of one turkey is probably less than $75, you can also buy a ham for Christmas for each of them! Just keep the total under $75 per recipient per year.

Tax Code:

See Code Sec. 274(b)(1) and Rev. Proc. 95-50.

"Giving is the business of the rich."
~ J.W. Goethe

Cafeteria Plans

Question:

How can I get a full deduction for day care? How can I deduct the full amount of my term life insurance?

Discussion:

A cafeteria plan is probably the answer to many of your questions. More and more employers are adding cafeteria plans. The secret they know is that cafeteria plans are easy to set up, cost little or nothing to administer and provide a savings from payroll taxes.

A cafeteria plan is an employer-sponsored benefit package that offers employees a choice between taking cash or receiving qualified benefits. A predetermined amount is withheld before taxes from an employee's paycheck that can then be used by the employee for qualified benefits. These qualified benefits include day care for children or adults, group term life insurance, medical insurance or medical expenses.

The reason that many employers like these is that the amount withheld for cafeteria plans is not subject to any payroll taxes, either by the employee or the employer. Usually your medical insurance carrier will provide a cafeteria plan for you, free of charge. Employees love the plans because they can deduct the full cost of items such as medical insurance or day care when these deductions are usually limited on their Form 1040. There are certain items that are specifically excluded, such as scholarships, education assistance and specific excludable fringe benefits. See Code Secs. 117, 127 and 132 for further information or discuss this with your insurance carrier.

How do I get this deduction?

You must have a written plan, and there are reporting requirements. Your best bet is to see your insurance agent and use one of the standard plans available. Reflect the adoption of the plan in your corporate minutes. The withholding is done out of employee checks, prior to any taxes withheld.

Tax Code:

See Code Section 125, Proposed Reg. 1.125-1, Code Secs. 117, 127 and 132.

Dependent Care

Question:

Can my corporation pay for my dependent care?

Discussion:

Your company can pay up to $5,000 ($2,500 if you are married, filing separately) in dependent care services. Amounts over these limits are taxable to you. To qualify for this benefit, the dependent must be: 1) under 13 years old, 2) physically or mentally incapable of caring for himself or herself, or 3) a spouse who is physically or mentally incapable of self-care. In addition, you can't discriminate as to who gets this benefit. In other words, if your corporation has two employees, then both must have this benefit. There are some additional requirements discussed in the following section.

Note that you cannot take this deduction if the dependent is aged 13 or over. If this is true for you, consider the cafeteria plan.

How do I get this deduction?

First, you must have a written plan. Additionally, the employee benefiting from the exclusion must report the taxpayer's identification number of the provider. Get the identification number before you give the provider anything! I have found that it can be impossible to get someone's social security number after the fact. Finally, have a good accounting system to track expenses.

Tax Code:

See Code Secs. 129 and 21(b)(1).

Dividends-received Deduction

Question:

I have heard that I can reduce the amount of taxes I pay on dividends received by having my corporation receive dividends. How does this work?

Discussion:

A corporation can take a special deduction from gross income for dividends received from domestic corporations that are subject to income tax. This deduction is:

- 70 percent of dividends received from a corporation owned less than 20 percent by the recipient
- 80 percent of dividends received for a "20 percent owned corporation" or
- 100 percent of qualifying dividends received from a member of the same affiliated group

If your corporation owns stock in corporations that are completely unrelated to your company, then you pay tax on only 30 percent of the amount of the dividends you receive. If your corporation owns 20 percent to 80 percent of the stock of the company, then you pay tax on 20 percent of the amount of dividends you receive. If your corporation is part of an affiliated group, i.e., 80 percent or more of common ownership, then you do not pay tax on any of the dividends received.

There are some special rules for foreign corporations that vary and are based on specific circumstances. If you have a concern, see Code Sec. 245(a) and (b) and talk to a tax professional.

In total, your company cannot take a deduction of more than 70 percent of its taxable income without regard to any net operating loss, dividends-received deduction, capital loss carry back or adjustment for non-taxed portions of extraordinary dividends received.

You are not allowed a dividends-received deduction for stock held by your corporation for 45 days or less. If the stock is cumulative preferred stock, it must be held at least 91 days to qualify for the deduction. Further, the dividends-received deduction is reduced by dividends received from debt-financed portfolio stock by a percentage related to the amount of debt incurred to purchase the stock. Finally, make sure that you don't fall into the personal holding corporation definition.

How do I get this deduction?

This deduction is simply taken at the time that you file your tax return. Make sure your tax preparer is aware of this seldom-used corporate advantage.

Tax Code:

See Code Secs 243, 246(c), 246A and Reg, Sec. 1.243-2.

Education Assistance

Question:

How can I deduct the cost of my advanced degree?

Discussion:

A corporation can pay up to $5,250 per year per employee for tuition, fees, books, supplies, etc., and the employee can exclude it from his or her income! Further, the exclusion is available for both undergraduate and graduate degree programs and applies even if the employee is not seeking a degree. The courses covered by the plan need not even be job-related and could be courses involving sports, games or hobbies if they involve the employer's business or are required as part of a degree program. Any excess greater than $5,250 would be included in the employee's gross income and be subject to payroll taxes and federal income tax.

How do I get this deduction?

You must have a written plan, retain records (who took what course and a brief description of the course) and file an informational return for the plan. Adopt the plan in your corporate minutes and (what a surprise) track the expense with a good accounting system.

Tax Code:

See Code Sec. 127 and 6039D and Reg. Sec 1.127-1.

Group Term Life Insurance

Question:

Can my corporation pay for my life insurance premiums?

Discussion:

Your corporation can provide $50,000 worth of term life insurance per employee. Any excess more than that amount is added to the employee's income based on a table showing the cost per $1,000 of insurance. (The current table is available through your insurance agent.) The amounts that must be included are generally minimal. It is important to note that you can't discriminate against any employee of the company with regard to this benefit.

How do I get this deduction?

See your insurance agent for a term insurance policy. Reflect the approval of the purchase of life insurance for employees in the corporate minutes. Then keep track of the expenditure with a good accounting system.

Tax Code:

See Code Sec. 79 and Reg. Secs. 1.79-1 to 1.79-3.

Health Insurance

Question:

Can my corporation pay for my health and accident insurance?

Discussion:

Health insurance is fully deductible for your corporation, as long as your plan does not discriminate against employees. Note that there are special requirements (and restrictions) for the amount of deductibility of insurance if your business is anything other than a C corporation.

How do I get this deduction?

See your insurance agent for a health plan. Then simply keep track of the expenses with a good accounting system.

Tax Code:

See Code Sec. 106 and Reg. 1.106-1.

Medical Expenses

Question:

Can my corporation pay for preventative health care items, such as vitamins or weight loss programs?

Discussion:

Corporations can deduct 100 percent on many medical expenditures if the corporation authorizes them.

How do I get this deduction?

Adopt a resolution to implement a medical reimbursement plan that covers all your preventative and ongoing health care needs. This is non-discriminatory and must be offered to all employees.

Tax Code:

See Code Sec. 105(b) and 105(h)(6).

62

Application of Golden Tax Secrets to Specific Business Situations

The Home-based Business of Leslie Smith

In Reno Nevada, the heart of the old west, it's usual for clients to have horse or dog boarding, breeding and/or training facilities. The following case study is actually a conglomerate of facts for a number of cases. I've changed the details to make it a dog grooming and boarding facility owned by a fictitious person, Leslie Smith. While I've taken a touch of literary license, the facts remain similar to many familiar cases and perhaps even your own.

Home is where the money is:

My new client Leslie Smith had a talent with animals. Leslie had successfully raised and shown her prize Bedlington Terriers. She was known as a specialist in the special clip necessary for the lively animals. And, finally, one day she decided to make the plunge and start her own boarding and grooming facility. First, she converted the garage into a complete grooming facility and set up more kennels on her acre of land. She had many of the tools for grooming already. And she formed a corporation for her new venture. Now what?

Tools:

First, Leslie listed all of the tools that she contributed to her business. These included the tables, clippers, cages and other such equipment. She then assigned a fair market value (based on what she knew they could sell for on the open market). These assets were then "sold" to the company for a promissory note, which she can then draw against (tax-free) as her company becomes profitable.

Expenses:

She kept careful track of her expenses: cost of incorporation, cost of remodeling, business cards and the like. Leslie paid some of these expenses before she started her company. The company will pay her back for these expenses and take the deduction.

Chart of Accounts:

After consulting with her CPA, Leslie set up a chart of accounts that best fit her company. She did this on a carefully selected software packet on a new computer, which was deductible. By doing this she was sure to track all of her deductions.

Filing System:

She set up a filing system to file her receipts so that she could be sure to keep all of her deductions in case she was audited.

Athletic Facility Expenses:

These allow a corporation to deduct the cost of providing athletic equipment for employees. Leslie felt that it was important for her to keep in shape so that she could

"Place yourself in the middle of the stream of power and wisdom which flows into your life."
~ Ralph Waldo Emerson

more safely handle the animals. The corporation authorized the purchase in its minutes, and she could then write off the equipment!

Office Rent Expense:

She quickly discovered that she needed to convert a spare bedroom into an office. With that addition she had 1/3 acre in kennels, her double car garage (480 square feet) and a spare bedroom (144 square feet) utilized for the business. She then perused the newspapers to determine a comparable rent for the space used by the business. She found that "storage" on bare land was the most comparable to her 1/3 acre in use for the kennels.

The bare land generally rented for $250 per month. The double car garage was most comparable to warehouse space at $0.60 per square foot — total $288 for 480 square feet. And, finally, she found that a gross (including utilities and janitorial) lease averaged $1.45 per square foot in her area (total $208.80). This all totaled $746.80 per month that the corporation would pay her for use of her home. This would be rental income to her, against which she could expense a pro-rata portion of her mortgage interest, property taxes, homeowner's insurance, utilities, janitorial expenses and depreciation for that portion of her expense.

These deductions are rental expenses against rental income on her personal income tax return. Leslie kept good records of her personal expenses for her year-end personal tax return.

Telephone:

The IRS code in Section 262, specifically states that the main telephone line cannot be a business deduction. Leslie added a second line for her business in the name of her corporation. The cost of this line is fully deductible.

Leslie was now receiving equipment, meals and $746.80 per month in rent from her corporation. These benefits are all either at greatly reduced tax rates or completely tax-free!

As her company began to make more money, we discussed the benefits of becoming an employee of the company. At some time, practically all owners will have to draw a paycheck from their corporation. Admittedly, it can be a hassle to calculate payroll taxes and make mandatory tax deposits. Leslie learned that it wasn't very hard to do and that the benefits greatly outweighed the hassles.

Of the many benefits available to employees, Leslie selected the following:

Auto Allowance:

After weighing all of the possible alternatives (buying or leasing a car herself or having the corporation buy or lease the car), she determined to buy a van, personally, and then have the corporation pay her an auto allowance. While it could have been equally beneficial to have the corporation buy the van, it would have been necessary for her to finance the van in her name because the corporation was new and couldn't qualify for credit. Also, the corporation could not take the full Section 179 deduction. This is because she had already hit the limit with all of the new additional grooming equipment, kennels and cages, tables, desk, filing cabinet, and computer and printer.

Her decision would probably have been different if the corporation had not already hit the Section 179 limit.

She estimated her miles as 1,000 per month. The corporation then began paying her an auto allowance of $300 per month. This is not reportable income to her, but she is responsible for tracking mileage and reporting it to the corporation on a steady basis. She pays for the gas and the maintenance for the van.

Achievement Award:

During her first year of business, Leslie gave herself an achievement bonus of $400 because she'd worked so hard. The $400 paid for a luxury weekend (for herself) away from the family. This was tax-free to her, a deduction for the corporation and a very welcome break!

Education Assistance Plan:

Leslie's daughter had just graduated from high school and was interested in pursuing a degree in Biology. She went to work for her mother cleaning cages and drew a small salary that helped with her out-of-pocket expenses. The salary was deductible for the corporation and, because of the daughter's low tax rate, barely taxable for the daughter. Leslie set up an education assistance plan that went up to the legal maximum of $5,000 per year for all employees. Her daughter then went to college on the company!

Group Term Insurance:

Leslie purchased a low cost term insurance policy to cover both employees. This valuable benefit was tax-free to the employees and a tax deduction for the corporation.

Health Insurance:

The corporation paid for health, vision and dental insurance for Leslie, including full dependent care. The health insurance plan also included disability insurance.

Fiscal Year-End:

One of the real benefits of a corporation is the ability to use a fiscal year-end. Leslie set up her year-end as March 31. She could have selected the end of any month, but the nature of her business lent itself to using this fiscal year-end. Her busiest time generally began about May and ran through the summer. By closing the year out just before her busy time, she would have time to catch up on accounting for her tax planning. She has also set up the year-end so that she can bonus herself in March and have a full nine months before her "individual year-end" (December 31).

Lower Corporate Tax Rate:

In February, she had compiled her income and expenses for the first 10 months of business and, from that, determined that she had about $20,000 of income left in her corporation. Since this income was taxable at the lowest corporate rate of 15 percent and additional income to her (at her individual rate) would be taxed at the higher 28 percent, we decided to not bonus additional money to her. However, she qualified for a pension plan. She contracted her local stockbroker and set up a simplified employee pension (SEP) plan for a nominal fee. She had to cover all employees who worked more than 1,000 hours in that year. Leslie was the only employee who had worked that much, so she could contribute 15 percent of her salary. This is a deduction for her company, too.

Future Plans:

As the years go on and her business grows and prospers, she will likely pay more to her children as she brings them into the business. In the second year of business, she will buy more equipment or perhaps a truck for the business in order to make full use of the Section 179 deduction.

Leslie will succeed. As she prospers, she will also likely investigate methods of asset protection and estate planning. Any of us can experience this kind of exciting future. We just need to begin to take control of it!

As you can see, the home-based business as a corporate-run entity has many tax benefits. The storefront business also has advantages if it is incorporated, as the following information will show.

Storefront Business

First, let's start with a definition of a "storefront" business. Generally, this term is used to describe a business that has a location other than your home. This is a place where you meet most of your clients or customers.

How Is a Storefront Different?

The general expenses discussed in the preceding chapters are applicable for your corporation, no matter where your business is located. Also, the beneficial deductions available to employees are available to all corporations. Obviously then, a major difference is that a corporation with a storefront cannot usually pay you rent for a location unless, of course, you directly or indirectly own it.

Source of Income:

The second issue to consider is the "source" of income. This issue is especially important to business owners in high income tax states, such as California. If you have a business selling goods that is located in Sacramento, California, it doesn't matter if you have a corporation that was started in another state. You still owe California source tax!

On the other hand, if you have a business that provides services all over the United States, such as through the Internet, you probably do not have California source tax. These are complicated issues involving controversial tax strategies that will vary based on your personal circumstances. Make sure you check with your own tax advisor regarding your own special circumstances.

Tax Traps of the Storefront:

Besides the issue of source tax discussed above, the deductibility of tenant improvements has continued to be a sore spot for taxpayers. The tax code (IRC Section 168(1)(8)) states that you must depreciate tenant improvements made to real property over the same length of time that real property should be depreciated. This is regardless of how long your lease term is. In other words, if you lease a space for two years, you can still only depreciate the improvements over 39 years. If you move out at the end of the two-year lease, you can write off the rest of the improvements.

How to Avoid this Trap:

The definition of capital improvements versus repairs becomes important in this case. A deductible expense is one that maintains property in a normal and efficient condition. A capital expense is one that adds value to the property or significantly increases its life. A deductible expense is currently expensed — deducted in the year the expense is paid. A capital expense must be depreciated over a specific term. In the case of tenant improvements, it's a long time! Note: It is not the size of the expenditure that determines if it is expensed or capitalized. Study the following chart for examples of capitalized and deductible expenses. Remember the key is to make the expenses deductible, where possible. Obviously, it will not be possible in all cases:

Capital Expenses are for Improvements that:	Deductible Expenses are for Improvements that:
1. Are materially added to the value of the property	1. Are incurred to keep the property in operating order and do not add to the value of the property
2. Prolong the life of the property	2. Do not prolong the life of the property
3. Adapt the property to a new and unforeseen different use	3. Are incurred because an event makes an asset worthless
4. Are incurred for piecemeal fashion	4. Repairs

Tenant Improvements:

When having repairs done that might be considered as reconditioning or renovation, have the work done at different times and preferably completed in different tax years instead of all at once. In this way the work may be considered currently deductible.

See the case of American Bemberg Corp (10TC 361, Aff'd 177 F2d 200), Private Letter Ruling 9411002 and IRC Section 168(I)(8) for specific points regarding these issues.

Corporate Year-End

Timing is Everything

Saved by the year-end! One important aspect of tax planning is to take a close look at projected income within your corporate year-end. For a manufacturing client, we looked at projected income within the client's two corporations before the corporate year-end. The owner's two separate corporations were located in two different parts of Nevada and produced different items.

We had decided earlier to have two different fiscal years. Corporation #1 (the older and more stable of the two) had a year-end of June 30, and Corporation #2 (only in business for two years) had a year-end of September 30. The new manager at Corporation #2 miscounted the inventory by $100,000 in September. We didn't catch it at that time due to the lack of historical information with which to compare. Suddenly, Corporation #2 had $100,000 more income than anticipated. Luckily, there had been a sale of assets from Corporation #1 to Corporation #2 just prior to September 30. We were able to justify a higher sales price than we had originally thought. This reduced the income in Corporation #2 by shuffling it off to Corporation #1. Because Corporation #1 had nine months until its year-end, we had time to plan for it — all with no tax penalty. This demonstrates just one of the many reasons for making use of fiscal year-ends for your corporation.

Fiscal Year-End:

One of the greatest benefits of a corporation is the fiscal year-end. Use the fiscal year-end (a year-end other than a calendar year-end) to defer tax on payments to you for up to 11 months. By using fiscal year-end, you can stagger payments between corporations to maximize deductions and provide a safety net for tax planning. You'll get better advice if the year-end does not end during your accountant's busiest time!

Select a Fiscal Year-End:

Your corporation can have a year-end of any month-end date. It is generally easier, as a practical matter, to have a year-end that is on a quarter-end — for example, March 31, June 30 or September 30.

New Corporation:

If you are setting up your corporation, use form SS-4, Request for Employment Identification Number. On Form SS-4, fill in the date you have selected (3/31, 6/30, 9/30, etc.). That is now the year-end for your corporation. The tax return will be due 2.5 months after the closing date. An extension can increase the due date by six months.

Existing Corporation:

If you have already selected a calendar year-end and wish to now change it, you may if:

- the corporation has not changed its accounting period at any time within the six calendar years ending with the calendar year that includes the beginning of the short period required to effect the proposed change;

- the short period required to effect the change is not one in which the corporation has a net operation loss;
- the taxable income for the short period is, when annualized, at least 80 percent of the taxable income for the preceding tax year;
- the corporation is a personal holding company, a foreign personal holding company, an exempt organization, or a nonresident foreign corporation and has had the same status for both the short period and the preceding tax year; and
- the corporation does not try to make an S corporation election for the tax year that immediately follows the short period required to effect the change

If you meet these required conditions, file Form 1128 before the due date (including extensions) of the short period return. A return is then filed for the short period.

Avoid Potential Corporate Traps

Don't make this mistake! It was the first time I had prepared a return for my new corporate client. And, like so many others, he had the mistaken idea that all a CPA did was take his numbers and put them on a form. There hadn't been any advanced planning. So what we saw was what we got! I was totally dismayed to discover that my new client, an ophthalmologist, had a C corporation with a calendar year-end.

He ran the sales of eyeglasses through the same company. The net income from the sale of the eyeglasses was small compared to the bulk of his income (from personal service). This meant his income within the corporation was subject to the higher personal service tax of 34 percent. The lack of prior planning for my client didn't help him for that year, but we made changes for the next year.

First, we created a new corporation for the sale of eyeglasses (Corporation #2) with a year-end of June 30. We had Corporation #2 pick up a pro-rata portion of office overhead, but little other expense. The pro-rata split was based on actual square footage. We then changed the year-end of Corporation #1 to March 31 and ran the remainder of overhead and the doctor's salary against this corporation. The plan was to minimize income on Corporation #1 and allow enough time (from March 31 to December 31) to defer taxes if we needed to do a large bonus to the owner. We had also utilized the lower tax rate for corporations for Corporation #2 by setting up a corporation that was exempt from the personal services tax. Finally, we staggered year-ends for future tax planning opportunities.

"Jumping at several small opportunities may get us there more quickly than waiting for one big one to come along."
– Hugh Allen

Who Says Accounting Isn't Fun?

There are two corporate traps of which you need to be aware: the personal holding company and the personal service company. A brief description follows.

Personal Holding Company

In addition to the regular tax on corporate income, a special 39.6 percent tax is imposed on the "undistributed personal holding company income" of a personal holding company.

Definition:

A personal holding company is any corporation in which: 1) at least 60 percent of adjusted ordinary gross income for the tax year is personal holding company income and 2) at any time during the last half of the tax year more than 50 percent of the value of its outstanding stock is owned, directly or indirectly, by or for not more than five individuals.

Personal Holding Company Income:

Personal holding company income consists of dividends, interest, royalties, rents (unless they constitute 50 percent or more or the adjusted ordinary gross income, and the sum of: a) dividends paid during the tax year, b) dividends considered to be paid on the last day of the tax year, amounts received by a corporation from contracts for personal services, including gain from the sale or other disposition, and other non-earned income.

Adjusted Gross Income:

In determining whether 60 percent or more of a corporation's adjusted ordinary gross income is personal holding company income, the following adjustments must be made:

- Rental income must be reduced by depreciation, taxes, interest and rents
- Royalties must be reduced by depreciation, depletion, taxes, interest and rents

All capital gains are excluded in determining whether the 60 percent test has been met.

This is just a brief encapsulation of the special rules regarding a personal holding company. If you may fall into this area, seek professional tax advice.

Personal Service Company

Definition:

A personal service company is a corporation in which the principle activity is the performance of personal services that are substantially performed by employee-owners. An employee-owner is any employee who owns more than 10 percent of the outstanding stock of the corporation. Further, a personal service corporation is specifically identified as any corporation "substantially all of the activities of which involve the performance of services in the fields of health, law, engineering, architecture, accounting, actuarial science, performing arts or consulting." The Internal Revenue Code is quite specific in Sections 269A and 448 as to the definition of personal service corporations.

So What if Mine is Considered a Personal Service Corporation?

The corporate tax rate for a personal service company is a flat 35 percent. There is no graduation of tax rates such as in a regular corporation. I have one client where the wife is a high-income physician and the husband is a high-paid consultant. In their case, a personal service corporation was a great solution. This was because their marginal tax rate from the wife's income was 39.6 percent and with the corporation the couple could pay 4.6 percent less tax and get many corporate advantages. However, under most circumstances most people would want to avoid a personal service corporation designation.

How do I Avoid this?

For many people, such as the ophthalmologist in my example above, there is no way around the personal service corporation designation for a portion of their income. Some people can redefine exactly what their corporation does, and thereby change the tax implications. See your tax advisor if you are concerned about this aspect of your corporation.

Conclusion

- Remember: the tax code is constantly changing.
- Always consult with your accountant to verify that the figures you are using are current and to ensure compliance with any special rules governing each deduction.
- Use the Golden Tax Secrets given in this chapter as a guide.
- The federal government and the IRS make it possible (they actually help you) to function profitably as an entrepreneur. However, you have to know how to use the tax codes effectively in your business. To gain the maximum benefits from the tax codes you need to incorporate your business.
- If you operate a storefront business, you will need to incorporate in your home state.
- You can use the multiple corporate strategies and other entities to help you minimize your taxes.
- Plan your corporate year-end to your advantage.
- Be aware of potential corporate tax traps, which include those related to a personal holding company and a personal service company.

Section Three:
Advanced Strategies for Corporations
Navigating Your Corporation

Chapter 1:
The Who, What, When, Where, Why and How

- Who gets the income? Take advantage of the dual tax rate and discover how it can make a huge difference in your taxes.
- What type of income? How to change the characterization of income.
- When do you get income? How to set up your company with the proper timing.
- Where do you receive the income? When can a Nevada corporation earn the income?
- How can you benefit from even more tax advantages?

Chapter 2:
Avoiding the "Traps" of Corporations

- Double taxation — how to set up your company so you never face this danger!
- Personal holding company — why and how you should avoid it!
- Controlled group status — when controlling everything and owning nothing really counts!
- Accumulated earnings taxation — just when you thought everything was going great, here's a new tax to worry about! Plus, how not to worry about it.
- When not to use a C corporation.

Chapter 1:
The Who, What, When, Where, Why and How

One of the biggest advantages of C corporations over all other forms of business structures is that they are not flow-through entities. That means that a corporation pays its own tax on its own income. Consider what that meant for Mike, the owner of a construction company, in 1998:

Before:

Mike was the successful owner of a small construction company, operating through a Limited Liability Company. In 1998, after all businesses expenses, he still had taxable income of $120,000. Mike had two teenage children who helped out, but he had never employed them in his business. Mike discovered how he could use a corporation to his advantage after the tax year was finished. He learned quickly how much he would save the next year, with the right structure!

Taxable Income after business expenses	$120,000
Taxes: Self-employment Tax	$11,696
Federal Income Tax	26,813
State Income Tax	5,899
Total Taxes	$44,408

After (as a C corporation):

Mike immediately began his new tax strategy as a C corporation using the value of tax rate differences. He employed his children in the business so that he could take advantage of the lower tax rates they had. He drew a reasonable salary and then left taxable income within the corporation for investments. In this way, he took advantage of all the lowest tax rates possible.

Justin (age 16) — Salary $6,200 — P/R Taxes		$992
Megan (age 15) — Salary $6,200 — P/R Taxes		992
Mike — Salary $50,000 — P/R Taxes		$8,000
Federal Income Taxes	$8,500	
State Income Taxes	$1,700	
Corporation — Taxable Income		$120,000
Justin		(6,200)
Megan		(6,200)
Mike		(50,000)
P/R Taxes (all three)		(4,649)
		67,392
Corporate Taxable Income		$52,608

Taxes Now

Payroll Taxes (Corporate and Individual)	$9,984
Corporate Federal Income Taxes	$8,152
Corporate State Income Taxes	$4,208
Personal federal Income Taxes (Mike)	$8,500
Personal State Income Taxes (Mike)	$1,700

Total Taxes Paid	$32,544
Before Corporation	$44,408
After Corporation	$32,544
Tax Savings	$11,864

Or over 26 percent reduction in taxes!

The tax savings come from distributing income from one big tax bracket to three others. The other three brackets were those of Mike's two children, Justin and Megan, and that of his corporation. The only tax for his children came from payroll taxes on the salary they drew. He then paid tax on the amount he drew as a salary, and the corporation paid tax on the income left after the salaries were paid.

United States income taxes are calculated based on a rate table. While the "threshold" amounts vary from year to year, the concept has been the same almost since the beginning of our federal income tax system.

The "threshold" refers to the amount by which the rate changes. For example, the first $50,000 of a corporation is taxed at 15 percent and the next $25,000 is taxed at 25 percent. That means if a corporation earns $60,000 the first $50,000 is taxed at 15 percent and the rest is taxed at 25 percent. The threshold amount in this case is $50,000. When the income exceeds that amount, the tax rate on the excess portion goes to 25 percent.

"One of the secrets of life is to make stepping stones out of stumbling blocks."

~ *Jack Penn*

The secret in determining who gets the income is to take advantage of lower tax brackets. In Mike's case, the income was spread over his, the corporation's and his children's tax brackets.

What was the result?

He saved over 26 percent in taxes — just by taking advantage of the tax rate tables!

Conclusion

- Identify all possible tax rate schedules — corporations, children, parents, etc.
- Reduce tax liability by spreading income over available tax brackets.
- Maximize the use of the lowest percentage tax brackets.

What Type of Income?

You know what income is, right? It is the amount of money you make! Well, it's not as simple as it used to be, ever since the 1986 Tax Reform Act came along. Now income is grouped by type of income. Congress turned a relatively tough tax code into an unbelievably tough tax code in 1986. That's why accountants called it the "full employment act."

However, the concept of income groups really isn't that difficult. Besides, learning the difference in these groups can save you a lot of tax dollars! The first step in tax planning is to identify the type of income you need and the type of losses you have, as Joe and Sara learned.

Sara was employed as a veterinarian and Joe had his own computer consulting business. Sara's wage income put them into a higher tax bracket with no ability for tax planning. Luckily, Joe's business allowed them flexibility in their tax planning. Joe and Sara learned that there are three types of income.

Earned	W-2 wages
	Self-employed wages
Passive	Rental
	Royalties

Partnership and S-Corporation income

Portfolio	Interest and Dividends
	Capital gains/losses

Income and losses in these three categories, for the most part, stay in those categories. For example, passive losses offset passive income, capital losses offset capital gains and investment (portfolio) income. You are limited in how much additional loss you can take against earned income.

"You are never given a wish without also being given the power to make it come true. You may have to work for it, however."
~ Richard Bach

Trap of the W-2 Wage Earner

The typical W-2 wage earner only has earned income. He or she might attempt to diversify earnings and buy investments that he or she is told will "create" losses for them. In most cases, these losses are not allowed to offset against the earned income. The losses become "suspended," held for future use against hopefully future gains in the right area.

Before

Although Joe had his own business, he had set up his business so he took income as a self-employed person with a Schedule C, sole proprietorship. That meant that he had only earned income, just like his wife, Sara, did.

They wanted to diversify into a real estate partnership. They knew that one of the benefits of real estate ownership is the depreciation that is created providing tax losses, even though there is actual cash flow. But not for them!

At tax time, Joe and Sara realized that the tax loss they received from the investment was not available to them. So year after year, the benefit of real estate depreciation was suspended and held for future conditions that never occurred.

At the end of five years, the total amount suspended was: $9,090

The $10,000 investment provided no tax benefit at all to them.

After

As Joe and Sara learned about the different groups of income, they realized that they needed passive income to offset the lost (until now) passive loss. First, Joe incorporated his business in order to take advantage of all the special corporate deductions.

Next, Joe looked at his business location. Joe was renting office space for his business and he and Sara had been talking about investing in more real estate in their economically developing area.

They located a small commercial building that was about three times larger than current needs demanded. By buying this investment, Joe was able to rent out the other two-thirds of the building to cover the mortgage payment. His business began paying a fair market rent and created an expense for his business. This created passive income for Joe and Sara, as the building owners. But the passive income was offset by the passive loss from their other investment.

They had changed the character of the income received from Joe's business. Before, they had earned income — subject to self-employment tax and without the benefit of the tax loss from their passive investment. However, when they bought a building for the business and began paying rent to themselves, they lowered the earned income and created passive income.

What did this mean for their taxes?

Additional rent paid (annually)	$12,000
Reduction in self-employment tax	$1,696
Passive loss offset tax benefit	$564
Total	$2,260

But this is only the beginning! Joe and Sara now fully enjoy the benefits of real estate investing, being able to further offset the rent they receive by the depreciation on the building, and they can participate in the tax-free or tax-deferred building appreciation. The cash flow from the investment is greater than the taxable income. In addition, self-employment tax is lowered and they now make use of passive losses previously unavailable to them!

Change the Type of Income

You can receive income from your corporation in a number of ways. This often-overlooked benefit can make a significant difference on your tax return. For example, if you have:

Carry-Forward Capital Losses

Look for ways that your company can create a capital gain for you. Can the corporation buy an asset from you at a price that creates a gain for you? This asset can be depreciated or expensed by the corporation to provide even greater deductions!

Carry-Forward Investment Expenses

Do you have margin interest expenses or other investment expenses that you have been unable to write off? One of the easiest ways to create investment income is to loan money to your corporation so that the company is obligated to pay you interest. The interest is a deduction to the corporation and is investment income to you, not subject to self-employment tax, and can be used to offset those investment expenses (such as the margin interest)!

Conclusion

- Identify unused potential or current losses on your tax return.
- Structure income you receive from your corporation to turn "lost" losses into real gains.

"If we all did the things we are capable of doing, we would literally astound ourselves."
~ Thomas A. Edison

When to Pay Your Taxes

Tax planning is all about eliminating tax or deferring tax. In the happy past, one of the effective ways to defer tax was to move taxable income out as far as possible. By moving the tax, you could then take advantage of the time value of money. A dollar today is worth a lot more than a dollar tomorrow. So if you can move tax into the future, then you effectively pay less tax.

All business owners used to take advantage of this timing difference by having the year-end for their business different than the calendar year-end. That way, if their business year-end was January 31 and they discovered during pre-year-end tax planning that their business had too much income, they could bonus out to themselves. The deduction for the bonus happened before the business year-end at January 31, but the owner had 11 months, personally, to pay the tax!

Tax planning became very different after the enactment of the 1986 Tax Reform Act. That is because all business structures, with one exception, were forced to take a calendar year-end. The one exception, of course, is the C corporation.

What is the benefit of different year-ends?

Marie had a successful manufacturing company that, luckily, was in a C corporation with a year-end of March 31. Near the end of March, she discovered that she had made a mistake in counting inventory that increased the company's income by nearly $100,000. If her business had been held in an S corporation, an LLC, partnership or as a sole proprietorship she would have had no choice but to pay tax at the higher rate as the amount added on top of her regular income.

\But Marie owned a C corporation. She was able to pay a bonus to herself. And, as most business owners can relate, she needed to loan the money right back to the company. But the expense had been recorded on the corporation's books and so the tax due for the year-end at March 31 was what we had anticipated.

Marie would owe income taxes on the $100,000 additional that she had paid to herself, so what had she gained? She gained breathing room. She had nine months to restructure her tax planning and accommodate that income. In her case, she was able to reduce the corporation's taxable income and not pay any more tax personally. She was able to "even out" her taxes simply through the use of the different tax years.

How Much Money Did She Save?

If she operated her business as an S corporation, the additional money would have been taxed at her personal level, and there would have been no tax planning. The cost for her would have been:

If S Corporation:

Federal taxes	$39,600
State Taxes	$7,920
Total Taxes	$47,520

Because she had the time to plan for additional income, she paid no taxes.

This tax savings wouldn't be true in every case though. It is possible that the taxes would still have been due, just nine months later. An average savings based on the time value of money would be $3,500.

Possible Tax Savings	$3,500 to $47,530

The Key Advantage is Time!

The best benefit of being able to pick year-ends is that you simply give yourself more time. With multiple corporations, not under controlled group status, and alternating year-ends, you have the ability to stagger taxes.

Conclusion

- Select a year-end for your C corporation different than the calendar year-end.
- Schedule tax planning in advance of year-ends to minimize tax rate and maximize timing flexibility.

Where Do You Receive Income?

Do you live in a state that taxes your business income? You may be able to legally reduce or eliminate that tax and receive better asset protection.

In the example below, my clients have had good success with using Nevada as their corporate headquarters. Nevada has no disclosure of shareholders, allows one person to serve as a director and officer (who can be a nominee), no state income tax, and no disclosure of assets or income with any other state or with the IRS.

Direct Marketing Business

Tim and Carly had built a successful direct marketing business. They lived in California and ran their business through a corporation based there. In 1988, when I first met them, their taxes were:

Taxable Income   (after expenses) $100,000

They ran their business as a sole proprietorship, located in California, so they paid a substantial amount of taxes:

Self-employment Tax	$14,130
Federal Income Tax	$22,495
California Income Tax	$8,298
Total Taxes	$44,923

One of the huge advantages of a multi-level marketing business, besides the true passive income stream, is that the income can be legitimately earned anywhere the company office is!

Tim and Carly contacted the MLM company with which they were affiliated and learned what was necessary to transfer the income stream to the Nevada corporation. They set up a legitimate business office with phone, fax, physical address, etc. in Nevada and then allowed the income to be received in Nevada, which has no state income tax.

Tim and Carly continued to reside in California, so the personal income they received was taxed at their individual income tax rate. But because they received so many non-taxable benefits from the company — health care, car allowance, etc. — their personal income did not need to be very high to meet their living expenses.

In this case, they were able to legitimately take only $1,500 per month in salary. This meant $420 per year in California state income taxes.

The savings in California taxes was: $7,878

The saving of over $7,800 in California income tax is in addition to the other tax savings of over $25,000 possible through incorporation techniques discussed in the previous chapter. That means a total tax savings of almost $33,000!

Texas Consulting Company

Amy had a marketing consulting company located in Austin, Texas. She had developed a program for real estate professionals that helped them find and retain clients. This systematic program was written and held in multiple binders. Amy worked with real estate offices, teaching the techniques to the agents and developing in-house programs.

Could this Consulting Firm Be Moved to Nevada?

One of Amy's first questions to me was whether she could incorporate in Nevada to reduce or eliminate the Texas income tax on the business income. The answer, unfortunately, was that she could not. Business income is earned based on where the product or service is located and where the order is placed. In Amy's case, she performs a function at her client's site exclusively in the Texas area, receiving payment in Texas. It differs from the direct marketing company where once established, passive income goes directly to a company located where you wish.

Upstream Income

There was still a solution possible to Amy, however. She was able to "upstream" income to Nevada.

In her case, a separate C corporation was established in Nevada. This business was held separately from her Texas business, so that no controlled group status existed. The Nevada business held ownership of the product — the manual training system. A royalty was paid to the Nevada corporation for each use of that system. This royalty was income to Nevada, but a deduction to her Arizona business.

Texas					Nevada
Income					
(Expense)	=		=	=	Income
Reduced Income					Income — Nevada

In other words, her Texas taxable income was reduced by the amount that was earned in Nevada. She upstreamed income from Texas to Nevada.

"Take action. Seize the moment. Man was never intended to be an oyster."

– Theodore Roosevelt

How Did She Do That?

There is nothing difficult about the technique of upstreaming. But there are important steps to follow in order to successfully upstream:

- There must be a legitimate business formed with a product or service to sell.
- The minutes of all involved companies must reflect the agreement of the Nevada business to sell the product or service to the other state.
- A written contract must be prepared to reflect the agreement.
- Invoices must be prepared by the Nevada company to charge the other state business.
- Payment must be made by the other state business to Nevada.

Two Techniques Using Nevada Corporations:

Tim and Carly used their Nevada corporation to run their business directly. In order to make use of the more favorable Nevada tax laws, Anne needed to form an additional corporation headquartered in Nevada.

Tim and Carly had income go directly into their Nevada corporation. Amy used the technique of upstreaming to move income from her home state into the Nevada corporation. This created the same effect that Tim and Carly found — that of reducing or eliminating the income in their home state. But it was necessary for Anne to use an additional corporation and upstreaming to accomplish that.

The two techniques demonstrated here are:
Single Nevada Corporation:

If it can be proven that income is earned within Nevada and there is no nexus (point of sale) within the home state, a single corporation can be set up within Nevada. Typically, the best use of the single Nevada corporation structure is with passive income.

Multiple Corporations:

If it is clear that income is earned in your resident (home) state, then it will be necessary to set up an additional corporation and use the principle of upstreaming.

Conclusion

- Determine if the Nevada corporate strategy is right for you.
- If so, identify which Nevada corporate strategy type is best in your circumstance
  — single Nevada corporation or multiple corporations
- Set up the corporation properly with a physical business presence within the state of Nevada.
- If upstreaming, follow additional steps:
  — determine a legitimate business purpose
  — document decisions with proper corporate minutes
  — prepare written contracts to reflect the agreements
  — prepare invoices to show legitimate expenses
  — make payments to show an accurate money and audit trail

Why Use a Corporation?

We are frequently asked, "Why do I have to use a corporation. I read on the Internet that an LLC was the best structure."

Or "I heard from my neighbor that I should use an S corporation for my business."

Or "I talked to my banker and he said that it wasn't worth the trouble to incorporate and that I should be a sole proprietor."

What Is So Special About C Corporations?

The C Corporation is the oldest business structure around and dates back to the days of the old sailing ships in England. Yet it is not outdated for tax planning today. The fact that there are years of tax law supporting the C corporation means that tax planning is much easier because it is clear how the courts will view certain strategies. That means we can be sure of the laws supporting a certain tax position, as well as the asset protection in place.

However, more importantly, the C corporation is the only truly separate "legal person." That means that the C corporation is just like another individual — it pays its own taxes at its own rate. And that tax rate, just as with your individual tax rate, is graduated. Only in a C corporation can you take the benefit of "who gets the income."

If you receive income from your sole proprietorship, it is always earned income. You cannot receive passive income from your active business. The same is true for a general partnership and, in most cases, an LLC. Only the C corporation gives you the full benefit of determining "what type of income."

The C corporation is the only entity that is able to select a business year-end different from a calendar year-end. Only the C corporation can decide "when to pay your taxes."

All other types of business structure are flow-through entities. This means that income received within these companies flows though to the individual business owner. They operate as a pseudo-self in business and, in some types of business setups, with dangerous liability, too! Only the C corporation is a separate entity.

How Can You Benefit from Even More Tax Advantages?

Up to this point in this section, we have discussed some possibly new ideas for you in tax planning using C corporations. But what next?

The next step is to take action. If you feel that the C corporation is the best structure for your business, then consult with the right advisors to set up the corporation and map out your personalized tax strategy.

And, of course, you continually want to increase your financial education to keep up-to-date on new tax changes or learn new twists on old tax laws. You can receive that financial education in many ways — be a frequent visitor to your local bookstore or library, read business and financial books and attend financial and taxation seminars to hear other ideas and perspectives. I personally recommend the fine educational products available from Sage International, Inc.

If you are like most people, all of that new information will create uncertainty. Great!

It's that uncertainty (and your resolve to work through it) that propels you to move your business and your financial health on to new levels.

After each new educational step, you need to take action. Consult with the right advisors and mentors regarding your business as you grow and move to the next level.

Conclusion

- Continue to learn more about business structures and tax planning strategies.
- Lock in your new education by consulting with the proper advisors to develop your personalized plan of action.
- Take action!

"By perseverance the snail reached the ark."
– Charles Spurgeon

Chapter 2:
Avoiding the "Traps" of Corporations

How to Set Up Your Company So You Never Face These Dangers

"A C corporation! That's the stupidest thing you could do. You would have double taxation!" Have you heard that? Have you thought that? Do you really know what double taxation is?

What Is Double Taxation?

The term "double taxation" refers to what happens when the corporation and the individual owner both pay tax on the same income. In other words, there is double tax paid.

When Does Double Taxation Occur?

Double taxation occurs only in a few select cases. Most expenses that a corporation pays are deducted against the income of the corporation, so there is no double taxation.

There is one notable exception — when dividends are paid to the shareholder(s). Dividends are not deducted against the corporation's income and they are taxable to the shareholder.

Liquidating Dividends

Double taxation can also occur when a corporation is liquidated. For example, if you sell off all the assets of your corporation and then dissolve the corporation, you receive something the IRS calls a "liquidating dividend." There is no deduction for the corporation because it doesn't exist anymore and you have to pay tax on the income.

How to Avoid Double Taxation

In the first case, the way to avoid double taxation is not to pay dividends. Instead, find other ways to compensate owners through salary and benefits.

In the second case, don't sell off the assets and immediately dissolve the corporation. In fact, if you are selling your qualifying small business corporation, there can be tremendous exclusions from capital gains if you do it the right way! Those exclusions do not occur for any other form of business entity except a C corporation.

Why Is Only a C Corporation Subject to Double Taxation?

Double taxation starts with the fact that a C corporation pays tax on its own net income. It is not a pass-through entity, such as an LLC, limited partnership, S corporation or limited liability partnership. After income is received, there are many choices for how the money (income) can be spent within the corporation — expenses, benefits, salaries, retirement plans or other tax-deductible expenses for the corporation … or it can be paid out in dividends.

All but one of these expenses are deductions for the corporation. That means if your corporation has taxable income in year one, and resulting cash left in the account, the corporation can pay the expenses that are deductions against year two's income. And if there is no income next year, the loss can be carried back to the previous year for a refund. Double taxation does not occur here because while tax is paid initially, there is a deduction against income as expenses are paid.

How to Always Take Advantage of Deductions

Following are two examples. In Example one, salary is paid to the owner in the second year and there is no income to offset in that year. The salary income is taxable to the owner and a deduction to the corporation.

Example One:
Year One

Taxable Income	**$50,000**
Tax at 15 percent	$7,500

Year Two Corporation					**Year Two** Individual	
Income	$50,000					
Salary (30,000)		=	=	=	Income	$30,000
Taxable	$20,000				Taxable	$30,000

Salary paid to the owner is a deduction to the corporation and income to the owner — no double taxation here!

In Example Two, there is no income in the second year, but salary is paid to the owner. The net loss is carried back to the previous year, resulting in a deduction to the corporation, even though there was no income.

Example Two:

Year one

Taxable Income	**$50,000**
Tax at 15 percent	$7,500

Year Two			**Year Two**	
Corporation			Individual	
Corporation				
Income	-0-			
Salary	(30,000)	= = =	Income	$30,000
Net Loss	(30,000)		Taxable	$30,000

Prior Year

Income — Year One	$50,000
Loss — Year Two	(30,000)
Income	$20,000
Tax Refund	$4,500

Salary paid to the owner is a deduction to the corporation that is taken in a previous year when there is income — no double taxation here!

Plan Now to Avoid Double Taxation

The examples above demonstrate (one with continuing business income and one without business income) how the double taxation issue can be avoided.

There are many other ways to compensate owners with benefits that are not taxable to the owner and, in effect, become double deductions! The key point regarding double taxation is that you need to plan at the beginning of each tax year to avoid this issue.

Get the Right Advisors

The C corporation is not the best solution for every type of business. As with all business planning issues, you must have the right advisors helping you with your overall plan. But above all, don't avoid the C corporation structure because of this easily overcome objection.

Conclusion

- Don't pay yourself dividends from your C corporation.
- Look for all the ways a corporation can pay you using legitimate tax deductions.
- Always check your tax strategy with experienced tax advisors.

Personal Holding Company — Why and How You Should Avoid It!

Special Dividend Tax Rate for Corporations

Joann was a successful real estate developer who loved to speculate. Yet for financial security, she would maintain a fairly conservative stock portfolio with plenty of blue chip stocks paying dividends to her. She was very excited to learn that her significant dividend income (and the resulting tax) could be lowered drastically through a C corporation structure. In fact, only 30 percent of the dividends received in a C corporation are subject to income tax.

What a C Corporation Could Mean

Joann's dividend income was $20,000 per year and was being added to her already high income. She paid the highest possible federal and state tax rates on that income.

Before:

Income		$20,000
Federal Income Tax	$7,920	
State Income Tax	$1,740	
Total Tax	$9,660	

Proposed:

Income	$20,000
C Corporate Deduction	(14,000)
Taxable Dividend Income	$6,000

Tax:	
Federal Income Tax	$900

(She also avoided state income tax by forming a Nevada corporation.)

Personal Holding Company

However, if Joann creates a C corporation only to hold her investments, then it is deemed to be a personal holding company. A personal holding company can not take the special dividend reduction and, even worse, there is a tax on "undistributed" personal holding income of 39.6 percent.

The IRS defines a personal holding company as a corporation that:
- has 60 percent or more personal holding income compared to adjusted gross income

and
- has five or fewer individuals owning 50 percent or more of outstanding stock

Personal Holding Company Income

Personal holding company income includes dividends, interest, royalties, annuities, rents (unless they constitute 50 percent or more of the adjusted ordinary income) and personal service contracts where the person performing the work is specified.

All other forms of income (including rent where 50 percent of more of the income comes from rent) are not personal holding company income.

How to Avoid Personal Holding Company Status

If Joann put only her dividend-paying stock into the corporation, she would have a personal holding company because 60 percent or more of the corporate income was personal holding company income and she was the only shareholder. She then passed the test of a personal holding company by meeting the two requirements. But this is one test she didn't want to pass.

In Joann's case, the question was how she could flunk the personal holding company test on purpose.

One way to fail was by having more than five people hold 50 percent of the stock.

She could also fail the test based on the income proportion. She knew her dividend income would be roughly $20,000 per year and the income she earned was clearly considered personal holding company income. So how could she create net income of at least $14,000 per year that was not portfolio income? (Adding $14,000 in income would equal $34,000, making the $20,000 only 58.8 percent — less than 60 percent.)

That was relatively easy for Joann to do by putting a portion of her real estate business into her C corporation. In fact, she saved even more taxes by moving that business into her C corporation.

Note: Personal holding company tests can be more complicated than in Joann's case.

It is always advised that you have a competent tax planner involved in creating your plan. It is imperative to specifically address personal holding company issues if you plan to hold portfolio income within your corporation.

Conclusion
- Plan to fail the personal holding company test!
- Have five or more stockholders own 50 percent of the stock

Or

- Ensure that at least 41 percent of the corporate adjusted gross income will not be personal holding company income.

Controlled Group Status

What It Is and How to Avoid It!

" I love the idea of moving my income to a C corporation and only paying 15 percent on the first $50,000 of income. In fact, I make about $200,000 per year, so I'll just set up four corporations to make $50,000 per year in each and only pay 15 percent tax rate on all the money!" exclaimed Tom, testing ideas for corporations for the first time.

Tom's Problem

Tom found out that he couldn't work his tax strategy quite like he had thought. The reason was because of the concept of controlled groups.

What Is a Controlled Group?

There are two types of controlled groups — parent-subsidiary and brother-sister. Following are the abbreviated definitions of the two types. There are more steps involved in determining controlled groups, but the purpose here is not necessarily to make you a complete expert, but rather to give you an overview. Use this information to see if there could be an issue and then seek the right advisors.

Parent-Subsidiary.

This exists if one corporation owns 80 percent of the stock of another corporation.

Brother-Sister.

This exists when five or fewer people own at least 80 percent of the voting stock of two or more corporations and these same people own more than 50 percent of each corporation. Both conditions must be met for a brother-sister relationship to occur.

What Controlled Group Status Means

When two or more companies are determined to have controlled group status, their income must be consolidated — as if there were only one company.

That means that there is only one graduated tax rate table, one Section 179 deduction, a limit on foreign tax credits and one accumulated earnings credit. All inter-company transfers of income and expenses must be eliminated. In other words, if one company sells a product or service to another company within the group, that transaction must be wiped out for both companies.

In some cases, it is beneficial to be under controlled group status. That is because the earnings of one company can be used to offset the losses of another,

Tom's Solution

Tom wanted to make use of multiple corporations and was resolved to find a way to solve the controlled group problem. In his case, he had unrelated (unrelated by blood or marriage) people in his life who had helped him along the way. He was very interested in partnering with them in these companies.

Tom ended up creating three corporations for his three separate businesses — a multi-level marketing company (which he headquartered in Nevada), a construction company and a real estate sales office.

He sold and gifted shares in the corporations (in varying amounts) to a total of nine people so that the ownership did not fall under the controlled group status.

Conclusion

* If using multiple corporations, investigate whether your companies would fall under controlled group status.
* Consult with tax advisors to determine if controlled group status is desirable in your case.

Accumulated Earnings Tax

Just When You though Everything Was Going Great, Here's a New Tax to Worry About!

Life was looking great to the ten owners of ABC, Inc. In the beginning they had a few years of struggling with income, but the past five years had been profitable. After paying all of their benefits and salaries, they still had $50,000 of income in each of the previous years.

Maximizing the tax rate tables, they "left" the $50,000 of taxable income in the company at the low 15 percent tax rate.

Well, life had looked great until they learned about accumulated earnings tax.

What Is Accumulated Earnings Tax?

Every C corporation runs the risk of being subject to this additional tax of 39.6 percent assessed on accumulated earnings in excess of $250,000 ($150,000 for personal service corporations). This tax is in addition to the regular tax paid by the corporation.

90

ABC, Inc. had just reached the $250,000 threshold ($50,000 x 5 years) and now had to face this tax. But first their Board wanted to find out more about accumulated earnings and, more importantly, how to avoid it.

What Is Accumulated Earnings?

This is a much-litigated portion of the tax code and, interestingly, the case law does not mirror the IRS Code and Regulations. The simple definition, from the IRS Code and Regulations, states that accumulated earnings are the previously taxed income in the corporation reduced by any capital gain. In other words, they are the retained earnings held by the corporation without any capital gains reflected.

There has been significant case law supporting the "Bardahl Formula," which basically states that accumulated income is actually the working capital of the company.

ABC's Solution

There are actually a number of solutions to the problem. First, the IRS makes a specific exclusion for an amount necessary for the running of the business. So first the accumulated earnings (however calculated) can be reduced by capital necessary for the business cycle. Examples of this would be additional inventory, down cycles in the business, additional equipment and future construction — as long as it relates to the business! A statement needs to be attached to the corporation's tax return that states the purpose of the accumulated earnings.

Another potential solution, and one especially favorable for owners, is the purchase by the corporation of a split dollar life insurance policy on the life of the owner. The insurance premium reduces the accumulated earnings and allows cash to grow, tax-free, on behalf of the owner.

There are many issues revolving around the split dollar life insurance and so it is important you have a very knowledgeable insurance agent involved in the development of this plan.

Conclusion

- Consult with your financial advisor if you believe accumulated earnings is a potential problem.

When Not to Use a Corporation

A tax strategy is something you can't just read out of a book and reproduce in your life. Each of us is different. We all have different goals, different living expenses and different obligations. A customized financial plan and tax strategy is essential to maximize our personal talents and provide for our needs and desires.

The C corporation structure is one of the tools that can be used to build your strategic tax plan — but it is not for everyone or for every circumstance! For instance:

- If your business will incur significant start-up and ongoing losses. Unlike the S corporation, you cannot take advantage of losses in the C corporation to write off your personal W-2 income. If you are only a W-2 wage earner, the C corporation will not help you with your personal taxes.
- Personal Service Corporation as indicated on page 67.
- Holding appreciating real estate. Capital gains are treated as an individual gain.

Robert Kiyosaki, the international best-selling author of "Rich Dad, Poor Dad" likes to say, "The S in S corporation stands for SMALL! The C corporation is for people who want to think big."

This really is true. In most instances, if you don't plan on creating a business with the greatest wealth producing capability, then the C corporation is not for you.

Requirements of a Proper C Corporation
The C corporation has some very strict requirements for those who form one:
- It must be run with and take on the attributes of a real business
- You must have a true business profit motive
- You must keep annual minutes
- You must keep true accounting records and, if computerized, use a business accounting software program such as Business Works or QuickBooks Pro
- You must have taxable income now or in the foreseeable future that you desire to shelter

Long Range Planning
As discussed earlier with double taxation, you must plan for stockholder distributions and the sale of your business. That means you must make a commitment to developing a plan for the long run. A savvy CPA who understands the tax code can offer such planning and/or a worthwhile exit strategy.

Does a C corporation have to last forever? No. But you should have an exit strategy in place that maximizes the tax advantages if you are planning to sell or close the business.

How committed are you to planning for you and your family's financial future, not only today, but for the long range?

Real Estate
There is one other area that does not work within the C corporation — the ownership of real estate. Do not confuse this with an LLC or LP that will own real estate and use the C corporation as partner in that business. As a partner, the C corporation can "own" real estate. But it is never a good idea to hold real estate directly within the C or S corporation.

Cost
The C corporation is a more involved structure to set up and maintain. If you are

92

running a true business with true income, then the tax savings will well outweigh the investment. But notice the word "if." If you are not dedicated to having a business, then the expense of the C corporation is really just that — another added expense.

Conclusion

- Verify that you have or will have sufficient non-wage income to justify a C corporation.
- Do not start a C corporation to own real estate.
- Verify that the tax benefits will outweigh the added cost and maintenance requirements needed to run a C corporation.

How Do I Know What Structure Is Right for Me?

Before you meet with your advisors, have a clear picture of where you are now and where you want to go.

Where Are You Now?

There has been many a time when an individual has called us and proudly told us of the steps he or she has already taken, and we in turn share with him or her that while the action was admirable, the steps he or she took could very well end up costing him or her thousands of dollars. Make sure you consult with a trained professional before blindly making changes to your family's finances.

Where Are You Going?

Your advisors need to know what your business plan is. For that matter, so do you. Spend the time to write up what your business goals are, what projected income and expenses are and a timeline of probable achievement. Of course, in the beginning you are really just guessing. But have you ever noticed in your life that if you write something down it has a tendency to come true? That is what happens frequently with these projections when you truly believe in them and work toward your goals. Your advisors need to have an idea what your vision is so they can best advise you.

What Then?

At some point, after you have made your mark on the world through your successful business, you will consider other life goals or retirement. What then? Do you want to sell your business? Or do you want to pass it on to your family? Perhaps your ultimate goal is to sell it to your employees. Your advisor needs to know this, too, so that he or she can give you the best informed advice for your individual situation. But the responsibility for doing the homework and choosing your advisors will always rest with you.

Careful selection of those offering direction, advice and their expertise should not be

"Do not follow where the path may lead. Go instead where there is no path and leave a trail."
– Muriel Strode

underestimated. The advisors you are choosing need to be qualified to advise about taxes, business structure, achieving goals and about your smooth and rewarding exit strategy.

Note: These are real concerns! But with proper planning and correct initial set-up structure, you can avoid the potential corporate pitfalls. You must have the right advisors to steer you through and keep you clear of potential land mines.

Do Not Make This Mistake!

Carl left our planning meeting for his home in Idaho excited about using a C corporation to its full advantage. He understood that he would be able to take advantage of timing differences and the dual tax rates (personal and corporate) as well as the special corporate tax deductions.

I didn't hear from him for a few months, until one day he called and told me he had finally gotten incorporated with his long-time attorney back in his small town in Idaho. As the conversation progressed, it came out that instead of a C corporation, the attorney had talked him into an LLC — telling him it was basically the same. But it wasn't. Carl was upset that he had spent money for an LLC and was determined that he would do the exact same thing with it that he could have with a C corporation. Of course, he couldn't.

The decision he then faced was whether to chalk up the substantial expense of the LLC to experience and create the correct structure or he could run his business as an LLC and eliminate all the benefits of a corporation. With either decision he had gone through added expense and trouble, because he did not listen to the correct advisors!

A Corporation Is Not for Everyone

The above example with Carl is not meant to imply that a C corporation is correct in every circumstance and for every person. It isn't. The point is that today it is common to see the LLC as recommended for every possible situation. This makes no more sense than recommending a C corporation for every situation. If they were all the same, there wouldn't be different laws defining them. Before you settle on a business strategy that will direct your operations for years to come, consider all the facts, tax ramifications, short and long-term goals and your exit strategy. Knowledge truly is power.

Conclusion

- Identify the type of income, projected income, growth and the ultimate exit strategy of your business.
- Locate tax, legal, financial and other specialty advisors to construct a wise plan.
- Listen to your advisors and weigh the recommendations carefully to determine your best plan of action. If there is conflict, seek additional advice.
- Spend the time now and get the most education possible to ensure the correct decisions are made later.

Knowledge + The Right Actions = Money

NOTES

Section Four:
Your Corporate Operation
Starting Smart by Running Your Corporation to Maximize all the Benefits

Chapter 1:
Your Corporate Charter is Born—Your Corporate Structure
- What is a corporate charter?
- Who are the players?

Chapter 2:
Care for Your Corporate Child: Danger Ahead — Don't Jeopardize Your Corporation by Ignoring Corporate Formalities
- Simple, easy and quick procedures you must follow to keep your corporation legal

Chapter 3:
Nurture a Great, Lasting and Successful (Profit and Protection-Centered) Relationship with Your Corporation
- Director, officer, employee — where do you fit in to get maximum benefits?

Chapter 4:
Warning: Don't Kill Your Corporate Protection and Benefits!
- Apply simple strategies to keep your corporate veil from being pierced

Chapter 1:
Your Corporate Charter Is Born —
Your Corporate Structure

- What is a corporate charter?
- Who are the players?

Case Study 5 (Bobby)

Bobby worked as an apprentice carpenter throughout much of high school. When he graduated, he got a job with a well-known construction company where he worked for close to ten years. One afternoon the owner of the company came to the job site to share some bad news. He was diagnosed with an incurable illness and had only one year to live. He had no desire to keep his company going and would shut down immediately following this job.

Bobby went home that night and shared the news with his wife. After her initial reaction she looked him straight in the eye and said, "You're an excellent carpenter, why don't you start your own company, be your own boss, never answer or depend on anyone else again." He was both scared and motivated by her proposal.

The next day Bobby called his brother who was an accomplished CPA. His brother suggested that Bobby operate from a corporation.

"But I'm small potatoes right now," he replied.

"Doesn't matter. You need the liability protection, the benefits and the peace of mind a corporation gives you."

"Peace of mind," he thought while conjuring up images of huge corporations and mountains of paperwork.

Because he trusted his brother's advice, he contacted a local company that sets up corporations. The process, he found out, was very easy and affordable. The hardest thing for him was to come up with a corporate name. He learned that he could be the president, secretary, treasurer and director of his own corporation. He didn't need anybody else. He felt like he was finally in control.

Bobby worked very hard in his business. In his first year he had hired three other carpenters and a bookkeeper who all stayed busy with the many projects Bobby lined up. His brother was a big help. He taught Bobby the importance of treating the corporation like a separate entity. This included the following:

- Never commingle funds
- Sign his name as president of the corporation whenever contracts were involved
- Have his letterhead, business cards and Yellow Page ad reflect the corporate name

There was no question that Bobby was operating correctly through a corporation. For the first time in his life he was putting money away for retirement and actually had more spending money in his pocket. Yes, his brother was right. He did have peace of mind.

Key Points
- A corporation is a separate legal entity.
- A corporation is formed by filing the articles of incorporation in a given state.
- The corporation is owned by the stockholders.
- The corporation is governed by the board of directors.
- Corporate action is performed by the corporate officers and employees.

A Corporate Charter Is Born
"In the beginning an idea formed."

You may already have an established business or are ready to go into business for yourself. Whatever the situation, you have come to the conclusion that a corporation is the best business structure to operate from due to its major tax benefits and the liability protection it gives you.

The incorporation process starts when an incorporator prepares and signs the articles of incorporation or, in some states, certificate of incorporation. The articles set forth specific information such as the name of the corporation, the principal place of business, the name and address of the incorporator and the name(s) and addresses of the first board of directors, as well as specific information relating to the type and amount of stock the corporation will be authorized to issue and director/officer liability protection.

On the day those articles of incorporation are filed in the secretary of state's office in the state in which it is operating, the corporation is born. In addition to filing with the secretary of state, some states require additional filing with a county clerk or publishing a copy of the articles in the local newspaper. If this applies to your state, you want to ensure these formalities are met prior to starting your business.

A corporation is a separate legal entity with a life of its own. It can conduct itself and act as any individual can, except it cannot vote or get married.

How Does the Corporation Think for Itself?

A corporation operates through a board of directors who are elected each year by the shareholders of the corporation. The directors, in turn, elect the officers who are responsible for carrying out the instructions as set forth by the directors.

Let's take a look at the different roles and management responsibilities of the corporate players:

Director(s):

It is the director's duty to manage the shareholders' investment through due care and diligence.

You, as the director, are the governing body of the corporation, and, therefore, you set corporate policy, actively manage the affairs of the business and select and supervise the officers who are responsible for handling the day to day business matters.

Officer(s):

As an officer, you perform whatever duties have been delegated to you by the board of directors, and you are generally responsible for the day-to-day management of the corporation. You are also held accountable by the same standard of conduct as the board of directors.

Shareholders:

Shareholders contribute capital for investment in the business in the form of cash, property or services. In exchange, they receive a stock certificate that represents their ownership interest.

This ownership gives them the right to vote, the right to receive distributions of dividends if declared by the directors, and the right to receive a proportionate share of the assets in the event of a dissolution. Shareholders do not have any say in the management of the business. However, they do have the power to elect the directors, who in turn elect the officers responsible for running the business, so indirectly, they can control corporate policy.

President:

The president reports directly to the board of directors, carries out their requests and is ultimately responsible for the actions of the other officers in the corporation.

Secretary:

It is the corporate secretary's responsibility to make sure that the corporation's actions are properly authorized and documented. This person is generally the one to prepare resolutions to bring to either a board of directors' or shareholders' meeting to be read and voted on. The secretary also serves as liaison between corporate management and the shareholders.

Treasurer:

The treasurer has responsibility for all financial records and transactions, including maintaining the corporate bank accounts, investments and liabilities. This information is vitally important to the board of directors so that it can make informed decisions in regard to the corporation's financial future.

Registered Agent:

The corporation must maintain a registered office and a registered agent within the state so that all legal or official matters pertaining to its corporate existence may be addressed there. You can be your own registered agent for any home state corporation. The primary responsibility of the registered agent is to receive any notices of litigation (service of process) on behalf of the corporation. By law, the corporation must maintain certain documents in their registered agent's file, such as:

a) a certified copy of the articles of incorporation and any amendments thereto
b) a copy of the corporate bylaws and any amendments thereto
c) copy of the original stock ledger or a stock ledger statement designating where the original is being kept

"If you have built castles in the air, your work need not be lost; that is where they should be. Now put the foundations under them."
– Henry David Thoreau

You are required to have a president, secretary, treasurer and director, and the same person can (in most states) serve in all four positions. However, you can expand your corporation to include a vice president if you choose, or you could have an assistant secretary and/or assistant treasurer if such positions would be helpful in the operation of your business.

Conclusion

- A corporation is born from an idea.
- The idea takes form through the articles of incorporation filed in a given state.
- The stockholders are the owners of the corporation.
- The board of directors determines the strategy, direction and action of the corporation.
- The officers and employees carry out the plan of action set by the board of directors.

Chapter 2:
Care for Your Corporate Child: Danger Ahead — Don't Jeopardize Your Corporation by Ignoring Corporate Formalities

- Simple, easy and quick procedures you must follow to keep your corporation legal

Case Study 6 (Emma)

Emma thought she knew it all. She was savvy, sophisticated and the sole owner of a successful advertising firm that she had incorporated more than five years pervious. She had started her business in her spare time in the upstairs bedroom of her townhouse. Within a few years, she had 15 employees and a beautiful office in the heart of downtown.

One afternoon while she was thinking quietly in her office, her secretary came in and dropped a large envelope on her desk. It was a summons to appear in court. An unhappy client was suing Emma personally as well as her company.

Emma immediately called her attorney who told her to get her corporate minute book to him right away. "My what?" she questioned.

"Your corporate minute book," her attorney repeated.

"You mean the black binder collecting dust on my bookshelf? Why do you need that?" she asked.

Her attorney went on to explain that the basis of the lawsuit was a contract dispute. Her attorney wanted her minute book to review the resolutions that had authorized Emma as an officer of the corporation to enter into a contract with this other company. Also, in order to dispute the fact that Emma was being sued personally, he wanted to make sure that she had properly established the corporation by electing the officers and directors each year, had in fact issued herself stock and had necessary paperwork to support the fact that she was indeed operating through a corporation.

Emma had procrastinated. She had never completed the organizational formalities. In fact, when she got her corporate minute book, she set it up on a shelf and never even looked at it. She always thought that she'd get to it later. In the back of her mind she knew that she was supposed to hold annual meetings to elect the officers and directors even if it was only she. She knew to document her important business decisions through the use of minutes and resolutions. But every year she just put it off, thinking, "Who will ever know?"

"One man with courage makes a majority."
– Andrew Jackson

Key Points

- Your corporation must create a paper trail of its important business activities.
- These records prove a corporation is run properly.
- Meetings are held by the directors and/or shareholders to determine action.
- Minutes are the records of these meetings.
- Resolutions are the actions taken or to be taken.
- Notices of meetings and the adoption of bylaws are also part of the paper trail necessary to keep a corporation legal.
- Ownership, disclosures, privacy and buy-sell agreements are part of the formalities that keep corporations legal.

A Journey Along the Paper Trail of Corporate Formalities

Before beginning on any corporate business venture, you should take stock of what has been accomplished so far, so that you are fully prepared for what lies ahead. Such as:

- How to keep it legal.
- How to use it most effectively to achieve the greatest protection and benefits your corporation affords you.

So what has taken place thus far?

- The articles of incorporation have been prepared and signed by the incorporator, who has filed them with the secretary of state.
- You know who will be serving as the first officers and director(s) of the corporation.
- You know what kind of business the company will transact.
- You know that in order to receive the liability protection you desire you have to look and operate as a corporation.

How are these steps accomplished?

Hey, Are We Ever Gonna Get Organized?

The first and most important step you must take in the formation of your corporation is the completion of the corporate organizational formalities. This should be done within the first 60 days of incorporation.

Without proper corporate records the protection of the corporate veil is jeopardized. In fact, persons who act for the unorganized corporation may be personally liable for contracts made by them as well as any personal injuries that may result from the course of business.

The business conducted at an organizational meeting will depend on whether it is a meeting of the incorporators, directors or shareholders.

The incorporator, during this organizational meeting, will present the filed articles of incorporation and a proposed form of bylaws. The incorporator, at this time, elects temporary director(s) to serve until formally nominated and elected by the shareholders.

Since there is no further business for the incorporator to conduct, the meeting will adjourn.

The director(s) who were temporarily elected to service during the incorporator's meeting have to hold their organization meeting as well.

Organization Meeting Agenda:
The following represents the agenda for this meeting:
   a) Presentation, acceptance and approval of the articles of incorporation
   b) Approval and acceptance of action taken at previous meetings (the incorporator's meeting)
   c) Approval and acceptance of the bylaws
   d) Approval and acceptance of the corporate seal
   e) Approval and acceptance of the form of share certificate
   f) Authorization to issue shares of stock
   g) Acceptance of share subscriptions (form of offer to purchase stock) as presented to the corporation for the purchase of shares (this determines who the shareholders will be)
   h) Form of offer to sell stock pursuant to Sec. 1244 IRC. If you sell the stock at a loss or it becomes worthless, you can take a full loss deduction of up to $50,000 per tax year ($100,000 on joint returns) against ordinary income as compared to taking it as a capital loss
   i) Authorization to pay expenses in connection with the formation of the corporation
   j) Election of corporate officers
   k) Acceptance of bank resolution (determines which financial institution the corporate funds will be kept and who is authorized to sign on the account)

Each issue is brought before the directors one at a time for acceptance and approval. Once approved, they are documented in the minutes of the meeting by the use of resolutions.

Minutes:
Minutes are the permanent, official record of the actions taken at a meeting of either the directors or shareholders.

Resolutions:
A resolution, on the other hand, is a document that records actions that the directors (sometimes shareholders) resolve to take on behalf of the corporation. Resolutions can be part of the minutes of a meeting or can be used separately and kept chronologically in the minutes section of the corporate record book.

More Excellent Reasons to Create a Paper Trail
The most commonly asked question I get is, "Do I need a resolution for that?"

When you're in business for yourself, it seems as though the paperwork that crosses your desk never ends.

The good news is that by operating through a corporation the amount of paperwork involved protecting the corporate status is very minimum. People often think that they have to have a resolution for everything. That's simply not true. In fact, you are required to hold only two formal meetings a year. They are the annual meeting of shareholders (which is held to appoint the directors) and the annual meeting of directors (which is held to elect the officers to serve for the ensuing year). At these meetings the acts of the directors and officers, respectively, can be ratified for the previous year.

Types of Meetings:

There are, however, actually three types of meetings that can be held by either directors or shareholders. They are organizational meetings, which have previously been discussed, regular meetings and special meetings.

The Annual Meetings of Shareholders and Directors:

These would be considered regular meetings since they are a required formality. The procedure governing this type of meeting is detailed in the corporate bylaws.

Special Meetings:

At any time during the year, additional meetings may be called by the directors or shareholders. These would be considered special meetings, and the procedures for calling a special meeting are also outlined in the bylaws. You would call a special meeting to discuss urgent times of business or to approve any legal or tax issues that seem to arise from time to time.

For example, a special meeting might be called to approve an S election recommended by the corporation's accountant to approve a loan to a corporate officer, to discuss the necessity of a bank loan or to approve a real estate transaction.

So How Do We Document These Decisions and Transactions?

Your meetings can be held in person, by phone, fax, e-mail, web or whatever method you find convenient.

1. Real Meeting with Minutes

The directors or shareholders hold a meeting to discuss and vote on items of corporate business. After (or during) the meeting, the secretary prepares written minutes showing the date, place, time and purpose of the meeting and the decisions (resolutions) approved and adopted by the directors or shareholders. This method should be used to document the annual meeting of directors and shareholders.

2. Paper Meeting with Minutes

This method allows directors or shareholders to informally agree to a specific corporate action. Minutes are prepared for the directors/shareholders to sign, as though the decisions were approved at a physical meeting. This gives formal documentation reflecting actual decisions made, without the inconvenience of holding a physical meeting.

"Nothing in life is to be feared. It is only to be understood."
– Marie Curie

Section 4 • Chapter 2: Care for Your Corporate Child: Danger Ahead — Don't Jeopardize Your Corporation by Ignoring Corporate Formalities

3. Action by Written Consent

The quickest and easiest way to document formal corporate action is called "action by written consent." This is the best method if you are a one or two-person corporation. Directors and/or shareholders sign this document containing the language of the decision (resolution) to be approved. Always make sure that all directors or shareholders sign the consent form. Keep all completed forms in the minutes section of the corporate minute book in consecutive date order.

Whichever method you choose to document formal corporate decisions is up to you. The key is to document your decisions, showing that you respect the separate legal entity of the corporation. In a small, closely held corporation the following terms may not seem relevant, but we will touch on them since they are an integral part of corporate operations.

Quorum:

For a shareholder meeting, this is the minimum number of shares required to be represented (in person or by proxy) and that are entitled to vote to conduct corporate business. Usually this is no less than one-third of the shareholders. Refer to your bylaws for specific corporate policy.

Proxy:

This is a written authorization of a shareholder directing another (the proxy holder) to vote the shareholder's shares in the manner directed by the shareholder.

Voting of Shares:

Each outstanding share, regardless of class, is entitled to one vote. This is called the one-vote-per-share rule. Please refer to the bylaws for exact corporate policy.

I'm Going to Have a Meeting with Myself?

Well, at least there shouldn't be any arguments! In a small, one-person or family-owned corporation this formality may seem silly, But remember, when you operate through a corporation, the corporation is a separate legal entity governed by state law, internal rules of procedure and established corporate formality.

Any business may come before a regular meeting. But a special meeting can't consider or transact any business other than that specified in the notice of the meeting. An exception to this occurs when all shareholders are present or represented by proxy and give their consent.

The time and place for a meeting are determined by the board of directors. You can hold your meetings (directors and shareholders) by telephone or anywhere in the world if this is specified in your articles of incorporation or bylaws. (The annual meeting makes for a great vacation, and it's completely tax-free when the corporation pays for it.)

Notice of Meeting:

This should specify the time, place, date and purpose of the meeting to be held. If you have outside shareholders, reasonable notice of the meeting must be given. Usually not less than 10 or more than 60 days is required. The bylaws will detail the specific time frame required in your corporation.

Waiver of Notice:

As a practical matter, most small, closely held corporations can rely on the use of waivers. This means that if a person is present (in person or by proxy) without any objection, to meet and discuss the issue at hand, the votes cast and the resolutions agreed to will be in full force and effect. The best method, however, is to get the signature of the stockholder and/or director on a waiver either before or after the meeting.

Since the bylaws have been mentioned over and over, you should have an exact definition of them.

Bylaws:

These are the rules and procedures that govern internal corporate policy. They are the road map for guiding your company. You will find written in the bylaws the answers to any questions you may have regarding shareholder meetings, board of directors duties and powers, corporate officers, shares of stock, dividends, amendment procedures and indemnification of officers and directors.

The bylaws should not be complicated with intricate procedures. They should, however, be as extensive and thorough in their description of the regulation and management of the corporation's affairs as deemed practical. The bylaws serve as the guide for corporate management. They can be altered, amended or repealed by the board of directors and/or shareholders pursuant to, of course, the bylaws.

I Hereby Resolve to...

The decisions you make on a daily basis do not require the approval of the directors. The decisions that really need director approval are key legal, tax and financial decisions. The following is a partial list of activities requiring a resolution. *

Activities Requiring Resolutions
- Opening bank accounts or establishing borrowing authority
- Written employment agreements
- Shareholder agreements, if the corporation is a party
- Tax elections, such as one to elect S corporation status
- Amendments to the articles or bylaws
- The purchase or sale of a business
- The purchase, sale or lease of property to be used by the business, including such things as an office building, computer system, company car or other items
- Loans, financing, bond issuance
- Reorganization, including mergers
- Dividend declarations
- Approval of plans to merge, liquidate or dissolve
- Employee benefit plans, including pension and profit sharing plans, health insurance and others
- Settlement of lawsuits and claims, indemnification of officers and directors
- Stock issuance
- Changes of registered agent or registered office
- Filling board or officer vacancies
- Authority to enter certain contracts

- Establishing committees or appointing members to serve on committees
- Redemption or retirement of corporate shares
- Salary matters pertaining to corporate officers
- Resolutions ratifying prior corporate acts by officers or directors

* Reprinted from "The Essential Corporation Handbook" by Carl R.J. Sniffen, The Oasis Press, 1992

All corporate records and documents should be maintained in consecutive date order so you see the progression of decisions made over the course of the business. Financial statements as well as corporate records should be maintained at the principal office of the corporation.

Limited Liability:

One very attractive characteristic of the corporation is that investors risk only the amount of their investment and are never held personally liable for corporate obligations, except when the corporate veil is pierced!

This limited liability means that corporate debts are limited to recovery only from corporate assets including the capital contributed by the shareholders. This protection of limited liability is the main reason people incorporate.

Similarly, officers and directors are not personally liable for corporate obligations unless they have exceeded their authority or breached their fiduciary duty to use good judgment and due care when incurring those obligations.

During the organizational meeting of the directors, the directors will accept written offers to purchase stock from the subscribers (any individual who wants to be a shareholder). The type of stock to be issued (usually common), the amount of shares requested and the consideration to be paid for those shares (cash, property, services) is detailed in each written offer. As soon as the board of directors has approved the issuance of stock to the individual subscriber, the corporation has a shareholder.

Upon the adjournment of the directors meeting it is time to hold the first meeting of shareholders. During their organizational meeting they will ratify (approve) all actions taken at both the incorporator and directors meetings. At this time they actually elect the first board of directors to serve for the ensuing year. (You were only serving as temporary board of directors during the entire organizational process until such time as the shareholders could hold their meeting and formally elect you.) After that, the meeting of shareholders adjourns.

Stock Issuance:

The last organizational formality is the issuance of stock. Each shareholder will be issued a stock certificate, which is the instrument that represents the ownership of shares in a corporation.

The articles of incorporation designate the type of stock to be issued (common, preferred, voting, non-voting, etc.) and the stated par value or no par value of those shares.

Shares with par value may be issued only for the consideration expressed in dollars, not less than the par value, as designated by the directors. For example, if the shares have a stated par value of $1, they can be sold for $5 if an investor is willing to pay that amount, but in no case can shares be sold for less than $1.

Shares without par value may be issued for whatever consideration may be fixed from time to time by the board of directors for any amount they deem reasonable in their good judgment. In other words, these are shares that do not have any minimum amount for which the shares can be sold to an investor.

You will probably not issue shares within a short period of time with major price variations ($1 today — $10 tomorrow). This brings up a question of breach in the directors' duty of due care when dealing with the shareholders and raises other securities issues best avoided. If you want to sell stock to a number of shareholders, you should consult with an experienced securities attorney.

Stock Ledger:

To record the issuance and transfer of shares, the corporation maintains a stock ledger as it's official record. Any transfer made between individuals must be registered in the stock ledger so that all rights of ownership are transferred as well. Otherwise, the right to vote and to receive dividends remains with the original holder.

Buy-Sell Agreements (Shareholder Agreements):

Another issue for consideration is the use of buy-sell agreements. This is a contract whereby the surviving owners (shareholders) or the entity (corporation) agrees to purchase the interest of a withdrawing or deceased owner. In a closely held corporation, failure to plan for either possibility can be disastrous.

This is an agreement between or among part-owners of a business that under stated conditions (usually severance of employment, disability or death) the person withdrawing (or his heirs) is legally obligated to sell the interest to the remaining shareholders of the corporation. This is dependent on the type of agreement. The agreement also specifies a price fixed either on a dollar basis or on a formula for computing the dollar value to be paid.

In summary, this agreement determines when an owner can sell his or her interest, who is eligible to buy his or her interest and what price a buyer must pay for that interest.

What Can Happen If You Do Not Have a Buy-Sell Agreement?

- A total stranger could end up working with you or, even worse, sharing control of your company, because one of the owners left and sold his or her interest to a buyer you don't even know.
- An owner divorces or dies, leaving you to work with a spouse or another family member.
- An owner files for personal bankruptcy and you find that he or she, without your knowledge, secured the loans with his or her ownership interest. Once filed, you and the bankruptcy trustee now run the company.
- Upon your death, your beneficiaries have a small business interest they will have a hard time selling.
- How do you determine a fair price immediately if an owner departs or dies? How do you deal with the heirs? What if you can't come to an agreement; how will the business continue doing business?

When to Amend the Articles

On rare occasions you may need to amend your articles. The most common reasons to amend are to:

- change the corporate name
- change the corporate purpose
- change the number of authorized shares
- change the stated par value
- create new classes of shares, such as preferred or common non-voting

The usual procedure for amendment is for the board of directors to adopt a resolution that sets forth the amendment provision. This is followed by submitting the provisions for a vote at an annual or special meeting of the shareholders. If adopted, an amendment is filed with the secretary of state.

For any jurisdiction that requires the articles be filed with the county clerk or published in the newspaper, the amendment must parallel those formalities.

There is no limit on the number of amendments you can file. As your business evolves, often so do the articles.

LLC Amendments

From time to time, LLCs may also need to amend their articles of organization. Any amendment to the articles almost always have to be approved by all or a majority vote of the members. It must be filed with the state if you are:

- Changing the name
- Changing the structure from member-managed to manager-managed or vice versa
- Adding, changing or deleting provisions
- Authorizing any special classes of membership interest, such as non-voting

Amending the LLC Operating Agreement

The operating agreement is a contract between the LLC and the members. Anytime you amend the Articles, you want to make sure that the agreement matches the changes approved by the members. This is especially true if you are going from member-managed to manager-managed.

You have two choices. You can either retype (or replace) the entire operating agreement which will include all of the approved changes, then have it signed by all current members (and their spouses if they signed the original). Or you can attach the resolution or written consent that contains the new language to the appropriate section of your current operating agreement, and then have all the members initial or sign the resolution to show their approval.

Conclusion

- A paper trail is required to document your corporate or LLC activities. These records prove that your business is run as a corporation, not merely an alter ego of the owner. If you want help, Sage Int'l prepares Annual Minutes & Resolutions.
- Officers and directors (or Members and Managers) are not personally liable for debts and obligations unless they have exceeded their authority or breached their fiduciary duty to use good judgment.
- Protect your business and the shareholders (or members of an LLC) with the use of a buy-sell agreement.

NOTES

Chapter 3:
Nurture a Great, Lasting and Successful (Profit and Protection-Centered) Relationship with Your Corporation

- Director, officer, employee — where do you fit in to get maximum benefits?

Case Study 7 (Fritz)

Fritz's grandfather was a printer; his father was a printer; and at age 29 Fritz found himself at the helm of the family corporate business. He'd started out as a young boy helping his dad after school and on weekends. It was a good, viable business. His father made enough money to send Fritz to college to earn a business degree.

When he returned from college, fresh-faced and full of ideas Fritz was amazed at how lax his father had been running the business. His dad was ready to retire, and so at the next board of directors meeting a unanimous vote confirmed Fritz as the new president.

He immediately felt some resistance from several employees. Maybe it was because he was having all the employees (including himself as president) sign employment contracts detailing their positions, titles and compensation. Or they were disgruntled because he took away everyone's authority to negotiate deals, enter into contracts or make trades without first receiving board of director approval.

Fritz knew what a lawsuit-crazy society we live in today and was taking no chances on losing the protection of the corporate veil simply by allowing any employee apparent authority to act on behalf of the corporation. As president, he had to answer to the board of directors who in turn had to answer to the shareholders. Fritz knew he had better know what was going on throughout the business.

Key Points

- What's best is to clearly define your activities as a director, an officer and as an employee.
- Any corporate transaction has to be performed by a director, an officer or an employee, not by you as an individual.
- If you and/or your corporation are having difficulty with the law or the IRS, neither you nor the corporation can transfer assets to another entity fraudulently. (Even if you are not in trouble with the law or IRS, fraudulent transfers are never a good idea.)
- Shareholders are usually not liable for corporate debts.

Director, Officer, Employee —
Which Are You? Are You All Three?
How Do You Keep the Activities/Duties Separate?

The Number one Question is, "How Do I Handle Money Transactions Concerning My Corporation?"

This is my most frequently asked question. A few typical follow-up questions include:

a) Should I become an employee of the company and take income as a salary?

b) Should I take profits in dividends as a shareholder?

c) Should I work as an independent contractor to my corporation?

These subjects will be addressed separately. However, care must be taken to follow the rules. If you don't, there are ramifications and some consequences you certainly do not want or need.

Employee of Your Corporation:

Let's say you've formed a corporation. You (and perhaps your spouse) are its sole shareholder(s), you (and your spouse) are the only one(s) working for the corporation. The ideal situation is to become employees of the corporation rather than operating as independent contractors. Let me explain why.

As an employee of the business you have access to many corporate benefits that are not allowable if you operate as an independent contractor or only show yourself as an officer and director. You must, in fact, be a W-2 wage-earning employee subject to the required payroll tax withholdings (Federal/FICA/SSI/Medi).

Once set up, the ultimate goal is to take a low salary so only the minimum amount is withheld. You then make up the difference by letting the corporation pay for all those wonderful tax deductible benefits, such as monthly car allowance, dependence care, health insurance, medical/dental costs, home office rent and the like. And you can start saving for retirement immediately.

Note: Since you are an employee of a corporation, your salary will be subject to any state income tax requirements in the state in which you reside. However, this should be minimum because of the salary you took.

Salary or Dividends

Being the owner of the corporation entitles you to certain rights and preferences. However, you have no voice (formally) in the day-to-day management of the corporation.

Most corporate owners acting as employees (W-2 wage-earners) take compensation in the forms of salary and benefits. In a small or family-owned corporation the issuance of dividends (income distributions to shareholders) is very unlikely, thereby avoiding any double taxation.

The board of directors has the sole discretion to determine the amount, cash or stock, which will be paid as dividends. Keep in mind, however, that dividends can only be paid from the net earnings and profits of the corporation. (To determine the earnings per share, you divide the net profit by the corporate shares outstanding.)

"Definite of purpose can, and it should so completely occupy the mind that one has no time or space in the mind for thoughts of failure."
~ Napoleon Hill

If there is no profit, dividends cannot be paid. When dividends are paid, they are taxed twice: once at the corporate level and again in the hands of the shareholder. If the board of directors decides not to pay any dividends, but reinvest back into the company, these funds are called "retained earnings."

Independent Contractor (IC)?

For yourself, you would be hard-pressed to convince the IRS you are an independent contractor in your own business. The most basic standards for qualifications as an IC are not present: you are working under the corporation's direction, not independently. You are working at the corporation's premises, not elsewhere. Even if you were an IC, you would not be eligible to receive any corporate benefits.

When Do I Pay Myself?

Initially, you will probably serve as the officers and director without any compensation. However, when the corporation has sufficient income to support your salary, then pay it! Then you can begin taking advantage of all the corporate benefits available to you.

Write Your Compensation Policy:

The rule of thumb is to determine your salary and bonus policy at the beginning of the year, formally and in writing. However, it can be determined that compensation is likely to vary based on the corporation's profits. The key is to have a formula that is followed year after year to show consistency in the way compensation is figured.

Place Your Spouse and Children on the Corporate Payroll!

To take advantage of valuable tax deductions place your spouse and even your children on the payroll. Of course, they have to actually work in the business, and payroll taxes must be paid regardless of their ages. This enables the corporation to pay money that would have been paid at a higher tax rate in salary or dividends and shifts it into your children's tax bracket that starts at 15 percent.

As an employee, your spouse participates in all the tax deduction benefits available through a corporation. With your children as employees you can begin saving for their college education tax-free!

How much Can You Pay Yourself?

Yes, you do it all and, as hard as it is to believe, the IRS may deem your salary to be too high. In closely held corporations the IRS scrutinizes compensation paid to shareholder-employees to see if some of it may really be dividends.

The courts tend to look at all the factors regarding your compensation to determine if the corporation is really getting its money's worth. Are you qualified (education and experience) for the job? How many hours do you work, and what are the duties you perform? What achievements do you have that show the business wouldn't have made it without you? What are key employees paid in similar businesses that offer similar services?

A court looks at the size of your company (based on sales), net income or capital value and the relationship between you and your corporation. The 9th Circuit Court of Appeals says it will look at a company's return on equity after paying compensation. If that amount satisfies any outside shareholders then there is a strong indication that profits are being siphoned off as salary.

Show Me the Money!

There are a variety of avenues to pull money out of the corporation. The goal is to have your corporation spend excess earnings on you, the owner-employee, as a deduction to your corporation and without tax implications. Note the following avenues to retrieve cash, compensation and benefits:

- Profits (dividends)
- Salaries
- Bonuses (established criteria early in the year based on sales or increased profits)
- Loans (shareholders often lend money initially to the corporation in addition to their capital investment)
- Leases (shareholders lease equipment, buildings, real estate to the corporation)
- Sale of corporate assets (shareholder sells assets to the corporation)
- Employee benefit plans
- Fringe benefits
- Expense accounts

Proper documentation is critical. Remember, the IRS can challenge and disallow claimed deductions if they view them as unreasonable.

Arm's Length Transactions:

When you operate through a corporation you have many hats to wear and many roles to play. Any transaction involving you and the corporation must be handled with a great deal of care. Keep in mind that the corporation is a separate legal entity, and the board of directors is required to use good faith and judgment. The board owes a duty to all shareholders, not just a majority of them. If the corporation is going to enter into a contract, lease a piece of equipment or buy a piece of land that ultimately benefits you as an individual, it needs to be handled at arm's length — just like you would if you were doing business with any other person or company. For example, if the corporation is going to buy a piece of property that you own personally, you would set the same terms that would prevail if the parties to the transaction were not related to each other in any way. The transaction should be fair and reasonable, not one-sided. Be sure to maintain a traceable paper trail to prove that all actions were performed by a corporation and not just by individuals.

Fraudulent Conveyance — Another Red Flag:

A corporation facing financial difficulties cannot simply dispose of its assets in order to avoid paying its creditors without first considering the fraudulent transfer laws.

If you are being sued as an individual, you may be tempted to transfer some or all of your assets to your corporation to keep the assets protected. This will ultimately get you in trouble. The courts refer to this type of transaction as "fraudulent conveyance," and this term is used to describe any attempt to improperly transfer assets for the purpose of avoiding lawsuits, liens and the claims of creditors. You should consult with an attorney before making any transfers to determine if such transfers will be considered fraudulent.

"The greater the obstacle, the more glory in overcoming it."
– Moliére

Personal Guarantees:

Certain debts, such as a bank loan or establishing credit with a supplier, which you may incur require you first sign a personal guarantee as a condition of the transaction. This removes any liability insulation for the corporation, and instead requires you to pay the obligation in the event the corporation can't.

While often signing a guarantee cannot be avoided, you should make sure you terminate any outstanding guarantees once credit has been firmly established with your corporation, or more importantly, if you ever sell your company to someone else.

Hot Tip

Make sure you remove yourself from any personal guarantees because they follow you, not the corporation.

Shareholder Liability:

By limiting their ability to the amount of their investments, shareholders become the economic foundation for encouraging business development and fostering stability in commercial transactions.

When a corporation is organized for lawful purposes and treated as a separate legal entity distinct from its owners (and absent special circumstances), owners generally are not liable for corporate debts.

Shareholders must make it very clear that they are, in fact, operating through a corporation. For example, if you have been operating as a sole proprietor for a period of time and later incorporate the business, you can be held personally liable to creditors that never received construction notice of the corporation and that still believe the business is being operated as a sole proprietorship.

The way to avoid this problem is to immediately begin operating in a manner that clearly identifies you are operating as a corporation featuring your new corporation designation (Inc., Corp. and the like). You do this by printing new letterhead and business cards, by signing contracts and other documents in your capacity as a corporate employee and by making it very clear that you are acting as an officer of the corporation, whether in person or on paper, by including your corporate title. This will eliminate the appearance that you are acting in an individual capacity.

If you, as a shareholder, officer or director undertake activities that breach your duty to the corporation, are negligent or allow the corporation to engage in unlawful acts, you will be held personally liable.

If the state of incorporation has laws that protect the shareholders from personal liability for corporate debts, you must be careful and cognizant of any laws (shareholder liability) in other jurisdictions if your corporation will be transacting business in another state as a foreign corporation.

116

How Can I Be a Foreigner If I'm Still In the United States?

When you incorporate, the state in which you incorporate is the domestic state and the corporation is a foreign corporation to every other state. If you are intending to conduct business in any other state, the rule is that a foreign corporation must qualify to do business (filing as a foreign corporation with the secretary of state in that state) prior to commencing business.

There is a traditional statutory test (Transacting Business Test) for determining whether a corporation must qualify in a foreign jurisdiction.

Many court cases have resulted from lack of a true definition of transacting business. Section 15.01 of the Model Business Corporation Act enumerates certain activities that may be conducted by a foreign corporation without it being considered to be transacting business.

These are:

- Maintaining, defending or settling any proceeding
- Holding meetings of the board of directors or shareholders or carrying on other activities concerning internal corporate affairs
- Maintaining bank accounts
- Maintaining offices or agencies for the transfer, exchange and registration of the corporation's own securities or maintaining trustees or depositories with respect to those securities
- Selling through independent contractors
- Soliciting or obtaining orders, whether by mail or through employees or agents or otherwise, if the orders require acceptance (fulfillment) outside this state before they become contracts
- Creating or acquiring indebtedness, mortgages and security interests in real or personal property
- Securing or collecting debts or enforcing mortgages and security interests in property securing the debts
- Owning without more (non-income-producing) real or personal property
- Conducting an isolated transaction that is completed within 30 days and that is not one in the course of repeated transactions of a like nature
- Transacting business in interstate commerce

Generally speaking, most states have adopted the 1984 Revised Model Business Corporation Act in its entirety and only a few remaining states may have some exceptions. It is suggested that you contact your secretary of state's office to request the statutes that govern foreign corporations in your home state.

Conclusion

- Even if a corporation consists of only one person, the duties and activities of the corporate directors, officers and employees must be kept separate and apart from one another particularly from you as an individual.

- Any transaction involving you and the corporation must be treated at arm's length — just like you would if you were entering into a transaction with an unrelated third party.

- There are at least 10 ways you can receive cash, compensation or benefits. There are different tax implications for each method. Consult with your CPA to determine which tax-savings strategies will work best for you.

- You must take great care to convey corporate assets legally, particularly if you are under some type of legal attack.

- Be aware of the legal ramifications if you sign a personal guarantee for any corporate debts.

- Your corporation is domestic to the state in which the articles of incorporation were filed. It is foreign to all other states and countries. You need to be aware of the legalities of running your corporation as a domestic or foreign corporation in your state.

NOTES

Chapter 4:
Warning: Don't Kill Your Corporate Protection and Benefits!

- Apply simple strategies to keep your corporate veil from being pierced

Case Study 8 (Lanny)

Lanny owns a quick-mart on the corner of a busy street. He bought the business several years ago from an aging couple that were ready to retire. He operated the business as a sole proprietorship, and after a couple of years, with the advice of his CPA, he incorporated. Lanny didn't adhere much to corporate formality. If he needed cash, he'd take money out of the cash register and never write it down. He would sometimes order things for his home and let the company pay for them. And other times he would pay personal bills with a company check. He didn't have any company letterhead or business cards that indicated he operated from a corporation. Annual corporate filings were always late and sometimes missed altogether until a "final notice" was sent from the secretary of state.

His CPA kept warning him that his current business practices must stop. But Lanny never listened.

One day a young woman came into the store to buy a soda. As she passed by the ice machine, she accidentally slipped and fell in a puddle of water. She broke her arm and hit her head on a canned food display.

Within a week Lanny had received notification he was being sued — not his corporation, him, personally. He immediately called an attorney to try to hide behind the corporate veil.

During the course of discovery the prosecuting attorney was able to show that Lanny never operated through the corporation. In fact, at no time could you ever tell the difference between Lanny and the corporation. The attorney was able to prove it was merely his alter ego. His negligence in both his store and his business practice cost Lanny his livelihood and his personal assets.

Key Points

- Run your corporation as a corporation or the corporate veil of protection could be pierced.
- If you have a variety of business activities, it is wise not to put them all in one corporation or one business entity.
- The IRS says you have to file a corporate tax return when your corporation is acting like a corporation.

Piercing the Corporate Veil

This is a judicial theory used to ignore the separate identity of the corporation and hold individual shareholders liable for all corporate debts.

When a shareholder conducts his affairs as though the corporation doesn't exist and where limited liability of the shareholder would produce inequitable results, the courts continually (40 percent of all cases) pierce the corporate veil. However, a party must establish that the shareholders' ownership combined with other factors, such as the commingling of corporate and personal funds, was prevalent before the corporate veil can be pierced.

A common thread that runs through these cases is gross carelessness of the owners. You can take various steps and can implement certain policies to minimize your risk. First, treat your corporation as an entity separate and apart from you and abide by the legal requirements for running it.

The following steps should be taken:
- Never commingle personal and corporate funds or other assets.
- Do not divert corporate funds or assets to other than corporate uses.
- Do not treat corporate assets as if they were your own.
- Whenever you are going to subscribe to or issue more stock, always get proper authorization by holding a special meeting of the directors.
- Never assert that shareholders are personally liable for corporate debts (personal guarantee).
- Maintain and update corporate records (annual meeting minutes, resolutions).
- To avoid confusion over which entity entered into a transaction, keep separate records for each business you own.
- Avoid identical equitable ownership in two corporations (control group issue).
- If you have more than one corporation:
    - avoid the appearance of total domination and control over both,
    - elect separate officers and directors,
    - use different offices and business locations,
    - hire different employees and legal counsel.
- Make sure you have enough capital and insurance to deal with any potential liability.
- Have a real business purpose.
- Never conceal or misrepresent the corporation's owners, management or financial interests.
- Adhere to all legal formalities and make sure all transactions between related parties are at arm's length.
- Never use the corporation as a shield when contracting with others if the intent is to avoid performance or to commit illegal transactions.
- Never use the corporation to avoid an existing liability for yourself or another entity.
- Keep the corporation in good standing by complying with annual state filing requirements.

"Opportunities are usually disguised by hard work so most people don't recognize them."
– Ann Landers

Commingling funds, adhering to corporate formalities and adequately capitalizing the corporation are the three most important issues on which we will focus.

Commingling Funds:

Where commingling occurs, the common patterns of behavior are that corporate assets and personal assets are treated the same without regard to corporate ownership. This means that the affairs of the corporation are indistinguishable from you personally. This occurs when all corporate decisions are dominated by debtor-shareholders and corporate funds and employees' moneys are utilized for your own benefit.

Corporate Formalities:

To be in compliance with corporate formalities, ensure that you maintain the division required by following these four principles:
1. Keep separate corporate records.
2. Issue stock.
3. Annually elect the officers and directors.
4. Properly document all inter-shareholder-corporate loans with notes and security instruments.

Capitalization:

This is another important factor considered by the courts. To determine whether a corporation is adequately capitalized, three methods are employed:
a. A comparison of the capitalization requirements of businesses in the same industry
b. Having sufficient assets or purchase liability insurance in sufficient amounts
c. A statutory minimum capital requirement (though some states have no minimum capital requirement)

To comply with these standards, you should establish your capital requirements in advance and maintain a sufficient level of liability insurance common within your industry.

Revoked Corporate Charter:

The secretary of state can revoke or administratively dissolve your corporate charter if you:
- do not file the annual report when due
- do not pay annual state filing fees
- do not maintain a registered office or agent within the state
- falsify information in the annual filings

Most states notify you if you are in default. You need to make sure you file on time every year. Contact the secretary of state for fees and filing requirements.

"A Tisket a Tasket:"

Never put all your eggs in one basket. Any time you operate more than one business, you should seriously consider incorporating each one separately. If one business venture fails, the other isn't jeopardized. It's the smartest way to eliminate losses and defensively organize your business enterprise.

How Do You Sign Documents?

When you or someone else is authorized to act on behalf of the corporation it is important how you sign. This indicates whether you, personally, or the corporation, are bound to the terms of the agreement. An example of the proper way to sign:

Sage International, Inc.

By: <u>Cheri S. Hill, President</u>

Using the Corporate Name:

All letterhead, business cards, purchase orders, invoices and any other sources of communication such as advertising and telephone listings should notify the world that it is dealing with a corporation and not you, personally.

The IRS Says...:

A company is considered a corporation, for tax purposes, when it acts like one. As far as the IRS is concerned, you are liable for a corporate tax return (Form 1120) when you made your first expenditure or received your first bit of income. Also, if you have been issued an employer identification number (EIN) from the IRS, you will be expected to file a return. However, if you have had no activity, you should file an informational return (Form 1120 with zero activity) to avoid unnecessary correspondence with the IRS. Consult with your CPA for professional assistance.

The Bottom Line:

The two words to always fall back on are "common sense." When you respect your corporation as a separate legal entity, you have a relationship that must be nurtured and developed. By using good practical judgment always ask yourself this question: "If I were entering into a transaction with an unrelated third party, how would I expect this transaction to be handled/documented?" Act no differently concerning your own corporation. The old adage, "put it in writing," was never so true. You can't over-document. The opposite can lead to intense scrutiny by the IRS, creditors, minority shareholders and the courts.

It is not common practice for the courts to pierce the corporate veil simply because a company fails due to mismanagement, poor judgment or bad luck. It is unlikely that the courts will make officers, directors and shareholders responsible for corporate debts. Only under exceptional circumstances (fraud and/or illegal operations) will personal liability result. By acting in good faith, you will generally escape personal liability.

Having chosen a corporation to conduct your business, I'm sure you're anxious to get started on the right track. If you follow the guidelines detailed throughout this section, you can have peace of mind knowing you are pursuing the right avenues and will benefit both personally and professionally.

Conclusion

- Your corporate veil can be pierced if you do not run your corporation as a corporation.
- Never put all your assets in one corporation or one entity.
- When your corporation receives its first income or makes its first expenditure, the IRS calls it an operating corporation.
- Use common sense to operate your corporation as a corporation, not merely an extension of yourself.

NOTES

Section Five:
Protecting Your Assets
Everyone Shows You How to Make a Million –
We Show You How to Keep It!

Chapter 1:
Be Prepared. Don't Let the World Kick You in the Assets!
- The Flaming Arrows of Challenge

Chapter 2:
Protect Your Personal Assets
- Homestead
- Home Equity Line of Credit
- Insurance
- Medicaid Planning Basics

Chapter 3:
Planning for Death (Yes, it is going to happen)
- Only Three Ways to Pass Your Wealth
- Joint Tenancy
- Common Myths About Avoiding Probate
- Difference Between a Will and a Trust
- Living Trust vs. Testamentary Trust
- Keeping Control of Medical Decisions

Chapter 4:
The First Layer of Your Wealth Foundation
- Factors We Consider When Developing A Strategy
- The Many "Tools" in Our Toolbox
- Irrevocable Trust
- The Limited Partnership
- Charging Order
- Limited Liability Company

Chapter 5:
More Ways to Protect Business Assets
- Business Insurance
- Separate Your Personal and Business Credit
- Shut the Door on Business Identity Theft

Chapter 6:
Protect Your Intellectual Property
- What is Intellectual Property?
- Copyrights
- Trademarks
- Trade Secrets
- Patents
- Legal Basis for Intellectual Property Laws
- Hold Your IP in an LLC

Chapter 7:
How Golden Will Your Golden Years Really Be?
- Individual Retirement Accounts
- Self-Directed IRAs
- Real Estate Investing with your IRA
- Employer Sponsored Retirement Plans

Chapter 8:
Our Precious "Fur" Children
- Pet Trusts
- States That Allow Simple Pet Trusts

Chapter 9:
The Exit Strategy
- Planning for Your Exit
- Potential Deal Forms to Consider
- Valuation Methods
- The Business Exit Planning Process
- Maximizing the Sale Value of Your Business

Chapter 1:
Be Prepared. Don't Let the World Kick You in the Assets!

- The Flaming Arrows of Challenge

Why Do You Need Asset Protection?

More than ever before, the bitter facts of life require people who have struggled to create financial security to take extra measures to protect their hard-earned wealth, their homes, their savings, their investments, their retirement plans.

You need to think about asset protection in the hopes that you'll never be attacked. It's kind of like a plunger. You don't buy a plunger hoping you'll get to use it. But if you ever needed one and didn't have one…well, you're going to find yourself knee deep in it and you're not going to be very happy.

I am going to show you how to protect your assets from outside attack and how to do so within the parameters of the law. Just as legislators and lawyers have come up with myriad ways for you to fall victim to a ruinous financial claim, they have also come up with an almost equal number of ways for you to protect your assets from those claims.

My goal is to make you judgment proof. That is you have no assets that can be reached by creditors or other claimants. This does not mean that you must render yourself broke, rather, it means that your assets are beyond the reach of a plaintiff or the courts, and that for the purposes of a lawsuit, you are considered poor.

"True Asset Protection can only occur if you take away the incentive to sue."

Key Points
- Asset Protection is both lawful and smart. You have an obligation to yourself and your family to protect and preserve what you have worked so hard to accumulate. It is important to set up legal and defendable plans using the law to your advantage.

128

The Flaming Arrows of Challenge

How many of you are aware that there are challenges lurking at every turn of success? These challenges are like flaming arrows ready to strike us at anytime.

Flaming Arrow #1 – Liability Exposure

Did you know the US has 80% of the world's lawyers? It's estimated that 50,000 lawsuits are filed in this country every day. In fact, almost 95% of all litigation in the world is initiated in the United States.

We are in a litigation explosion and the impact on every one is significant.

When patients sue doctors, the cost of health care rises. Manufacturers add a liability premium to the price of their products. Litigation cripples business. It is time consuming, expensive, and emotionally charged.

Right now, if you are engaged in any business activity or if you have a professional practice, chances are that sooner or later you will be sued. In fact, the average person will be sued five times in their lifetime.

Both you and I should be concerned that the legal system has no effective means of discouraging abusive lawsuits and that the court system is heavily weighted toward the sympathetic plaintiff, with the judges and juries playing Robin Hood with your money.

It is not uncommon for awards in malpractice and negligence cases to exceed $1 million dollars.

And reality in the legal system is that people are named as defendants in lawsuits not because they are at fault but because of their ability to pay. Attorneys consider whether a theory of liability can be developed against a party who can pay a judgment. This is called the search for the "Deep Pocket Defendant." This Deep Pocket will have substantial insurance coverage or significant personal assets.

All of you by now probably heard about the Bronx man who sued McDonald's, Burger King, Wendy's and KFC claiming they were responsible for his 272 pounds and both heart attacks he suffered. His diabetes, high blood pressure and high cholesterol would never have happened if he knew fast food was unhealthy. He thought that because they said it was 100% beef they meant it, no idea they were full of sodium and fat.

Who's the deep pocket here? Who really wins in a lawsuit? The Lawyers!

Do you realize that every year thousands of families are suddenly wiped-out? One lawsuit or business setback can cost you everything you own - your home, cars, business and personal assets, retirement savings - everything!

"The will to prepare to win is more important than the will to win. Preparing usually means doing those kinds of things that failures don't like to do. It means studying and learning. It means reading books, going to seminars. It means not being afraid to corner experts and ask foolish questions."
–Robert G. Allen, author of Creating Wealth

Section 5 • Chapter 1: Be Prepared. Don't Let the World Kick You in the Assets!

Ask yourself: Are you in a position right now to defend a claim for the sale of a defective product, an unfair or deceptive business practice, or a claim by an employee for a wrongful termination or sexual harassment?

What type of asset protection plan do you have in place for your business and personal assets so they are not at risk?

I hear people say, "If I get sued, I'll just give my assets away!"

Before creating any asset protection plan, you need to understand the legal restrictions on transfers that impair the rights of a creditor. For example, some people may physically hide their money and jewelry, or some may make gifts to friendly parties or relatives with some secret agreement to give the property back once the trouble has passed. So for the last 400 years, the courts have invalidated transfers made by a person with the actual intent to hinder, delay or defraud their creditors.

This is called a Fraudulent Conveyance. The transfer is ignored and the property is treated as if still owned by the debtor so it can be seized by a judgment creditor.

You might be thinking to yourself, how vulnerable am I really?

You may feel safe and secure, the simple truth is that you can never be certain that your lifetime's accumulation of wealth won't suddenly disappear tomorrow. No matter what our lifestyle or occupation, or how prudently we act, we all flirt with liability and financial disaster.

The key is Risk Recognition. In other words asset protection is based on the recognition of risk and the structuring of your holdings in a manner that will reduce your exposure to risk. The key to risk avoidance, is to recognize that attacks on your assets can come from virtually any direction such as,

- A costly uninsured motor vehicle Accident
- A major damage suit for injury around your home or business (someone falling down a flight of stairs)
- A tax audit and an outrageous IRS assessment
- Business Debts
- Breach of Contract Disputes
- Lawsuit with business partners
- Malpractice
- or how about a fine for violating any one of thousands of federal or state laws- such as environmental protection; Americans with Disabilities Act; or Fair Housing.
- Natural Disasters

And #1: Divorce! 70% of all marriages in America end in Divorce. Second marriages are even less successful. Have you or anyone you have ever known walked away with all of their assets after a divorce?

Asset Protection planning is both lawful and smart. You have an obligation to yourself

"All labor that uplifts humanity has dignity and importance and should be undertaken with painstaking excellence."
- Martin Luther King, Jr.

and your family to protect and preserve what you have worked so hard to accumulate. It is important to set up legal and defendable plans (before liability is incurred) using the law to your advantage. In fact, let me ask you, "When do most people install a security alarm system in their home or office?" 99% will say, "after they've been robbed!"

Is Estate Planning the same as Asset Protection Planning?

Well let's first clarify what is your estate? This is simply everything you own - your real estate, bank accounts, stocks, bonds and other investments; your IRA and other retirement plans or benefits; family heirlooms, collectibles and personal belongings; the benefits from your insurance policies, and any interest owned in LLC's, corporations, partnerships etc. So if you start adding it all up - especially the insurance benefits - you will find that you actually have a lot more than you think.

Estate Planning is done so you control who receives your assets when you die and if it's a good plan to also protect you at incapacity. It lets you-not the courts-maintain control of your assets. Most of us, of course, want that to happen with the least amount going to legal fees and taxes.

Asset protection planning on the other hand, is reducing your exposure to risk while you grow, protect and leverage your hard-earned wealth.

They are actually intertwined and here's why:

Flaming Arrow #2 - Probate

"Where There's a Will an Heir Will Pay!"

The word Probate is a Latin word that means laying open. This is a legal process through which the courts make sure that, when you die, your Will is valid and your debts are paid and your assets are distributed according to your Will, essentially they have laid your estate open. If you die intestate, that is without a Will, the courts will decide for you. So why do you have to go through probate? Why can't someone in your family do this instead of the court?

Because probate is the ONLY legal way to change the title on assets when the person listed as the owner cannot sign his or her name. If you are not alive, you cannot sign your name. And your family and friends can't sign for you, only the court can do it.

Also, the cost to probate your estate must be paid before your heirs can fully receive your assets. In addition to probate fees, there may also be taxes-both final income taxes (state and federal), estate taxes, and perhaps thousands due in unpaid medical bills and other debts. Also, if you own assets (especially real estate) in another state, your family will probably have to go through more than one probate, that is, one in each state property is held.

Elvis Presley when he died, his estate was valued at more than 10 million dollars. More than 3 million were paid in federal estate taxes and state inheritance taxes and

"It always looks as if the best way to solve a problem is to spend somebody else's money."
– Milton Friedman

almost 2 million were spent on administrative, executor and legal fees while his estate was in probate. By the time his debts and expenses were paid, less than 3 million was left for his heirs.

Flaming Arrow #3 - Estate Taxes

This is a federal tax imposed on assets after death.

In 2001, after 10 years of debate, Congress passed legislation that will gradually repeal the federal estate tax over the next ten years. This is a tax imposed on assets left by the nation's wealthiest residents. However, be aware that many states impose their own taxes and costs when residents die. Estates too small to trigger the federal tax can easily rack up thousands of dollars in state death taxes and probate costs. Far from being repealed if the federal tax is rescinded, this state burden is on track to rise over time.

In the past, most states haven't had to impose separate taxes to get a piece of their residents' estates. Instead, the states received a portion of what the estate owed the federal government. This "pickup" tax raised state coffers without the estates owing any extra. However, states are losing this boost. The federal law temporarily repealing the estate tax has already phased out the states' ability to take a portion of said tax. That translates to billions of dollars in lost state revenues which is why several states are pretending that the repeal isn't happening and taking from their residents' estates some of what they used to get from the federal government.

This is how the Estate Tax will Fade Away:

Under the law, the Estate Tax Exemption increases each year while, at the same time, the tax rate goes down. Finally, in tax year 2010, the tax no longer exists. Well not so fast, anyone dying after December 31, 2010, the tax is restored and the exemption reduces to $1 million.

This has created an estate planning nightmare, unless Congress chooses between now and then to change the law.

Year	Estate Tax Exemption	Gift Tax Exemption	Highest Estate & Gift Tax Rate
2002	$1 million	$1 million	50%
2003	$1 million	$1 million	49%
2004	$1.5 million	$1 million	48%
2005	$1.5 million	$1 million	47%
2006	$2 million	$1 million	46%
2007	$2 million	$1 million	45%
2008	$2 million	$1 million	45%
2009	$3.5 million	$1 million	45%
2010	Estate Tax Repealed	$1 million	top individual income tax rate (Gift Tax Only)

Section 5 • Chapter 1: Be Prepared. Don't Let the World Kick You in the Assets!

"Don't find fault, find a remedy."
  – Henry Ford

"Death and taxes and childbirth! There's never any convenient time for any of them!"
  –Margaret Mitchell

If you're married, estate tax is most likely to be an issue when the second spouse dies because when the first spouse dies, everything left passes tax-free. But if the second spouse owns all of the couple's property, and it is worth more than the estate tax exemption, estate tax will be due. So if you and your spouse own more than $1 million, you seriously need to think about using a family living trust, making gifts during your lifetime, or using other legal tax-avoidance strategies.

In other words, don't let Uncle Sam become your biggest heir!

Flaming Arrow #4 - Catastrophic Illness

"The single greatest fear of our senior citizens, and of all Americans is that a long-term catastrophic illness may strike and, because of the absence of public or private coverage, they will become destitute." - Claude M. Pepper, US Representative from Florida

The toughest decision you may ever have to make is to place your parent or spouse into a nursing home. No one ever wants to take that step. But there may come a time when there's just no choice. The statistics are horrifying: Five out of ten Americans over the age of 70 will require skilled nursing care for a minimum of two years.

Most people think of a catastrophic illness as a massive heart attack, a bone-crushing auto accident, or cancer. But the biggest catastrophe of all may well be the crippling, chronic conditions-such as senility, Alzheimer's disease, severe arthritis, osteoporosis, or the long-term effects of a stroke. These conditions require full-time care and attention, which you as the child or spouse simply cannot offer.

While issues like these create extreme emotional trauma, that trauma often pales in comparison with the financial shock of having to pay for long-term nursing care. With nursing home bills averaging $4,000 per month, a million Americans every year are forced into destitution. Medicare benefits cover only the first 100 days of skilled care. After that, the patient is financially "on their own." Nursing-home patients and their families often are stripped of everything: their homes, their savings, their dreams.

Why do our citizens have to bankrupt themselves, become dependent on the state and be robbed of their dignity and self-esteem because they suffer from "uncovered" or chronic illnesses?

What is most disheartening is that the financial devastation is unnecessary. Why do so many sit idly by while a financial nightmare becomes reality instead of planning ahead? Why doesn't the government promote planning? The answer is simple. It would cost Uncle Sam a lot of money. In fact, government bureaucrats will even go out of their way to prevent you from finding out how to protect yourself and your family.

Flaming Arrow #5 - Disability

Stress, diabetes, heart disease, chronic pain, cancer, auto accidents. 1 out of 7 people in America will experience it during their lifetime and the consequences can be devastating. The effects of a disability can cause a financial hardship to a loved one's family - often worse than the financial loss from a death.

Flaming Arrow #6 - the "T" word, TAXES!

"If Patrick Henry thought that taxation without representation was bad, he should see how bad it is with representation." - Old Farmers Almanac

Isn't it funny when congress talks about a slight tax increase it costs us $200 and a substantial tax cut saves us thirty cents!

Do you realize that the biggest chunk of money you will ever put in one place is the money you hand over to the US Government? If you were to make $50,000 a year over a 30 year career, you would pay about $600,000 in Federal, State and local taxes. The interest you would have made on that money over the years carries it easily over the million dollar mark.

The average person will give up $1,000,000 in taxes in their lifetime! That's sad, especially when you realize that most people die without ever amassing $100,000 in cash.

And when companies pay more in taxes they simply pass it onto us the consumer. For many decades, business owners have been facing overwhelming odds against their long-term survival due in large part to the oppressive tax system, which seems to stand in the way of a profitable business operation. More specifically, The IRS is the one powerful agency that can most quickly break a small business owner.

And what about the fact that an internal IRS Audit determined that over half a million taxpayers overpaid their taxes to the tune of three hundred and eleven million dollars. I repeat, a half a million taxpayers overpaid their taxes by $311,000,000. Why? Fear of the IRS! The IRS probing into your financial affairs seems to describe one of life's most dreaded experiences.

We're choking on taxes. And where has it gotten us? We've got a huge national debt with little family savings. And it's all related to taxes.

This is a game. You've been playing this game since you were born, except no one asked if you wanted to play. The game is the game of taxes. How many of you realize by now you can't quit this game? It's going to be played, and you're going to be a player, whether you want to play or not.

"The best use of life is to invest it in something which will outlast it.
~ William James

"Avoiding danger is no safer in the long run than outright exposure. Life is either a daring adventure, or nothing."
~ Helen Keller

The key is to learn to play the game of taxes so you can soon score huge financial gains!

What about Tax Professionals?

Every year Money Magazine sends out a tax situation to at least a hundred tax return preparers. Of the responses they received one year, they found a difference in tax liabilities anywhere from thirty-five thousand dollars up to sixty nine thousand dollars owed. What if you were the person who paid sixty nine thousand dollars? That equates to 100% of an overpayment in taxes! How would you know? Do you think the IRS is going to notify you if you overpaid your taxes?

What about Audits?

The chance of being audited by the IRS is 1 out of every 2 people and typically you will have some problem with your taxes at least once during your lifetime. Have you faced an audit? Received a bill for back taxes? Or had some other serious problem with the IRS?

Federal tax lien filings have tripled and IRS Enforcement Action is heating up.

Far too many accountants are intimidated by aggressive revenue agents and can very easily be pressured into giving damaging information about you, their client. Any number of practitioners who profess to be capable of representing clients before the IRS are more nervous about the confrontation than you.

Here's another fact I find interesting: Most people do not know how much income tax they pay during the course of a year.

Write down how much you paid last year in income taxes.

Write down how much you expect to pay at the end of this year.

Do you know your personal income tax bracket? Write it down.

Write down what you are doing right now to reduce your taxes?

And cheating is not an answer! In a national poll, one out of five Americans admitted to cheating on their tax returns. The IRS says that 17% of taxpayers don't fully comply with the tax laws on a regular basis. If you throw in people who cheat by not filing, the number is closer to one in four. Undoubtedly the figure would be higher if wage earners did not have taxes withheld by their employers and the self-employed did not have their earnings reported to the IRS on 1099 forms.

Realistically, cheating by self-employed people approaches 100%. It may just be a question of degree. Did you ever mail a personal letter with a business bought stamp?

"Progress always involves risk; you can't steal second base and keep your foot on first base."
–Fredrick Wilcox

Flaming Arrow #7 - Bankruptcy

The Bankruptcy Abuse Prevention and Consumer Protection Act of 2005 (BAPCPA) went into effect in October 2005. BAPCPA represents the most significant change in bankruptcy law since the Bankruptcy Code was first enacted in 1978. Its enactment followed nearly eight years of debate in Congress. Some of the more significant changes introduced to bankruptcy doctrine include:

· Increasing the amount of paperwork which must be filed by every debtor;

· Making it more difficult for individuals to receive a Chapter 7 discharge via a "means test";

· Allowing creditors to pursue collection remedies without court permission in various circumstances;

· Requiring that attorneys for debtors conduct investigations of their clients' filings and be personally liable for them.

Upon signing the bill, President Bush stated, "Under the new law, Americans who have the ability to pay will be required to pay back at least a portion of their debts… the new law will also make it more difficult for serial filers to abuse the most generous bankruptcy protections…the law will also allow us to clamp down on bankruptcy mills that make their money by advising abusers on how to game the system."

As an aside, I need to tell you that the First Circuit Court's decision to tie corporate veil piercing logic and arguments to bankruptcy proceedings is a landmark development. It significantly changes the dynamics of bankruptcy proceedings for business owners, making it all the more important to ensure you are maintaining proper corporate governance for your business entities. (After the "Inc." Dries…® in Minutes! is a service offered by Sage International, Inc. To learn more call 1-800-254-5779).

Women and Bankruptcy

In the last year alone, there were more than 1.5 million bankruptcy filings. That's up 15% from last year. A more startling statistic is that nearly 1 million of those filings were women and because of their likely role as caregivers in our society, these female filers bring almost 2 million children into bankruptcy court with them.

In fact, the bankruptcy filing rate is eight times higher than during the Great Depression - with one household in every 100 going the bankruptcy route.

On the flip side, reports show that about 200,000 women will be creditors in a bankruptcy proceeding, seeking child support and/or alimony payments from bankrupt filers. And even though these debts are not dischargeable in bankruptcy, these women will now be forced to compete on the same level with banks and credit card companies,

Section 5 • Chapter 1: Be Prepared. Don't Let the World Kick You in the Assets!

"Freedom means the opportunity to be what we never thought we would be."
~Daniel J. Boorstin

"Respond intelligently even to unintelligent treatment."
~ Lao-tzu

which have been elevated to a more secured status under the BAPCPA reforms that mandate repayment plans over liquidation.

If you sold all of your assets today could you cover all of your debt?

When is the last time you have done a complete financial inventory? Listing all of your assets, liabilities, personal property, bank accounts, retirement accounts, business interests, stock, bonds, planes, trains and automobiles? Do you know your true net worth?

Flaming Arrow #8 - Job Security

"Fail to Plan and You Plan to Fail"

More than 3 million jobs have been eliminated each year since 1989, for a loss of 43 million jobs since 1979 and every year over 8 million Americans become unemployed.

Average wages have stagnated since 1973, something they haven't done since the Civil War. Did you know that the average family income is substantially lower today than it was back in 1989? In fact, 95% of all Americans retire in poverty after working for 45 years!

Out of 100 people that start working at age 25, by age 65…1% are wealthy, 4% have enough money to retire, 3% are still working (they can't afford to quit), 64% depend on social security, friends or charity and 29% are dead.

If you retire at age 65 and live to be 85, you'd need $240,000 saved up to be on a fixed income of only $12,000 a year!

One fellow said that he thought the perfect retirement plan would be one where the only check that bounced was the one written to his undertaker.

Unfortunately, most of us have no idea how long either we, or our money are going to live.

Will your current plan give you more than that? Ask yourself, how golden will your Golden Years really be? Think about your retirement savings. For many of us, that nest egg is our single largest asset - and now that nest egg is under assault.

We are once again witnessing another huge wave of layoff announcements coupled with the never ending financial tragedies brought on by the big corporations.

"There is no business entity or individual…that 'has it made.' There is no business so successful and secure that there isn't the chance of a big surprise just around the corner. Success is a thing of the past, not the future, because you can never be sure what's coming. About all you can predict is that things will change and there will be surprises."

–From the Printer's Ink newsletter, published by Thomson-Shore, Inc

Flaming Arrow #9 – Unexpected Death

About 17 years ago we received a call from a couple who needed to set up a living trust immediately because the very next day the husband was going in for open-heart surgery. On their way to the hospital they stopped by the office to sign all of the trust documents. I felt a little uneasy because the husband obviously wasn't feeling well and his wife, a lovely woman in her late 40's was pacing back and forth, showing signs of extreme anxiety. After they left, I felt pretty good because we were able to help. A few days later we got a phone call from one of their relatives telling us that while the husband was in surgery his wife suddenly collapsed and died instantly from a massive heart attack. I was stunned! Both of them were so concerned about his survival and the totally unexpected happened: He lived and she died.

I've presented you with a lot of issues. Are there any solutions? I believe there is!

Conclusion

- Asset Protection planning must be a life-long process. Your financial picture constantly changes as you acquire or dispose of assets. Also the risks you are exposed to may change as well as your financial objectives and priorities. Thorough and periodic reviews will ensure your plan is updated and that you do not become vulnerable.

The Golden Years – *You need a lot of gold to get through them!*

"Man's mind, once stretched by a new idea, never regains its original dimensions."
– *Oliver Wendell Holmes*

NOTES

Chapter 2:
Protect Your Personal Assets

- Homestead
- Home Equity Line of Credit
- Insurance
- Medicaid Planning Basics

Case Study 9 (Josh & Anita)

The phone pierced the silence at 3:00 a.m. Grabbing his glasses, Josh picked up the phone and mumbled hello. "This is Sargeant Baker of the Reno Police. Do you own a 2001 Honda Accord?" Josh sat up straight, thinking about his daughter who had gone to a party that night, and quietly said, "yes".

"Your car was involved in a fatal accident. Do you know Tom Cashio, he was driving your car?"

"Yes, that's my daughter's boyfriend, what happened? Why was he driving my car? Is Katie o.k.?" A million questions were running through his head and a million knots in his stomach!

"Your daughter is fine and is in fact the one who reported the car missing." Sargeant Baker went on to say, "It appears Tom who was intoxicated, took the car without your daughters permission. He was clocked going 90 mph down Western Avenue, lost control and slammed head-on into a tree. He was pronounced dead on the scene."

(Melanie – Tom's Mom)

Overcome with shock and grief from the loss of her 19 year old son, Melanie vowed to do something. She was angry and decided to sue.

She sued Coor's Brewing Company because she felt they promoted underage drinking and she sued Josh & Anita, the parents of the young girl whose car Tom had taken without their permission, but as a result died that night.

Now let me ask you. Will Coor's Brewing Company be affected by this lawsuit? Probably not, they have a bank of attorney's on staff. Will the parents of the young girl who owned the car be affected? Positively, Yes! They easily could lose everything they own.

Key Points

- How your family's wealth is owned is something, which you must plan before liability is incurred. In other words, advance planning is much more likely to withstand a challenge than after the fact.

From Santa:

I'm writing this note to inform you
That taxes have taken away
The things that I find most important
My reindeer, my workshop, my sleigh.

So I'm making my rounds on a donkey
He's old and feeble and slow
So you know if you don't see me Christmas
I'm out on my ass in the snow!

Personal Assets

The first thing you need to look at is how you hold title to all of your assets?

- Your Home*
- Investment Property
- Bank Accounts
- Mutual Funds/Stocks
- Business Ownership
- All Other Types of Investments
- Intellectual Property (copyright, trademark, patent)
- Vehicles

To effectively insulate your assets, we need to legally change how you hold title to those assets so that you become separate from those assets. Remember, it's about control, not ownership.

When dealing with a personal residence it is not recommended that you re-title it into an LLC or a corporation because you will lose the few write-offs associated with taxes, mortgage interest, along with the $500,000 (married couple) or $250,000 (single person) federal capital- gains tax exclusion on your profit when you sell your home.

So everyone always asks me, how do I protect my home?

Homestead

Homestead exemption laws typically have three primary features:

1. They prevent the forced sale of a home to meet the demands of creditors;
2. They provide the surviving spouse with shelter;
3. They provide an exemption from property taxes which can be applied to a home.

For purposes of these statutes, a **homestead** is the one primary residence of a person, and no other exemption can be claimed on any other property anywhere, even outside the boundaries of the jurisdiction where the exemption is claimed.

In some states, homestead protection is automatic. In many states, however, the homeowner must file a claim for homestead exemption with the state, and will not receive the protections of the law until this has been done. Furthermore, the protection can be lost if the homeowner abandons the protected property by taking up primary residence elsewhere.

Homestead exemption, however, does not apply to forced sales to satisfy mortgages, mechanics liens or sales to pay property taxes.

Immunity from forced sale

States provide different levels of protection under their homestead exemption laws. Some only protect property up to a certain value, and if a home is worth more than that, the creditor can still force the sale of that home, but the owner can keep a certain amount of the proceeds of the sale.

What are homestead exemption laws?

Homestead laws were generally designed to protect the home from creditors, provides the right of occupancy given to a surviving spouse, minor children, and unmarried children of a deceased owner and also afford reduced property tax treatment. When people use the term "homestead exemption" they may be referring to the tax exemption or reduction, or the exemption from debts or execution for the payment of debts.

This page only discusses the exemption from debts aspect. Don't be confused.

The exemption does not mean that you cannot lose your home to creditors or that a lien cannot be placed on the home. If you borrow money on your home like most people do, the mortgage holder can foreclose and the exemption has no effect. If an unsecured creditor sues you and obtains a judgment, the creditor can enroll the judgment as a lien on your property. However, to the extent that you have a homestead exemption, the creditor cannot execute on the homestead and take the home.

Specific homestead laws vary from State to State. The homestead exemption may be used without filing a recorded claim in some States, while in others, a designation of homestead may be required. On the other hand, in virtually every State, in order to receive a homestead tax exemption the property must be designated as such.

Homestead exemption forms are usually available from the tax assessor in your county. If not, the tax assessor can provide you with the proper location.

State Laws

These laws are for your information only. You need to check the state codes for the most current version. All amounts are stated in general terms as specific variations may apply.

Alabama - Up to $5,000 in value, or up to 160 acres in area. - Code of Alabama, § 6-10-2

Alaska - Up to $64,800, no area limitation. - Alaska Statutes, § 09.39.010

Arizona - Up to $150,000, no area limitation Arizona Revised Statutes, § 33-1101

Arkansas - Up to $2,500 in value, or at least ¼ acre for city homesteads, 80 acres for rural homesteads Arkansas Code, §§ 16- 66- 210 and 218; Arkansas Constitution Article 9

California - Up to $50,000 in value. California Code Annotated, §704.730

Colorado - Up to $45,000 in value, no area limitation Colorado Revised Statutes Annotated, § 38-41-201

Connecticut - Connecticut General Statutes Annotated, § 52- 352b

142

Delaware - None - provided Delaware Code Annotated, § 4901- 3

District of Columbia - D. C. provides an exemption equal to owner's aggregate interest in real property (No monetary or area limitations) District of Columbia Code § 15- 501. DC does not call this a homestead exemption.

Florida - Exemption equal to value of property as assessed for tax purposes (No monetary limitations) - area limitations of ½ acre urban land or 160 acres rural land Florida Constitution, Article 10 § 4

Georgia - Up to $5,000 in value, no area limitation. Code of Georgia, Annotated, § 44- 13-1 and 44- 13- 100

Hawaii - Up to $20,000, but the head of a family and persons 65 years of age or older are allowed up to $30,000, no area limitation Hawaii Revised Statutes, §§ 651- 91, 92

Idaho - Up to $50,000 in value, no area limitation Idaho Code § 55- 1003

Illinois - Up to $7,500 in value, no area limitation. Where multiple owners, can be increased to $15,000 Illinois Compiled Statutes, Annotated, § 734 5/ 12- 901

Indiana - Up to $7,500 for residence, up to $4,000 for additional property, no area limitation. Co-owner, if also a joint debtor, may claim additional $7,500. Annotated Indiana Code, § 34- 55- 10-2

Iowa - No monetary limitation, but a minimum value of $500 - area limitations of ½ acre urban land or 40 acres rural land Iowa Code Annotated, §§ 561.2 and 561.16

Kansas - No monetary limitation - area limitations of 1 acre urban land or 160 acres rural land Kansas Constitution, Article 15 § 9 and Kansas Statutes, Annotated, § 60-2301

Kentucky - Up to $5,000 in value, no area limitation Kentucky Revised Statutes, § 427.060

Louisiana - Up to $25,000, but may include entirety of property in cases of catastrophic or terminal illness or injury. Area limitations of 5 acres urban land or 200 acres rural land Louisiana Statutes Annotated, § 20:1

Maine - Up to $25,000 in value, but may be up to $60,000 under certain circumstances, no area limitation Main Revised Statutes, Annotated, § 4422

Maryland - Up to $3,000, but in Title XI bankruptcy proceedings, up to $2,500, no area limitation Annotated Code of Maryland, § 11-504

Massachusetts - Up to $300,000 in value, no area limitation Annotated Laws of Massachusetts, § 188- 1

Michigan - Up to $3,500 in value - area limitations of 1 acres urban land or 40 acres rural land Michigan Compiled Laws, § 600.6023

Minnesota - Up to $200,000 in value, but up to $500,000 if used primarily for agricultural purposes- area limitations of ½ acre urban land or 160 acres rural land Minnesota Statutes, Annotated, § 510.02

Mississippi - Up to $75,000 in value - area limitation of 160 acres Annotated Mississippi Code, § 85- 3-21

Missouri - Up to $8,000 in value, no area limitation Annotated Missouri Statutes, § 513.475

Montana - Up to $100,000 in value, no area limitation Montana Code, Annotated, §§ 70- 32-101, 70- 32- 104 and 70- 32- 201

"There are two things to aim at in life; first to get what you want, and after that to enjoy it. Only the wisest of mankind has achieved the second."
–Logan Pearsall Smith

Nebraska - Up to $12,500 in value - area limitation of 2 lots, urban land or 160 acres rural land Revised Statutes of Nebraska, § 40-101

Nevada - Up to $350,000 in equity, no area limitation Nevada Revised Statutes, § 115- 010

New Hampshire - Up to $50,000 in value, no area limitation New Hampshire Revised Statutes, Annotated, § 480:1

New Jersey - No homestead exemption is provided, but an exemption for personal property of up to $1,000 is allowed New Jersey Statutes, Annotated, § 2A: 17- 1 and 2A: 17-17

New Mexico - Up to $35,000 in value, no area limitation New Mexico Statutes, Annotated, § 2-10-9

New York - Up to $10,000 above liens and encumbrances in value, no area limitation Consolidated Laws of New York, Annotated, CPLR § 5206

North Carolina - Up to $10,000 in value, no area limitation General Statutes of North Carolina, Annotated, §1C- 1601 and North Carolina Constitution, Article X

North Dakota - Up to $80,000 in value, no area limitation North Dakota Century Code, Annotated, § 47- 18- 01

Ohio - Up to $5,000 in value, no area limitation Ohio Revised Code, § 2329.66

Oklahoma - Unlimited in value - area limitations of 1 acre urban land or 160 acres rural land. However, where using more than 25% of property for business purpose, the value drops to $5,000. Oklahoma Statutes, Annoted, §§1 and 2

Oregon - Up to $25,000 in value - area limitations of one city block if within a city or 160 acres rural land Oregon Revised Statutes, § 23.240

Pennsylvania - No homestead exemption provided, but a general monetary exemption of $300 exists. Pennsylvania Consolidated Statutes, Annotated, §§ 8121, et. Seq.

Rhode Island - Up to $150,000 in value, no area limitation General Laws of Rhode Island, § 9- 26- 4.1

South Carolina - Although no homestead exemption is provided, an exemption for personal and real property of up to $10,000 in value may include property claimed as a residence Code of Laws of South Carolina, § 15- 41-30

South Dakota - No monetary limitation - area limitation of one dwelling house and contiguous lots used in good faith South Dakota Codified Laws, §§ 43- 31-1 and 43-31-4

Tennessee - Up to $5,000, but may be up to $7,500 if claimed by two persons as a homestead, no area limitation Tennessee Code, Annotated, § 26-2-301

Texas - No monetary limitation - area limitation of 10 acres urban land or 100 acres of rural land if claimed by a single person. A family may claim 200 acres of rural land Texas Property Code, Annotated, §§ 41.001 and 41.002 and Texas Constitution, Article 16 § 51

Utah - Up to $20,000 in value, but only $5,000 in value if property is not primary residence - area limitation of 1 acre Utah Code, §78-23-3

Vermont - Up to $75,000 in value, no area limitation Vermont Statutes Annotated, Title 27, § 101

Virginia - Up to $5,000, but may be increased by $500 for each dependant residing on property, no area limitation Code of Virginia, § 34-4

Washington - Generally, up to $40,000 in value, but may be unlimited if used against income taxes on retirement plan benefits, no area limitation Revised Code of Washington, Annotated, § 6.13.030

West Virginia - Up to $5,000 in value, but an additional $7,500 may be available in cases of "catastrophic illness or injury," no area limitation West Virginia Code, Annotated, §§ 38-9-1 and 38-10-4

Wisconsin - Up to $40,000 in value. No area limitation. - Wisconsin Statutes, Annotated, § 815.20

Wyoming - Up to $10,000 in value. Each co-owner is entitled to a homestead exemption. Wyoming Statutes § 1-20-101

Home Equity Line of Credit

HELOC stands for home equity line of credit, or simply "home equity line." It is a loan set up as a line of credit for some maximum draw, rather than for a fixed dollar amount.

For example, using a standard mortgage you might borrow $150,000, which would be paid out in its entirety at closing. Using a HELOC instead, you receive the lender's promise to advance you up to $150,000, in an amount and at a time of your choosing. You can draw on the line by writing a check, using a special credit card, or in other ways.

HELOCs are convenient for funding intermittent needs, such as paying off credit cards, making home improvements, or paying college tuition. You draw and pay interest on only what you need.

Since it is a lien (usually a 2nd mortgage) against your property it's a great way to tie up a chunk of equity, hence offering additional asset protection on your personal residence.

Interest on a HELOC

Because the balance of a HELOC may change from day to day, depending on draws and repayments, interest on a HELOC is calculated daily rather than monthly. For example, on a standard 6% mortgage, interest for the month is .06 divided by 12 or .005, multiplied by the loan balance at the end of the preceding month. If the balance is $100,000, the interest payment is $500.

On a 6% HELOC, interest for a day is .06 divided by 365 or .000164, which is multiplied by the average daily balance during the month. If this is $100,000, the daily interest is $16.44, and over a 30-day month interest amounts to $493.15; over a 31 day month, it is $509.59.

"You will never 'find' time for anything. If you want time, you must make it."
- Charles Bruxton

The Risks of a HELOC

The major disadvantage of the HELOC is its exposure to interest rate risk. All HELOCs are adjustable rate mortgages (ARMs), but they are much riskier than standard ARMs. Changes in the market impact a HELOC very quickly. If the prime rate changes on April 30, the HELOC rate will change effective May 1. An exception is HELOCs that have a guaranteed introductory rate, but these hold for only a few months. Standard ARMs, in contrast, are available with initial fixed-rate periods as long as 10 years.

Have Enough Insurance

The basic principle underlying all insurance is "shared risk". Simply put, a large number of people pay a small amount of money each to share the calculated risk of suffering a large financial loss through no fault of their own. As an example, you might pay $300 to insure a piece of property worth $100,000. If the property is totally destroyed, say by fire, the insurance company would pay the $100,000. The idea is that most of us can afford the comparatively small amount of money (premium) to pay for the insurance policy but could not afford the full loss, or even the partial loss, of the destroyed or damaged property. Obviously, not all insured property is going to be damaged or destroyed in any given year, or perhaps ever. That is the "risk" part of the equation and is determined by professionals called actuaries as the insurance companies determine how much each insured must pay as his or her "share" for the insurance.

The terms "property" and "casualty" mean the following:

Property means real property and physical property, that is things, like houses, cars, buildings, and so forth. It is the "stuff" side of insurance. Casualty refers to people and the injuries they may sustain. The casualty part of insurance is also called Liability because someone other than yourself may be injured through some act or fault of yours and you can now be legally liable for those injuries.

Homeowners insurance has three basic parts: dwelling, contents, and liability.

The dwelling part is pretty straightforward. It's based on the value of the home (not including the cost of the land). Be sure you get an optional coverage called "replacement cost". This option obligates the insurance company to pay for the cost of replacing (not improving nor enlarging) your home even if, due to current costs, the cost to replace exceeds the limit stated on the policy. The replacement cost option protects you against unanticipated spikes in the cost of building materials and labor.

The contents portion of a homeowners insurance policy covers things in the house: furniture, clothing, tableware, etc. It will also cover things like garden tractors and tools if in an outbuilding destroyed in the same occurrence. Typically, the dollar amount of the contents insurance is a percentage, usually 50% to 60%, of the value of the dwelling. You will want to get the replacement cost option on the contents as well. The reason for this is that partial claims are usually settled on an actual cash value basis. This means that a certain amount will be deducted from the payment for depreciation. For example, the

"It is good to learn what to avoid by studying the misfortunes of others." – Publius Syrius

water heater in your home springs a leak and ruins the carpet in the family room. The carpet store gives you a price of $600 to replace the carpet with like kind and quality. But the insurance claims adjustor points out that your carpet was five years old and showed considerable wear. Therefore the company will deduct 25% for depreciation. So subtracting the policy deductible of $250 and 25% or $150 for depreciation, the insurance company pays you $200. Be advised that this is fair. The insurance company did not agree to improve or better your situation. It agreed to pay for your loss. You lost a five year old carpet. The way to a happier settlement is to secure the replacement cost option on the contents as well as the dwelling. The deductible will apply in any case, but in the example above the replacement cost option would have put an additional $150 in your pocket.

There are some additional matters regarding contents you should consider. Let me give you an example. Your wedding ring is large, contains several stones of varying size, and in total is very expensive. One day you look down at it and realize that one of the diamonds in the ring is missing. You have no idea when or how the stone was lost. The occurrence (insurance jargon: mysterious disappearance) may not be covered under your homeowners insurance for jewelry because that insurance may be limited to only loss by fire or theft. Even if some coverage is available, without a written appraisal by a registered gemologist, it will be very difficult to establish value, and even if reasonable value can be agreed upon, it may exceed the limits of your policy. The solution: if you have an unusual circumstance, say some very expensive jewelry, valuable antiques, fine art, or expensive audio/visual equipment, consider putting such items on a schedule with appraised values for each.

The final part of homeowners insurance is liability insurance. This protects you and members of your immediate family in the event that someone should be injured on your property or that you do physical damage to the property of others. The service repairman who tumbles down your basement steps because of a roller skate carelessly left there, or your daughter's softball goes through your neighbors window and shatters a $1,000 antique vase are just some examples of instances where your homeowners liability insurance would come into play.

In addition to the standard homeowners liability insurance you may want to consider two additional coverages: The first is a "personal injury" endorsement. Personal injury means claims arising out of issues like false arrest, malicious prosecution, libel, slander or defamation of character, invasion of privacy, wrongful eviction or wrongful entry. If you are engaged in volunteer work or gratuitous civic or public service activities, this can be a vital addition to your insurance.

The second addition to consider is a "personal liability umbrella" policy. This is insurance which is over and above, like an umbrella, the dollar limits of your homeowners liability insurance. The dollar limits of the liability umbrella are usually $1,000,000 or $2,000,000. This umbrella can be significant if you have high value assets such as expensive real estate, a valuable stock portfolio or high value collectibles which could be at risk in an expensive lawsuit. (Dogs and swimming pools involve additional liability risks. Consider higher liability limits and make sure you are in compliance with insurance company requirements regarding fencing, etc.)

Renters Insurance

Many people who rent apartment units or other housing mistakenly assume that the owner's insurance policy will cover the loss of personal property after a devastating event (fire, flood, break-ins, etc.). The reality is that renters are not automatically protected - the landlord will only be reimbursed for the structure itself, not the renters' belongings.

Renters insurance is similar to homeowners insurance except there is obviously no insurance on the dwelling since that is owned by someone else. Renters insurance provides protection for contents and liability, including injury and damage to the property of others. Many renters overlook this insurance because they feel their situation is "temporary" and because they believe their furniture and belongings are of relatively little value and not worth insurance. If that is your opinion you may want to price some new furniture and appliances. However, even if you are correct, you still face the liability issues.

Many renters discover that the liability coverage provided by renters insurance is even more valuable. Landlords are generally responsible for accidents and dangerous conditions on public property, but this protection ends right at the renters' sidewalks or doorways.

After all, when your friend's grandmother visits your apartment slips and falls breaking her hip on the new rug you failed to secure, you can't blame the landlord. If a visitor slips and falls on a renter's floor then decides to sue for damages, renters insurance should cover the medical expenses. This may just be an exchange of information between insurance companies, not an actual civil law proceeding.

If you are a renter, you need renters insurance!

Automobile Insurance

Collision and Comprehensive

An automobile insurance policy is typically divided into four parts: physical damage, liability, medical payments and uninsured/underinsured motorists.

Collision, one part of the physical damage coverage, is the part you probably think of first. It is the insurance that pays for damage to your automobile as the result of an accident. If you have financed the purchase of your vehicle, the bank will require you to carry this insurance and they will be listed as the party to be paid if damage results in a total loss. The dollar amount of the insurance is not determined by you, it is determined at the time of loss by calculating the actual cash value of your vehicle using industry wide reference sources such as the NADA guides or Kelly Blue Book. (If you own an older vehicle which is paid for you may want to check Kelly Blue Book or other sources to

"Experience is not what happens to a man: it is what a man does with what happens to him."
–Aldous Huxley

determine the vehicle value. It may not be cost effective to pay several hundred dollars a year for physical damage coverage on an older low value vehicle). If you are involved in an auto accident and your insurance company pays for the damage to your vehicle, you will be required to pay a part of the cost which is known as the "deductible". Typical are $250 or $500. The higher deductible you select, the lower your cost for the insurance. This is not a dollar for dollar trade-off. Think carefully about selecting a $1000 deductible which saves you $60 a year in premium. Also, if you finance your vehicle, the bank may set a maximum on the deductible you can choose.

There is a second part to automobile physical damage insurance. This is called Comprehensive. It pays for damage that is not the result of an accident such as, hail, vandalism, a rock smacking your windshield, or contact with a deer.

The second important part of an auto insurance policy is known as Liability. This refers to your liability if you are involved in an auto accident which is adjudged to be your fault and your insurance company pays. The dollar amounts of liability insurance are frequently listed on the insurance policy as "per person" and "per accident". Thus you may find your auto insurance policy lists $100,000/$300,000 liability limits. This means that the maximum your insurance company will pay for one damaged auto and one injured person is $100,000. The maximum they will pay for any one accident, regardless of the number of autos or persons involved, is $300,000. Auto Liability insurance covers not only the damage which you may do to another persons vehicle, but also to the injuries which the other driver and passengers may sustain. Costs for medical care, permanent disabilities, loss of limbs or eyes, and the cost of lost wages, not to mention the costs of litigation, can far exceed the costs to fix damaged autos. It is generally advisable therefore to choose the highest liability limits available to you. In other words, don't scrimp on Liability limits.

A widely misunderstood part of auto insurance is the third part, Medical Payments. It is not to be confused with Liability discussed above. Medical Payment insurance covers you and in some instances your passengers for injuries that you sustain that are not covered by the other driver's insurance. In some instances, Medical Payments may come into play if the other driver's limits of liability have been exhausted. Medical Payment insurance is not frequently used, but it is inexpensive in cost. This insurance generally has low limits and may be optional.

The fourth part of an auto insurance policy is Uninsured and Underinsured Motorist. This insurance protects you in the event that you are involved in an accident caused by another driver who either has no auto insurance or has insurance with limits of liability so low that they are exceeded by your injuries. Why, you ask, should you have to pay for insurance that the other guy should be paying for? The answer is: you shouldn't. However, the facts are that there are many folks out there driving (illegally) without auto insurance or with insurance with the minimum possible liability limits, typically $20,000 per person and $40,000 per accident. Ironically, the underinsured drivers or those driving without insurance are frequently those with the poorest driving records. Consider your Uninsured/Underinsured insurance limits carefully. It is you and your family you are protecting.

"All men dream but not equally. Those who dream by night in the dusty recesses of their minds wake in the day to find that it was vanity; but the dreamers of the day are dangerous men, for they may act their dream with open eyes to make it possible."
–T.E. Lawrence

Life Insurance

Life insurance is unique in that it is solely for the protection of others. Those "others" are your spouse, your children, or at least other members of your family. When you die it can pay for all those outstanding bills, loans, legal costs, and burial expenses. Unfortunately, dying is expensive. Unless you want those expenses to come out of retirement funds, savings, or from a 2nd mortgage on the house you just paid off, you will need some type of life insurance when you die.

Disability Insurance

Disability insurance provides a continuing income stream over an agreed period of time in the event that you become disabled and are temporarily unable to work. Although both will involve answering health related questions on the application, health insurance and disability insurance are not the same thing. Health insurance may pay for the treatment of any injury or disease that disables you, but it will not help pay for your ongoing living expenses while you recuperate and before you can return to work. Health insurance pays your medical providers, disability insurance pays you.

So called "accident" insurance is also not disability insurance. Such policies pay only for a disability which is the result of any accident and pay for only a short period of time. Most people overlook disability insurance because they haven't done the math. If your monthly and annual budget requires two incomes, how well and how long could you survive on one, or on none?

Long-Term Care Insurance

The impact that long term care costs can have on you and your family should not be ignored. Roughly 1 out of 4 Americans between the ages of 55 and 79 is severely disabled. Forty percent of persons 65 or older will spend some time in a nursing home.

The average monthly cost of a nursing care facility in around the U.S. is $4,000. Most people do not have or are unable to qualify for long term care insurance. In addition, long term care policies usually provide only partial coverage and/or coverage for a limited number of years. Consequently, many people will be faced with using their entire life savings to cover the costs of long-term care.

With proper estate planning, however, this unfortunate result can be avoided.

With so many long-term care insurance policies to choose from, insurance companies are attempting to distinguish themselves and their products from one another. One marketing strategy is to offer policies with a laundry list of special features, discounts, riders, and expanded benefits. As insurers develop new long-term care products to appeal especially to baby boomers, they'll add all types of bells and whistles to entice you. Coverages within a long term care insurance policy can include nursing home care, home health care, assisted living, and adult day care.

When you're shopping around for long-term care insurance, try to compare the exact same level of coverage from policy to policy. You'll find that isn't always easy, because long term care policies differ enormously from company to company. Complicating matters is the fact that some companies include certain benefits in a basic policy, while others add them through riders. A rider will frequently add valuable benefits, but the key is determining which riders are worth the extra money. Watch out, though, some riders add to the cost without a corresponding increase in benefits to you.

Home health care rider

Sometimes you need to buy a rider to add home health care coverage if it's not part of a basic long-term care policy — and it's an extremely important benefit to purchase. With home health care, you may be able to avoid going to a nursing home or assisted living facility even if you're no longer able to care for yourself.

According to Kathleen Ligare, senior vice president with GE Financial Assurance's Long-Term Care Division in San Rafael, Calif., all of their policies have home health care coverage "baked" into them. She believes that home health care is a core benefit that should be included in every long-term care policy. In contrast, some insurers offer home health care coverage only as a rider to a nursing home policy.

While most people prefer to be cared for in their own home, nursing home care may be the only option in some areas. Jeff Sadler, president of SDS Inc., an insurance marketing, training, and sales firm in Ormond Beach, Fla., notes that in thinly populated states like North Dakota, you may experience great difficulty finding a quality provider of home health care in remote areas. Thus, you won't benefit from having home health care coverage. Most people, however, do need a policy that pays for home health care.

Nonforfeiture benefit rider

State insurance regulations often require that long-term care insurers offer nonforfeiture benefit riders. Furthermore, this option must be offered if you're buying a tax-qualified policy. As the name suggests, this rider assures that you won't forfeit all of your benefits even if you stop paying premiums before making a claim. However, Kim Purnell, a long-term care specialist in Palm Bay, Fla., and marketing director for Bankers United/Goldencare LTC Insurance Division, calls nonforfeiture benefit riders "a joke." You will pay premiums that are 40 percent higher (or more) for a policy with this rider. It will probably require that the policy be in force for a specified length of time before any benefit is available, your benefit will be lower or payable for a shorter period than it would be if you had continued paying the premium.

According to the United Seniors Health Cooperative, an independent consumer advocacy group, you'll pay in the neighborhood of 40 percent more for a policy with a nonforfeiture benefit rider attached to it. Ligare says all companies are required by insurance regulations to offer nonforfeiture benefit riders, but they're not purchased by many policyholders.

Return-of-premium rider

A return-of-premium rider is considered to be a type of nonforfeiture benefit. Your estate or a designated beneficiary will be entitled to the return of some or all of your premiums if the policy isn't used during your lifetime. With certain versions of this rider, after a specified number of years, you can drop the policy altogether and receive some portion of your premiums back. Return-of-premium riders are not available from all companies nor in every state. Some experts argue its value. The rider allows people to hedge their bets by buying the insurance coverage and get money back if they decide long-term care isn't necessary. Still others contend that you're paying more for the privilege of dropping the policy at a stage in life when there's a greater risk of needing long term care.

Return-of-premium riders are "typically not a good buy," says Sadler of SDS. The cost of purchasing this rider is significant, and you'd probably earn much more by investing the extra premium money yourself.

Shared-benefit rider

A shared-benefit rider lets you extend the duration of your benefit if both spouses have coverage. If both the husband and wife have a policy, the rider lets either draw from the other's policy if their own benefits are exhausted. Ligare says GE Financial Assurance builds this "shared care" feature into certain policies without using a rider and permits couples to share one single pool of benefits. It's less expensive than buying two separate policies.

Inflation rider

No matter which long-term care policy you buy, an inflation rider is an important option. These riders help ensure that your long-term care policy payments keep pace with the escalating cost of care. Because this coverage is so important, insurance regulators in many states require any purchaser of a long-term care policy to specifically reject the inflation rider.

Shop around for a policy in your state that has the benefits you want at a cost you can afford.

How to Be A Savvy Insurance Buyer – You and Your Agent

1. Assess your relationship to the agent. How comfortable does he or she make you feel? Are they using a lot of technical jargon, or explaining the insurance in a language you can understand? Is the agent answering your questions? Are they asking you enough of the right questions to determine what you really need or merely trying to sell you something? If you don't feel comfortable with this agent, then seek out another one.

2. Come prepared to the meeting with your insurance agent. Don't be afraid to make a list of the questions and issues you want to discuss. Better to consult a list than to remember later an important question you forgot to ask.

3. Don't be afraid to ask questions. There are no dumb questions in the purchase

"The question for each man to settle is not what he would do if he had means, time, influence and educational advantages; the question is what he will do with the things he has. The moment a young man ceases to dream or to bemoan his lack of opportunities and resolutely looks his conditions in the face, and resolves to change them, he lays the corner-stone of a solid and honorable success."
–Hamilton Wright Mabie

of insurance. If the agent appears impatient, or unsure of the answers, it may be time to find a different insurance agent.

4. Try to imagine real life situations and ask questions accordingly. For instance, if your home is partially damaged by a fire, but is uninhabitable because of the loss of critical facilities (water, power, heat) would your homeowners insurance pay for the cost for you and your family to live temporarily in a hotel or apartment?

5. Don't buy insurance from whoever answers the phone. Seek out an agent and try to find one with the most expertise in the insurance you are seeking. Also avoid buying insurance through the mail or by phone using 800 numbers. **If you don't consult an agent, you dramatically increase the chances of having uncovered claims.**

Things You Need To Do

Think about the type of insurance you need to buy. Become familiar with the general concepts and terminology which applies.

When your insurance policy is delivered READ IT. At least make sure, for instance, that all of your autos are listed. If the policy has beneficiaries, confirm that all the names are spelled correctly and relationships to you are correct. Confirm the coverage limits, face values, are those you discussed with the agent. If you chose options or "riders", make sure they are with the policy. Remember, the people who process insurance policies are human too!

If you are facing a major life event: marriage, birth of a child, divorce, a new business venture, etc. consider the implications for your personal insurance. The time to discuss such events with your agent is before, not a year after, they happen.

Video inventory your home and office.

Remember that insurance is a major purchase. Shop around and compare policy features, appropriateness for your needs, company ratings and price. Approach the purchase of insurance in the same way you would the purchase of any other significant cost long term purchase involving a contract full of legalese. In other words, don't shop by price alone.

MEDICAID PLANNING BASICS

Medicare vs. Medicaid

Just because you may be entitled to Medi**care** benefits does not mean you are entitled to Medi**caid** benefits. The **Medicare** program pays for hospital and physician costs for seniors and the disabled. The **Medicaid** program covers long term care costs, subject to certain income and asset restrictions.

Unfortunately, many nursing home residents end up exhausting their assets on long-term care. But it doesn't have to be that way. The best time to plan for the possibility of nursing home care is when you're still healthy. By doing so, you may be able to pay for your long-term care and protect assets for your loved ones. How? Through Medicaid planning. You worked hard all of your life to pay off your mortgage and build a retirement fund. You expected to live off your savings in the comfort of your own home, and you planned to leave something to your kids at the appropriate time. Suddenly, the unthinkable happens—you suffer a stroke at age 70 and must spend the rest of your years in a nursing home. What will happen to your life savings?

Eligibility for Medicaid depends on your state's asset and income-level requirements

Medicaid is a joint federal-state program that provides medical assistance to various low-income individuals, including those who are aged (i.e., 65 or older), disabled, or blind. It is the single largest payer of nursing home bills in America and is the last resort for people who have no other way to finance their long-term care. Although Medicaid eligibility rules vary from state to state, federal minimum standards and guidelines must be observed.

In addition to you meeting your state's medical and functional criteria for nursing home care, your assets and monthly income must each fall below certain levels if you are to qualify for Medicaid. However, several assets (which may include your family home) and a certain amount of income may be exempt or not counted.

Medicaid planning can help you meet your state's requirements

To determine whether you qualify for Medicaid, your state may count only the income and assets that are legally available to you for paying bills. Medicaid planning helps you devise ways of making your assets and income inaccessible. Along with qualifying you for Medicaid benefits, Medicaid planning seeks to accomplish the following goals:

- Sheltering your countable assets
- Preserving assets for your loved ones
- Providing for your healthy spouse (if you're married)

Over the years, attorneys have developed several strategies to rearrange finances and legally shelter assets from the state. These strategies—and the Medicaid rules themselves—can be complicated, so you should consult an *experienced elder law attorney* if you wish to take steps to protect your assets from the state.

According to Timothy L. Takacs, a Certified Elder Law Attorney he recommends you **do not** make the following:

Ten Asset Protection Mistakes with regards to Long-Term Planning

Mistake #1: Relying solely on a will or a living trust. A will takes effect only upon your death, and a living trust, although preferable in some cases, will not protect your assets from the government and nursing homes.

Mistake #2: Relying on Medicare or health insurance. Neither Medicare nor health insurance pays for the cost of long-term care in a nursing home. With the average cost exceeding $4000 a month, without a Plan most families will quickly run through their life savings.

"It is not work that kills men, it is worry. Work is healthy; you can hardly put more on a man than he can bear. But worry is rust upon the blade. It is not movement that destroys the machinery, but friction."
– Henry Ward Beecher

Mistake #3: Transferring all assets to children or other relatives. This almost always results in lengthy, unnecessary periods of ineligibility when Medicaid or other public assistance is applied for. And the tax consequences can be devastating. Often, it's wiser to do nothing.

Mistake #4: Placing all assets into joint ownership with another family member. This is often regarded the same as a transfer and can result in lengthy disqualification periods. Or it may not shelter assets at all. It can also create unfortunate legal problems for families.

Mistake #5: Selling the family home to pay for nursing home care. This is almost never required. Yet many still believe that a person must sell his home to pay the nursing home.

Mistake #6: Not taking Medicaid estate recovery seriously. The government can and does sell your home after your death to recoup benefits paid out on your behalf.

Mistake #7: Applying for a conservatorship or guardianship. This court-supervised method of dealing with a person's incapacity is time-consuming, costly, burdensome, and restrictive. With proper planning, you avoid the need to go to court.

Mistake #8: Relying on family members to "do the right thing" when critical health care and financial decisions need to be made. In the absence of a Plan to protect assets and other planning documents, this is an awful burden to place on the members of your family.

Mistake #9: Not seeking the advice of a specialist in elder law and asset protection planning. Medicaid and other government benefits programs are a highly complex area of the law; the law varies from state to state and even within a particular state. Very few attorneys and advisors know and understand the laws and rules that apply.

Mistake #10: Doing nothing. Unless you have no assets to protect or you are unconcerned about how decisions will be made in the event of your disability or incapacity, you should take steps now to protect yourself.

Conclusion

- Take stock of your property to paint a complete financial and legal picture.
- Prioritize your objectives and be prepared to compromise. How important is liquidity, control, taxes, return on investment. To what extent is one factor more significant than another? Only you can decide. And in many cases your asset protection plan is usually a catalyst for more effective total financial planning.
- Remember that insurance is a major purchase. Shop around and compare policy features, appropriateness for your needs, company ratings and price. Approach the purchase of insurance in the same way you would the purchase of any other significant cost long term purchase involving a contract full of legalese. In other words, don't shop by price alone.

"Little minds are tamed and subdued by misfortune, but great minds rise above them."
    – *Washington Irving*

Chapter 3:
Planning for Death (Yes it is going to happen)

- Only Three Ways to Pass Your Wealth
- Joint Tenancy
- Common Myths About Avoiding Probate
- Difference Between a Will and a Trust
- Living Trust versus Testamentary Trust
- Keeping Control of Medical Decisions

**I feel a warmth around me
like your presence is so near,
And I close my eyes to visualize
your face when you were here,
I endure the times we spent together
and they are locked inside my heart,
For as long as I have those memories
we will never be apart,
Even though we cannot speak no more
my voice is always there,
Because every night before I sleep
I have you in my prayer.
- Louise Bailey**

Case Study 10 (Groucho Marx)

Groucho had a Will. But he didn't plan for incapacity. The end of his life became a public circus – the court declared him incompetent, and his companion and family members battled for control over his money and his care. Court hearings were open to the public, and the press had a heyday reporting details about Groucho's personal life and his finances. Everyone had attorneys, of course – and Groucho had money. The ordeal certainly seemed to take its toll on Groucho, who was wheeled in and out of court. Only days after a relative was appointed by the court to care for him, Groucho died.

The same thing can happen to you. Without proper planning, the court can take control of your personal and financial affairs – regardless of the size of your estate.

Key Points

- Do not depend on the legal system of this country to take care of you, your family, and your estate.

No one likes to think about their own mortality or the possibility of becoming incapacitated. That's why so many families are caught off guard and unprepared when incapacity or death strikes.

When you die money will go to two of these:
- Attorneys (Courts)
- Taxes
- Family
- Charity

You have to decide which two you want.

In fact the federal government has passed laws requiring all Americans to donate a considerable portion of their family's wealth to the general welfare of this country. No one can be born in this country, grow rich in this country or die rich in this country without contributing a substantial portion of his or her accumulated wealth to others. However, what most families do not recognize is that you actually have a choice in how you support the general welfare of this country. You can do so as an involuntary philanthropist which, most Americans select as their default by simply overpaying their taxes or worse paying estate taxes by failing to do any type of estate planning. That's how you transfer all of your authority to the government and allow them to decide how to spend your hard earned dollars even though you may fiscally, morally or ethically oppose how our government will use your voluntary contribution.

Or you can choose to be a voluntary philanthropist, which means you retain control to self-direct your social capital to the causes and organizations you would like to support.

The sad truth is that upon your death, estate and inheritance taxes can destroy the very estate that you have worked so diligently all your life to create? Estate Tax is a federal tax levied on an estate when the owner dies. Inheritance tax is a state tax on the right to inherit.

Only Three Ways to Pass Your Wealth

- By Law: Joint Ownership with Right of Survivorship.
- By Will: This is the legal process (Probate) to validate a Will and handle the transfer of property to your heirs after all debts and taxes owed are paid. Probate is the only legal way to change title on a deceased person's assets.
- By Contract: This includes Life Insurance, Annuity Contracts and Trust Agreements because each has a named beneficiary and a contract to pay the proceeds to the heirs which means no Probate.

"I worked my way up from nothing to a state of extreme poverty."
~Groucho Marx

Joint Tenancy

A number of assets are commonly held jointly, such as homes and bank accounts. While jointly owned property may be useful in some situations, many people are unaware of the potential pitfalls of holding assets jointly. In fact, joint assets are a frequent source of litigation.

Joint tenancy of an asset arises when there is co-ownership of an asset among two or more persons. Joint assets are typically held in three different forms: *(1) tenancy in common; (2) joint tenancy with rights of survivorship; and (3) tenancy by the entirety.*

Tenants in common hold a proportionate undivided interest in the subject property. That portion of the property can be unilaterally sold, transferred, gifted or transferred by will.

A joint tenancy with rights of survivorship is similar to a tenancy in common; however, a co-owner decedent's share of the property will pass to the surviving joint tenant(s) and not through the decedent's will or by intestacy (when the decedent does not have a will).

A tenancy by the entirety arises presumptively when a husband and wife obtain assets jointly. A tenancy by the entirety also has rights of survivorship, but affords tenants additional protections such as limiting the ability of one spouse to sever the co-ownership and some creditor protection.

Pitfalls of Joint Ownership

A widow put all of her property, including her house, into Joint Ownership with her married daughter. She did this thinking that when she died her property would automatically go to her daughter without the need for Probate.

Several years later, her daughter and her husband separated and the widow decided to sell her house so she could move in with her daughter. But she soon discovered that she could not sell the house without her son-in-law's signature on the deed. The son-in-law was still legally married to her daughter and was entitled by law to a marital interest in the property. The title company would not insure clear title to the buyer without the son-in-law's signature because it was not clear what his interest would be. Her son-in-law refused to sign unless he got part of the money when the house was sold. The widow was stuck! She didn't know that Joint Ownership with a married person can include that person's spouse. And, because the widow had placed her house in Joint Ownership, she lost control of her own home!

When a Joint Tenant can't perform...

Most married couples own their property jointly, and they assume that if one of them becomes disabled or incompetent, the other can continue to take care of their personal and financial affairs without interruption. But look at what happened to this couple.

They were successful and responsible adults. They made safe investments and planned carefully for their future. They owned everything jointly and even had Wills, leaving everything to each other. But in just seconds their lives changed dramatically.

"To himself everyone is immortal; he may know that he is going to die, but he can never know that he is dead."
~Samuel Butler

The husband was in a tragic car accident and suffered extensive head injuries and brain damage. The wife could continue to write checks and pay their day-to-day bills because only one of their signatures was required on their checking account. But soon the cash started running out, and she was unable to sell any of their jointly-owned property without both signatures, and since her husband could not sign his name, the only way she could sell their property was to place her husband into Probate Guardianship and have the court sign for him. Her husbands Will was no help at all because he was still alive.

The wife had no idea how expensive and cumbersome this legal Joint Ownership could be. Not only did she have to deal with her husband's situation and the effects of this tragedy on their personal lives, but she had to deal with an impersonal court system. She was especially frustrated when she had to pay for the court to approve the sale of their own property and then get the court's approval on how her husband's share of that money would be used, even when it was used to pay for their personal bills and take care of him! When he finally died more than five years later, she found herself back in Probate Court - this time to Probate her husband's Will.

Things You Should Know About Joint Tenancy

Be aware that a joint owner has the ability to exercise ownership rights. A joint owner may have the ability to withdraw up to 100% of an account's funds. He or she may also be able sell their interest without the consent of the other joint owner(s) (this is not so with a tenancy by the entirety).

Joint ownership may result in an unintended lifetime gift and/or the accidental distribution of assets to an unplanned beneficiary.

Creditors may have the opportunity to not only reach the share of a debtor joint owner, but may attempt to reach the non-debtor co-tenant's portion as well.

Older adults often benefit from a reduction in real estate taxes because of their age. Adding another person to the deed who is under the age of eligibility for the tax reduction may disqualify the older adult from receiving the reduction in property taxes.

In the context of Medicaid planning, the establishment of joint ownership in an asset may constitute an uncompensated transfer which can affect Medicaid eligibility.

Common Myths About Avoiding Probate

Myth 1: "I have a will, so my family won't have to go through probate when I die."

False – Having a will does not avoid probate. In fact, a will is a one-way ticket to probate.

A will can have no effect unless it goes through the probate process – it must be admitted to the probate court to be legal and enforceable. Your will must be validated as being authentic before ownership of your assets can be transferred to your heirs, and the probate court is the only way this can be done.

Myth 2: "My will has a trust in it, so it won't have to go through probate."

"Let him who would enjoy a good future waste none of his present."
– Roger Babson

False – Many people think if they have a trust in their will, the trust lets them avoid probate. But, as I just explained, all wills – even those with trusts in them – must go through probate. The trust can't go into effect until after the will has been probated.

Myth 3: "I don't have a will, so there will be no need for my family to go through probate when I die."

False, again – Even if you haven't written a will, the state has written one for you. Every state has laws for the distribution of property for those who die without a will. So, if you don't have a will when you die (or if your will is not accepted by the court), the state has to make sure your debts are paid and your property is distributed according to the laws of that state – which may or may not be the way you would have wanted. Consider, for example, the true story of the famous movie actor James Dean:

His mother died when he was a small child, and his father sent him to live with an aunt and uncle who raised him. James, who had grown very close to his "new" family, had talked about wanting his aunt and uncle to receive most of his property if something happened to him, and particularly had expressed wanting to provide for his young cousin's college education – but he never got around to making out a will. When he was killed suddenly in a car accident, his estate went through probate. Since he did not have a will, his property was distributed according to California law (the state's will). Everything he owned was given to his father because he was his closest surviving relative, even though there had been little contact between them over the years. Under the terms of the state's will, his aunt and uncle (who had devoted years of their lives to raising and loving him) and his cousin received nothing.

Myth 4: "I have a power of attorney, so I don't need a will or joint ownership to avoid probate."

False – Some people give power of attorney to a spouse or adult child, thinking it will allow titles of their property to be transferred without probate when they die or if they become physically or mentally incapacitated. But a power of attorney is automatically revoked at death or incapacity, so it won't be of any use then.

Myth 5: "I'll just give it all away to my kids before I die so there won't be anything to probate."

True, there won't be any probate – but, depending on the size of the gift, there may be a gift tax involved. For example, if you transfer $30,000 in stocks to your son, you are making a gift. And if you make a gift of more than $13,000 per year per person, you have a potential gift tax liability.

Also, if you're giving your children titles to real property, you could be giving them a substantial income tax problem. That's because the property you give away would not receive a "stepped-up basis."   The "basis" of property is the value which is used to

"Death leaves a heartache no one can heal, love leaves a memory no one can steal."
– *Written on an Irish Headstone*

determine gain or loss for income tax purposes – in other words, what you paid for it versus what you receive for it when it's sold. If you give the property to your kids while you are still living, it keeps your basis (what you paid for it). But if they receive it as an inheritance (through a will or a trust), it receives a new "stepped-up" basis – and the property is revalued as of the date of your death.

For example:

Let's say you purchased a piece of property in 1985 for $100,000 and it's worth $300,000 when you die. If your children receive it as an inheritance, the basis for this property would now be $300,000. And if they sell it for $300,000, they would pay no income tax. But if you transferred title to your children while you were alive, the basis would be $100,000 (what you paid for it). If they then sold the property for $300,000 they would pay income taxes on the $200,000 gain – about $52,000.

Bottom line, giving property away just isn't nearly as simple as you may think it is – and it can cause both you and your children some serious tax problems.

Wills & Incapacity

As Groucho found out, a will doesn't provide any protection if you become incapacitated. Because a will can only go into effect when you die.

Whenever I ask anyone if they have a will I ask them to look at the following chart.

Difference Between a Will And a Trust

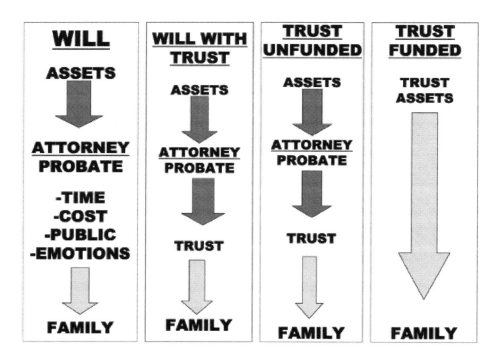

"One way to get the most out of life is to look upon it as an adventure."
– William Feather

See that last one? A fully funded Trust. My friend Tim Taylor (Estate Planning Schools of America) explains the Revocable Living Trust this way.

The most popular of all trusts in America is the Revocable Living Trust. It is nearly universal in its appeal and effectively resolves several serious problems instead of allowing your estate to be subject to the State and Federal taxes, fees, and long delays.

Living Trust Versus Testamentary Trust

A Living Trust is any trust established during your lifetime, hence the term intervivos, or living trust. Therefore, nearly every trust you may think of is considered a Living Trust.

Revocable and Amendable: Much of the appeal of the Living Trust is that it is capable of being revoked or amended with ease in the future.

Taxes: This form of trust does not have to file any taxes. It uses your Social Security number and all gains or losses are applied directly to your income tax forms. It is called "Living" because you form it while you are alive. This differs from "Testamentary" trusts formed by a Will at your death.

Control: You may act as your own trustees (who manage all trust assets and make all decisions). In the event you are not able at a later date to run your affairs, you have named successor trustees to take over without the need of court supervision. A Power of Attorney is added to non-trust matters.

Probate: Since you have predetermined the eventual transfer of your estate, your estate will not need the unnecessary costs and delays of Probate. This greatly reduces those problems inherent in the open ended process.

Federal Estate Tax: Married couples may DOUBLE their exclusion from Federal Estate Tax through a Living Trust's ability to preserve both tax credits. Single grantors keep their $1.2 million exclusion and a married couple may obtain a $2.4 million exclusion from this 37-55% tax. That's huge!

Capital Gain Tax and Gift Tax: Numerous families are currently in violation of the Gift Tax rules and will leave a Capital Gain Tax problem to their children by holding real estate and other assets in joint ownership with their family members. Gift tax is a tax imposed on the transfer of property by gift (without consideration). Such tax is imposed upon the donor of a gift (included in their gross estate) and is based on the fair market value of the property on the date of the gift. A Living Trust offers transfer without violating or incurring such taxes that penalize your heirs instead of helping them.

Of course, you only get all of these benefits if you actually "FUND" the trust. That means actually transferring (re-titling, recording, registering) all of your assets in the name of the trust.

Conversely, a **testamentary trust** is established at your death, generally by the demand of a Will. I have discovered that there are people under the belief that they have a trust, when they in fact, have only a Will that establishes a trust at their death. The cost to the individuals may be significant, especially for those who have a higher net worth due to their loss of their unified credit against lifetime gifts and Federal Estate Taxes.

Let's look at some famous people who failed to plan and what it actually cost them.

Estate Shrinkage Of Famous People Who Failed To Plan

Estate Shrinkage of Famous People Who Failed to Plan

Name	Gross Estate	Total Settlement	Net Estate	Percent Shrinkage
W.C. Fields	$884,680	$329,793	$554,887	37%
Nelson Eddy	$472,715	$109,990	$362,725	23%
Franklin Roosevelt	$1,940,999	$574,867	$1,366,132	30%
Humphrey Bogart	$910,146	$274,234	$635,912	30%
Clark Gable	$2,806,526	$1,101,038	$1,705,448	30%
Dean Witter	$7,451,055	$1,830,717	$5,602,338	25%
Henry J. Kaiser	$5,597,772	$2,488,364	$3,109,408	44%
Al Jolson	$4,385,143	$1,349,066	$3,036,077	31%
Gary Cooper	$4,948,985	$1,520,454	$3,454,531	31%
Myford Irvine	$13,445,552	$6,012,685	$7,432,867	45%
Walt Disney	$23,004,851	$6,811,943	$16,192,908	30%
William E. Boeing	$22,386,158	$10,589,748	$11,796,410	47%
William Frawley	$92,446	$45,814	$46,632	49%
Hedda Hopper	$472,661	$165,982	$306,679	35%
Marilyn Monroe	$819,176	$448,750	$370,426	55%
Elre Stanley Gardner	$1,795,092	$636,705	$1,158,387	35%
Cecil B. DeMille	$4,043,607	$1,396,064	$2,647,543	35%
Elvis Presley	$10,165,434	$7,374,635	$2,790,799	73%
J.P. Morgan	$17,121,482	$11,893,691	$5,227,799	69%
John D. Rockefeller	$26,905,182	$17,124,988	$9,780,194	64%
Alwin C. Ernst, CPA	$12,642,431	$7,124,112	$5,518,319	56%
Frederick Vanderbilt	$76,838,530	$42,846,112	$33,992,418	56%
Howard Gould	$67,535,386	$52,549,682	$14,985,704	78%

A Living Trust Story

Case Study 11 (Don and Marge)

Don and Marge set up one Living Trust together as Co-Grantors, and named themselves as Co-Trustees. They named their son Kevin as Back-up Trustee.

When Don suffered a stroke, Marge continued to take care of their financial affairs privately, with no court interference. She could concentrate on spending time with Don – instead of spending time in court. When Don later died, there was no probate. Marge met with their professional advisers to make sure their tax planning was done properly, and continued to handle all financial affairs without outside interference.

Several years later, Marge had a heart attack. Her son Kevin stepped in and handled everything. When Marge was able to manage her affairs again, Kevin stepped aside. Everything was done privately, with no court interference.

When Marge died, Kevin stepped in again and followed the instructions in Don and Marge's Trust. He paid their debts, met with their advisers and made sure that all tax returns were done properly. He worked with their attorney and bank trust officer to make sure everything was set up properly for the grandchildren. Then he distributed the remaining assets to family members and the church, as designated in the Trust.

Keeping Control of Medical Decisions

All this time I have been talking about how to keep control of your assets – now, at incapacity and after your death. What you need to know is that good estate planning is also about keeping control over decisions about your health care.

There are several other documents you will need at the time you set up your Living Trust:

Living Will – Better known as the "Right-to-Die Clause." This document says in effect that, if your life is being sustained solely by artificial means, it is your desire – (a decision made when you were competent) – that the plug be pulled. It lets others know how you feel about life support in case of terminal illness. One other point, living wills are absolutely crucial if family members do not agree on treatment of an ailing family member. (This point was recently driven home by the case of Terri Schiavo in Florida. There is no doubt in my mind that if Terri had a living will or health care power of attorney or both, Judge Greer, in the face of the family's disagreement, would have followed the directions in those documents to the letter and there never would have been multiple appeals to the courts and recourse to the Congress, all of which only guaranteed that Terri would have no dignity in her death.)

Durable Power of Attorney for Health Care – This is the second and more powerful "medical" document. This lets you choose the person you want to make ANY medical decisions for you – including life support – if you are unable to make them yourself. It is legally valid and enforceable. And it keeps the court from interfering in these private decisions.

Other ancillary documents should include a Durable General Power of Attorney (for decisions other than health care); Appointment of Guardian (minor children); Appointment of Conservator (who is responsible if you become incompetent); Assignment of Personal Effects (everything other than real property); Anatomical Gift (Organ Donor).

The good news is that a Living Trust can be designed to include just about anything you want. It is extremely flexible and gives you lots of control over what will happen to your possessions and to you if you become physically or mentally incapacitated and when you die.

The best time to set up a Living Trust is right now, while you are healthy and don't think you need one. Too many people put estate planning at the bottom of their priority list, when it really should be at the top.

And my last word of advice. Do not do this on your own. Depending on the size or your estate and your situation, you may need additional planning.

For example, you may have children from a previous marriage and could unintentionally disinherit or perhaps you have minor or adult children with special needs. I cannot emphasize enough about selecting and working with a qualified Estate Planning Attorney. Contact Sage International for a referral to someone in your state.

Conclusion

- By understanding the risks involved with the more common methods people use to try and avoid probate. A living trust has none of these risks. It completely avoids all probate and lets your plan stay your plan – it won't be altered by the court, unforeseen legal technicalities, or greedy relatives.

- Make sure you have all the ancillary documents included with your Living Trust to satisfy every potential contingency – now and in the years to come.

- Estate Planning is critical. By utilizing properly funded family living trusts, family limited partnerships, LLCs, corporations and irrevocable trusts you can avoid probate, create significant estate tax savings and have an effective method for removing assets from your estate.

- Learn everything you can about The Right Way and The Wrong Way of Leaving Money to Your Children (and others). I recommend the following books: Beyond the Grave by Gerald M. Condon, Esq. and Jeffrey L. Condon, Esq.; The Living Trust and How to Settle Your Living Trust by Henry W. Abts III; Best Intentions by Colleen Barney, Esq. & Victoria Collins, Ph.D., CFP

- If you don't like your children and family, then you should do absolutely nothing!

*"You can shed tears that she is gone,
or you can smile because she has lived.
You can close your eyes and pray that she'll come back,
or you can open your eyes and see all she's left.
Your heart can be empty because you can't see her,
or you can be full of the love you shared.
You can turn your back on tomorrow and live yesterday,
or you can be happy for tomorrow because of yesterday.
You can remember her only that she is gone,
or you can cherish her memory and let it live on.
You can cry and close your mind,
be empty and turn your back.
Or you can do what she'd want:
smile, open your eyes, love and go on."*

–David Harkins

NOTES

Chapter 4:
The First Layer of Your Wealth Foundation

- Factors We Consider When Developing a Strategy
- The Many "Tools" in Our Toolbox
- Irrevocable Trust
- The Limited Partnership
- Charging Order
- Limited Liability Company

Case Study 12 (Fred and Linda)

This couple contacted me last year to find out information about establishing a family foundation. After I gave them some information about the mechanics of a private foundation, I asked them how they created their wealth. What did they do for a living that now gives them the ability to share that wealth with others?

They proceeded to tell me they own 146 gas stations in California, Oregon and Washington. They own a fleet of trucks that hauls the gas to each location and they do it all as a sole proprietorship. (I nearly fell out of my chair!) They did go on to say they were recently sued and that also prompted them to start thinking about how to protect their hard-earned wealth. (Deep Pocket?) Oh, I almost forgot, they also told me they have 35 employees that do nothing but work on their personal tax return and they live in California (a high tax state!).

Key Points
- There is no one answer – no silver bullet – no magic formula that solves it for everyone.
- There are many tools in the toolbox and if you know they exist and how to effectively use them, you will be able to build a solid Foundation for Freedom.

"The avoidance of taxes is the only intellectual pursuit that still carries any reward."
–John Maynard Keynes

168

Factors We (Sage International) Consider When Developing a Strategy

1. We have to define your objectives and determine how soon you want to achieve them. Are you developing an exit strategy, retirement plan, or estate plan?
2. We have to be clear about your comfort level with a lot of new information and requirements.
3. We need to find out just how conservative or aggressive you want to be.
4. You need to tell us how much you are willing to invest (the cost) to complete the entire strategy.

Now, I could not take this couple (in their late 60's) and create 146 corporations. That would completely overwhelm them and of course, cost a ton of money. So what I told them at the very least is to separate each state. Form a Washington, Oregon and California corporation, to first segregate the assets according to each state but more important, to keep all of that income from flowing directly into the State of California. Over 65% of their money is earned outside the state of California, so why drag it all into the state to pay personal income taxes on?

Only the money they take as salary from those corporations would have to be declared on their personal income tax returns for the state of California.

Second, we need to form a couple of entities to hold the trucks. Once again, getting those high liability assets out of their personal name.

Third, set up the foundation and a couple of other types of trusts to start removing their highly appreciated assets from their estate. Besides having huge liability issues, major tax issues, they have to start thinking now about the estate tax issues as well. If they don't do something before they die, 3 nasty probates (CA, OR, and WA) will completely consume their family's time, energy and hard-earned wealth.

Is that their entire strategy? No. Without a lot more fact finding and specific information shared, no one can help these folks get structured.

The key is to start somewhere. Think about what keeps you up at night? That's where you start. Step-by-step, adding each piece of the strategy until it's complete. It could take weeks, months, even years. It's up to you. The bottom line through all of it is that you understand what you are doing, how all the pieces tie together, that you achieve the results you desire and most important, you have peace of mind because you know you are doing all the right things to protect and preserve everything you have worked so hard to create.

What I need you to understand is there is no one answer – no silver bullet – no magic formula that solves it for everyone.

That's why every strategy we develop is unique to our client.

"It's tough trying to keep your feet on the ground, your head above the clouds, your nose to the grindstone, your shoulder to the wheel, your finger on the pulse, your eye on the ball and your ear to the ground."

I can't even begin to tell you how many wealth building seminars I have been to, and have watched some attorney stand up on stage holding a nice little silver suitcase. And in his shiny suitcase sits all the documents to form a Corporation, Family Limited Partnership, and a Charitable Remainder Trust. This he declares: "is the answer to all of your problems." I am always amazed as I watch people rush to the back of the room and plunk down $2500. Please don't do that.

99.99% of the audience has absolutely no idea what a Charitable Remainder Trust is, what it is supposed to do, how it has to be treated, let alone how to properly set it up. Here's the caveat: In your shiny little suitcase there's a business card that states, "If you are having any problem setting up your entities, please call our toll free 800#. Bottom line: When all is said and done, another ten grand will be spent. This absolutely infuriates me!

Here's why:

The Many "Tools" in Our Toolbox

- Corporations ("S" and "C")
- Nonprofit Corporation/Private Foundation
- Professional Corporation
- Limited Liability Company
- Professional LLC
- Real Estate LLC (The BEST in the nation!)
- Series LLC
- Self-Directed IRA/401k owned 100% by an LLC
- Limited Partnership
- Limited-Liability Limited Partnership
- Domestic Asset Protection Trust
- Land Trust
- Charitable Remainder Unitrust (CRUT)
- Charitable Remainder Annuity Trust (CRAT)
- Charitable Lead Trust (CLT)
- Charitable Gift Annuity (CGA)
- Irrevocable Life Insurance Trust (ILIT)
- Qualified Personal Residence Trust (QRPT)
- Grantor Retained Unitrust (GRUT)
- Grantor Retained Annuity Trust (GRAT)
- Grantor Retained Income Trust (GRIT)
- Qualified Domestic Trust (QDOT)
- Beneficiary Trust
- Catastrophic Illness Revocable or Irrevocable Trust
- Children's Trust
- Generation Skipping Trust
- IRA and Qualified Plan Trust

And I know I didn't list them all…..

"I don't want to know what the law is, I want to know who the judge is."
– Roy Cohn

Until we know exactly where you are and where you want to go (are you going to sell it, give it away, pass it on to your family and friends, or spend it all?) can we lay out a strategy that's right for you. We have to select the right tools, resources, and additional experts necessary to accomplish the goals and objectives you've outlined.

With that being said, let's continue our education.

Irrevocable Trust

One of the truly fascinating features of a trust is its facility for passing money and property from generation to generation. Indeed, this is the intent of most trusts created by persons of power, privilege, and wealth. They regard their trust arrangement as a mechanism for creating ongoing life into eternity. Property- and the income from it – is passed on and on. In the generational process, the initial trustee is replaced by a successor trustee, who in turn is replaced by a successor trustee…and so on.

Over time, we have run across a lot of situations that surpass the limits of the Living Trust. These needs stem from ongoing changes in the federal tax code, state tax changes, and special needs to protect our children, protect individuals with special needs, and to protect our assets and/or business from potentially devastating consequences.

Very quickly a living trust (created while you are alive) may be defined as either a grantor type or non-grantor type trust. If it is a grantor trust, all of the income and tax liability remains with the grantor. With a non-grantor trust, which is also known as an **"Irrevocable Trust"**, you remove yourself from direct and indirect ownership and relinquish all the true control over to an independent trustee.

No matter how much money and property a trustor may have, no matter how clear and specific his trust instrument is, the success of a trust rests squarely and exclusively upon the trustee. A trustee must be loyal to his trustor while, at the same time, he is duty bound to the beneficiaries. The result is that every trustee is placed "in the middle" of all trust operations, once the trust property becomes irrevocable therein.

Three Pitfalls to Avoid with Irrevocable Trusts

1. You cannot reserve any power to revoke, rescind, or amend the trust or retain any rights, either directly or indirectly, to reclaim property transferred to the trust. Simply put, there can be no strings attached.
2. Gifts to trusts are given the most scrutiny under fraudulent transfer laws – because there is no "for value" exchange as there is with LLCs or FLPs. Often, for asset protection purposes, these tools are superior.
3. You, as the trust's grantor, cannot be its trustee. Nor can you appoint a trustee not considered at arm's length. Those who do not qualify for "arm's length" include your spouse, any close relative, or even a close personal friend. Courts closely examine the relationship between the grantor and the trustee to determine whether the trustee is only the grantor's "alter-ego." If there is such a relationship, courts will ignore the trust and allow creditors to reach the trust assets.

Tip: A corporate trustee, such as a bank or trust company, is much less likely to be judged as an alter-ego, thereby giving your trust an added layer of security.

These types of trusts can cause such a division of assets from the person that any liability and taxes are not laid at the feet of the grantor. Be advised however, there is a price to be paid for the advanced forms of trust. Anyone wishing such advanced planning should be fully prepared for the demands required for such protection.

Let's talk about some of our most widely used tools to hold assets:

The Limited Partnership

San Francisco Chronicle – November 25, 2006 – Nancy Gay Staff Writer

> Raiders general partner Al Davis' protracted attempt to sell a minority interest of the team – which he obtained from the heirs of deceased former limited partner Edward W. McGah – continues to go nowhere. For months, Davis has been offering for sale the 31 percent stake in the franchise he reportedly purchased as part of a 2005 franchise settlement with the heirs of one of the Raiders' co-founders, E.W. McGah, including daughter-in-law Barbara McGah and great grandson Sherratt Reicher, both of whom sued Davis in October 2003.
>
> Davis reportedly owns about 67 percent of the team's shares, and the 77-year old maverick owner-who is in poor health-has shown no inclination that he will surrender his controlling power over the franchise. And the 31 percent former McGah family interest that Davis is peddling has not generated much interest from buyers, sources said, because Davis is not including any form of franchise control in the transaction, either now or upon the event of his death. "Al Davis currently has, and will continue to have, **total control** of the Raiders, and that will continue into perpetuity."
>
> The Raiders' ownership is said to be split among the heirs of the eight original general partners of the Raiders, with Davis slowly building his majority share from the original 10 percent he purchased for $18,000 in 1966, when he became the team's third general partner, along with E.W. McGah and Wayne Valley.
>
> The original McGah family lawsuit wanted the partnership dissolved or Davis removed from his role as the team's managing general partner, alleging mismanagement, wrongful misappropriation of funds, fraud and breach of contract.
>
> E.W. McGah died in 1983, and his son Edward J. McGah received his father's interest in the Raiders as part of a family trust, becoming a limited partner. He died in 2002. The raiders claimed that the McGah heirs became "assignees" upon E.J. McGah's death, giving them no voting rights.

A reporter outside of a courtroom asked a defendant clad only in a barrel: "Oh, I see your attorney lost the case!" The defendant answered, "No, we won."

An Alameda County Superior Court judge later ruled that the McGah heirs could not have Davis removed from power as the team's managing general partner unless they had the backing of the remaining ownership interests in the team's partnership.

On Oct 19, 2005, the Raiders and the McGah family reached a settlement, which reportedly included the sale of the families' shares to Davis.

A limited partnership is much like a general partnership except for one important, fundamental difference. The limited partner is protected by law in that this person's legal liability in the business is limited to the amount of his or her investment. It enables this special type of investor to share in the partnership profits without being exposed to its debts, in the event the partnership goes out of business.

A limited partnership needs at least two partners. A General Partner, which has full control and full liability for the debts of the business. And a limited partner, which has no control and limited liability.

The general partner has total control as to how the assets in the limited partnership are managed. They also maintain control as to how the income of the limited partnership is distributed. The general partner can also receive a salary for their services.

The general partner does not have to be an individual. A corporation can serve as the general partner. It will be liable for the debts of the limited partnership to the extent it has assets.

So can you tell me the one down side of a limited partnership? "No Control." The role of the limited partner is very restricted (which is what the McGah family learned in the story illustrated above). In return for that limited participation, the limited partner enjoys complete protection against liability for the debts of the business. In fact, you only risk the investment you made in the business.

Because it has the benefit of limited liability for its limited partners, a limited partnership can be created only if it files a Certificate of Limited Partnership with the state.

A limited partnership does not have a limited life span. The death, retirement or insanity of a limited partner does not end the existence of a limited partnership - nor does the assignment of a limited partner's interest. However, if the general partner dies, retires or goes insane, the limited partnership can end unless the certificate filed with the state provides that the business will be continued with a new general partner. The good news is, the assets will remain with the limited partners and a properly drafted limited partnership agreement will permit the limited partners to select a new general partner.

Another valuable feature is the ability to restrict the transfer of limited or general partner's interest to outside persons. Through your limited partnership agreement, rights of first refusal, prohibited transfers and conditions to permit transfers are instituted to restrict free transferability of partnership interests.

"Lawyers are the only persons in whom ignorance of the law is not punished. "
-Jermy Bentham

" If anything is certain, it is that change is certain. The world we are planning for today will not exist in this form tomorrow."
-Philip Crosby

A limited partnership is a pass through entity for income tax purposes. The Limited Partnership files IRS Form 1065 which is an informational tax return. Each partner will receive a K-1 to file with their individual tax return. So the partners, not the limited partnership, report and pay the taxes. In other words, all profit or loss is passed down to the individual limited partners in proportion to their limited partnership interest.

For example, let's say the limited partnership earns twenty thousand dollars for the year. If I own 10% of that limited partnership, my tax liability is going to be on two thousand dollars worth of income.

One other point I want to make is the characterization of that income. If the partnership earned all of its income as long term capital gains, it is going to pass through to the partners as long term capital gains. If the partnership earns that income as ordinary income, it is going to pass through to the partners as ordinary income.

Now let's talk about asset protection with a limited partnership. First, I want to clarify there are two types of attack.

Internal Attack

What do I mean by an internal attack? Let's say you have four rental properties and one day somebody slips and falls on one of your properties. They break their back. They are unable to work and they can no longer provide for their family of 7. If you own those properties in your own name, and they sue you and win a massive settlement in a lawsuit, what can they come after? Everything you own.

Now the same scenario with a limited partnership. Each of the four rentals is held separately in its own limited partnership because each property has over a hundred thousand dollars worth of equity. Now someone slips and falls on property one. They win a lawsuit. How much can they come after? Who can they come after? They can come after the owner, who in this case will be a limited partnership and we have literally stopped the liability from spreading any further. The most they can do is go after that one piece of property. The most someone can get whenever they sue a limited partnership is the assets inside the limited partnership as well as the assets of the general partner. So for this example, we would use a corporation as the general partner. That's an internal attack and do you see how strong and effective the asset protection is here?

External Attack

Now let's talk about an external attack. I still own the four properties. All of which are held separately in four different limited partnerships. I come to Las Vegas. I love to gamble. I get carried away at the blackjack table and lose hundreds of thousands of dollars which I don't have. Then to make matters worse, on my way back to my hotel room, I bump into an elderly lady, knocking her down a flight of stairs. She never gets up. She now must spend the rest of her life in a nursing home. The lawsuits soon follow. They win and try to start collecting on the millions of dollars in judgments they have against me. The first thing the lawyers want to do is go after the assets inside the limited partnerships. Can they march right through and take those assets from the limited partnership? The

"Let our advance worrying become advanced thinking and planning"
– Winston Churchill

answer is no they cannot. Those assets are owned by the limited partnership, not me as an individual. The most they can try and do is take away my ownership of the limited partnerships, however, states have laws that say this: If somebody loses a lawsuit, and they own units of a limited partnership, somebody cannot take away those units of the limited partnership. Instead, the most they can get is something called a charging order against those units.

Charging Order

A charging order is basically a garnishment action against the limited partnership. In other words, if the limited partnership ever makes a distribution of money to me personally, the judgment creditor who won the lawsuit can stick out their hand and grab that cash away from me and put it into their pocket. It doesn't go into mine.

Here's my favorite creditor booby-trap regarding a charging order. As the assignee of the debtor's interest in the partnership, the creditor can be forced to personally pay all income taxes due from the seized partnership interest - even if the creditor received no payment. The creditor is then forced to pay money when his objective was to receive money. You have got to love that! Your partnership agreement should contain a provision that at the election of the general partner, the limited partners will pay their proportionate share of tax on any profit-whether or not they actually received the profit. Talk about fantastic leverage to negotiate a settlement for probably pennies on the dollar. That's how you turn the creditors' asset into a liability!

(Nevada becomes the first state to provide an additional level of protection to shareholders in closely held corporations. The corporation itself still can be required to pay a judgment, but a lawyer can't demand disclosure of the identities of the shareholders – a "reverse piercing of the corporate veil" in lawyers terms – to come after the stock that they own. The registered agents association, (for which I am a founding member), began seeking legislation to protect shareholders of closely held corporations during the 2005 legislative session. We argued that individual owners in other types of business formations – LLCs and Limited Partnerships, for instance – already enjoy similar protection in lawsuits. Publicly traded companies are not affected by the change in state law nor does the law protect closely held corporations from lawsuits such as product liability actions. A creditor still can win a judgment that assigns him the profits from a corporation but can't foreclose on the stock or take control of the corporation's operations. Gov. Jim Gibbons signed the law on June 13, 2007, and it applies to any legal action begun after July 1.)

Limited Liability Company

The principal attraction of the LLC is the liability protection for its members. The members of the LLC are not subject to personal liability for the contractual and other obligations of the LLC. Unlike a General Partner who has personal liability with a limited partnership.

The LLC can be member-managed, by one or all of the members or by an outside

"Planning is bringing the future into the present so that you can do something about it now."
~Alan Lakein

non member, which is called manager-managed. One example is you may want to have a manager if you or other members only want to invest and not be concerned with the day to day operations of the business. The key is that the management is internal and therefore not exposed to outside liabilities.

LLCs also offer restrictions on transfers as well as the charging order protection from creditors like the limited partnership.

One of the most significant benefits of the LLC, and the main reason for its existence, is that it is also a pass-through tax entity. All of the profits and losses of the business flow through the LLC without tax. They flow through to the members' tax return and are dealt with at the individual level. Be aware, however, that on a trade or business that generates income, the LLC members can be subject to self-employment tax.

Here's something interesting. The IRS has made it possible for LLCs and LPs to be taxed as corporations so that they can retain, instead of distribute, profits to meet future business needs. The advantage of this is that members or partners can now pay individual income taxes on only the profits actually paid to them. The business then pays taxes on any retained profits at the reduced corporate tax rates. I highly recommend you talk with your CPA before filing such an election because once the election is made you cannot return to flow-through taxation for a period of five years. In addition, you will in essence become corporate employees subject to federal and state withholdings on your wages.

I want you to look at the following chart. This is one example of how we might begin building the First Layer of Your Wealth Foundation.

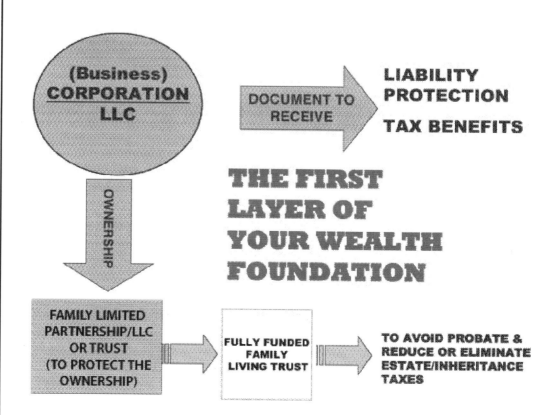

Conclusion

- Not every approach will work for every person. No two individuals share identical financial situations, family relationships or potential hazards. Your plan must respond to each of these considerations.

- Build a Team. Asset protection is a team approach. Not only will your family be involved, you should utilize knowledgeable individuals that can bring their special professional skills into the planning process.

- Peace of Mind can be achieved when you start putting all the pieces in place!

Chapter 5:
More Ways to Protect Business Assets

- The Importance of Business Insurance
- Separate Your Personal and Business Credit
- Shut the Door on Business Identity Theft

"There is no incentive for insurance companies to do what is right, such as live up to the promises made in their policies. Tort reformers fueled by insurance money think big business and the insurance industry need to be protected against "runaway juries." It's the other way around. Big business and the insurance industry have always been able to take care of themselves. The little people need protection from them. This country was founded on the common law right of the little guy to get into court with his hired gun to fight the oppressor, be it big government or big business. Take that away and we have nothing left. Look around. It's being whittled away, bit by bit, caps on damages here, restrictions on jury trials there. It won't end until we recognize the enemy and join together to take a stand against them. It will take the little people to do this together".

Louis G. Fazzi, Esq. Attorney & Counselor At Law

Key Points
- Get the best from insurance service people by learning how to select the right agency and to increase your business insurance knowledge.
- Good credit is the lifeline of your business.
- Take steps today to avoid business identity theft.

The Importance of Business Insurance

Whether you are a start-up business looking for a first-time policy or an existing business looking for better rates, every insurance buyer should be prepared to approach the insurance marketplace so he or she can get the best possible coverage and service for a reasonable amount of money.

Buying business insurance is among the best ways to prepare for the unexpected. Without proper protection, misfortunes such as the death of a partner or key employee, embezzlement, a lawsuit, or a natural disaster could spell the end of a thriving operation.

"I don't want to tell you how much insurance I carry with the Prudential, but all I can say is: when I go, they go too."

–Jack Benny

Ranging from indispensable workers compensation insurance to the relatively obscure executive kidnapping coverage, insurance is available for nearly any business risk. Considering the multitude of available options, business owners must carefully weigh whether the cost of certain premiums will justify the coverage for a given risk.

All businesses, no matter how small, need insurance coverage to protect from loss. You've invested so much in your business to get it where it is today. Insurance is like a silent partner who watches your back so you can focus on the business of doing business. In some cases, insurance may be required in order to comply with state and federal laws. As the size of your business grows, your focus shifts, and activities change, business insurance coverage must be evaluated. So, where to start?

The first thing business owners should do is review their existing coverage, to make sure what is and is not covered. For instance, most business owners do not know that basic hazard insurance does not cover flood damage. The National Flood Insurance Program provides current coverage to property owners, and you can get more information on that at www.floodsmart.gov. And when shopping for insurance, think about property damage and the loss of revenue as well as the extra expenses that arise while the business is shut down.

Thousands of business owners found their vital records destroyed after last year's hurricane. How should these records be protected? Business owners should make back-up copies of critical records and store them at a remote off-site location; the farther away, the better. Documents and CDs should be stored in fireproof safe deposit boxes or any other disaster-resistant locations. Another good idea is to send back-up data to a trusted third party office that can make sure you have your data when you need it.

Let's review some of the basic types of insurance available:

Business Owners Policy (BOP)

This type of policy combines property and liability coverage in one policy and generally includes additional coverage at no additional premium.

- Business Property Coverage: Get solid protection for your buildings, equipment and other business property.
- Business Liability Coverage: Many business owners buy general liability or umbrella liability insurance to cover legal hassles due to claims of negligence. These help protect against payments as the result of bodily injury or property damage, medical expenses, the cost of defending lawsuits, and settlement bonds or judgments required during an appeal procedure.

Business Auto Insurance

This type of business insurance provides coverage for automobiles, trucks, and vans used for business purposes. Major coverages are the same as personal auto insurance coverage. Auto insurance policies pay for damages due to an accident, or damages cause by fire, theft, flood, and vandalism. Also included is liability coverage for injuries you cause to other people and damages you cause to other property when you are at fault in an accident.

Umbrella Liability Insurance

Umbrella Liability Insurance provides additional protection for your business against catastrophic losses that are covered under liability policies, such as the Business Auto Insurance policy, commercial general liability policy, watercraft, and employer's liability coverage. If a claim payment on an underlying policy exceeds the limit of the policy, or if the total of claims on a policy exceeds the annual aggregate limit, umbrella liability policies can provide excess limits. It can also protect against some claims that are not covered by the underlying insurance policies.

Errors & Omissions Insurance

Errors and Omissions Insurance protects your company from claims if your client holds you responsible for errors, or the failure of your work to perform as promised in your contract.

Coverage includes legal defense costs - no matter how baseless the allegations. Errors and Omissions Insurance will pay for any resulting judgments against you, including court costs, up to the coverage limits on your policy. This coverage extends to both W2 employees and 1099 subcontractors, and can be worldwide in scope.

It is generally recommend E & O Insurance be at the foundation of every company's insurance portfolio. Usually it is wise to purchase the coverage prior to product launch, or when you have customers.

It is usually required by investors, particularly VC's.

Most Importantly: E & O Insurance might save you from extreme embarrassment, a lost client, or worst of all, a bad reputation.

Director's and Officer's Liability

Whenever you serve as a director or officer of a corporation, manager of an LLC or a nonprofit entity, you expose yourself to legal actions from those you serve. You may be liable for damages caused by your negligence in the performance of your duties. (Enron is an example of how the officers and directors were held personally liable and responsible for negligent corporate acts). Commercial general liability forms exclude this type of exposure, so you need to obtain special director's and officer's liability coverage. If this exposure exists in your situation, be sure to include it in your coverage specifications, and obtain quotes. The board of directors of your company needs this coverage too, even if it is a closely held company, as claims can arise between close associates. Such insurance provides coverage against expenses and to a limited extent fines, judgments and amounts paid in settlement.

"He that hath lost his credit is dead to the world."
– George Herbert, 1639

Product Liability

Every product is capable of personal injury or property damage. Companies that manufacture, wholesale, distribute, and retail a product may be liable for its safety. Additionally, every service rendered may be capable of personal injury or property damage. Businesses are considered liable for negligence, breach of an express or implied warranty, defective products, and defective warnings or instructions.

Home-Based Business Insurance

Contrary to popular belief, homeowners' insurance policies do not generally cover home-based business losses. Commonly needed insurance areas for home-based businesses include business property, professional liability, personal and advertising injury, loss of business data, crime and theft, and disability.

Internet Business Insurance

Web-based businesses may wish to look into specialized insurance that covers liability for damage done by hackers and viruses. In addition, e-insurance often covers specialized online activities, including lawsuits resulting from meta tag abuse, banner advertising, or electronic copyright infringement.

Workers' Compensation Insurance

Most people have a form of disability insurance because of their employment. I am referring to the Workers' Compensation laws which vary from state to state. They are designed to provide an employee compensation if that employee is injured "on the job". It can pay for rehabilitation and recovery costs, medical bills, and lost work time. In addition, Workers' Compensation includes death benefits that are provided to surviving spouses and dependent children of workers who are killed on the job. Workers' Compensation is not a substitute for health or medical insurance; employees are only covered for on-the-job injuries. If you are cleaning the gutters on your home and fall off the ladder breaking your back, you have no coverage under Workers' Compensation.

The amount of insurance employers must carry, rate of payment, and what types of employees must be carried varies depending on the state. In most cases, business owners, independent contractors, domestic employees in private homes, farm workers, and unpaid volunteers are exempt.

There are two important points to remember here. The first is that this form of insurance relates to employees. The self employed individual is not automatically covered unless they elect and pay for it. Second, Workers' Compensation is not well designed for the very highly compensated, specially skilled, professional.

Criminal Insurance

No matter how tight security is in your workplace, theft and malicious damage are always possibilities. While the dangers associated with hacking, vandalism, and general theft are obvious, employee embezzlement is more common than most business owners think. Criminal insurance and employee bonds can provide protection against losses in most criminal areas.

Business Interruption Insurance

Business interruption insurance can be as important as fire insurance. According to the Institute for Insurance Information, business interruption insurance is not sold separately but added to a property insurance policy or included in a package policy. Business interruption insurance compensates you for lost income if your company has

"An amazing thing, the human brain. Capable of understanding incredibly complex and intricate concepts. Yet at times unable to recognize the obvious and simple."
~ Jay Abraham

to vacate the premises because of a natural disaster, fire, and other catastrophes that may cause the operation to shut down for a significant amount of time. It covers the profits you would have earned based on your financial records if the disaster had not occurred. It also covers operating expenses like electricity that can continue even though the business is temporarily shut down. A good disaster plan may help lessen the impact of the disruption, which can lead to cost savings for out-of-pocket expenses related to recovery as well.

Key Person Insurance

In addition to a business continuation plan (Buy-Sell Agreement) that outlines how the company will maintain operations if a key person dies, falls ill, or leaves, some companies may wish to buy key person insurance. This type of coverage is usually life insurance that names the corporation as a beneficiary if an essential person dies or is disabled.

Malpractice Insurance

Some licensed professionals (e.g. doctors, lawyers, accountants) need protection against payments as the result of bodily injury or property damage, medical expenses, the cost of defending lawsuits, investigations and settlements, and bonds or judgments required during an appeal procedure.

Small Business Health Insurance

If you own or belong to a business or organization with less than 50 people small business health insurance has lots of benefits for you. Besides providing medical care for yourself and your employees, a small business health insurance plan helps spread the financial risk between all the members, which usually means lower premiums and more extensive coverage for everyone. But group health insurance has tax advantages too. Employer contributions to a small business health insurance plan are generally 100% tax deductible, and employees save on payroll taxes. Small businesses (and certain organizations, like non-profits) are generally eligible for group health insurance so long as they can show two or more full-time taxable employees.

Stay in Contact with Your Agent

The insurance marketplace is simply too large for any one person to be aware of all the possible solutions for every situation. Further, the gargantuan size of the marketplace dictates that no single agent can know all there is about where to find the best possible deal for your account. With hundreds of insurance companies, and the corresponding number of individual retailers, it is unlikely you will stumble into the best bargain on your first insurance purchase.

Experienced agents realize that the marketplace is bigger than they are. Because there are so many opportunities to find bargains, and because the entire marketplace is in a constant state of change, no single individual can have all the answers.

The work you need insurance people to handle will only get done if you make sure it gets done. Their actions or inactions can be a financial detriment.

With so many hats to wear, most small-business owners look at insurance as more of a nuisance than a vital component of their company's success. That attitude can change in a heartbeat however, "After a storm or a fire, I've never heard a business owner say they regretted the time they took to buy the right insurance."

Where To Find A Business Insurance Broker

The yellow pages, the Internet, your banker, or your accountant can usually be a good source of where to find a broker for your business. You can also ask your friendly competitors whom they use, if your businesses are the same as far as liability or small business coverage is concerned. Sometimes an association you are a member of can lead you to an excellent fit for your business insurance needs. Ask around and see if the same names begin to surface. This is a good indication of a possible answer for this business need. Special needs may be harder to find, and your state insurance commissioner may be a source of help.

In any event, asking around is a start to discovering a business insurance agent with whom you can develop a client-provider relationship.

Separate Your Personal and Business Credit

Good credit is the lifeline of your business. It enables you to obtain funding for things like expansion, capital expenditures, research and development, and staffing. It is the principal contributing factor to your business's future growth, not to mention the cash necessary for survival. Good business credit also allows you to keep the cash you have to cover your cost of doing business; such liquidity lets you respond quickly to time-sensitive requirements, without halting or compromising operations.

According to Dunn & Bradstreet: A business's creditworthiness is ultimately determined by what are known as the "4 C's of Credit" — character, capacity, capital and conditions — most of which can be found explicitly or implicitly in a company's credit report.

Character includes factors such as: size, location, number of years in business, business structure, number of employees, history of principals, appetite for sharing information about itself, media coverage, liens, judgments or pending law suits, stock performance, and comments from references.

Capacity assesses the ability of the business to pay its bills, i.e., its cash flow. It also includes the structure of the company's debt—whether secured or unsecured—and the existence of an unused line of credit. Any defaults must also be identified.

Capital assesses whether a company has the financial resources (obtained from financial records) to repay their creditors. In general, this portion of the credit report is the one most closely reviewed by the credit analyst. Heavy weighting is given to such balance sheet items as working capital, net worth and cash flow.

Conditions consider the external factors surrounding the business under consideration - influences such as market fluctuations, industry growth rate, political/legislative factors, and currency rates.

A credit manager or loan officer will answer these questions by locating and reviewing:
- requests for credit information
- customer supplied information
- bank information
- trade information

These factors are also taken into consideration by other service providers, such as insurance companies to set premiums. More than ever, companies are using automated decisioning, which means they input scores and ratings that summarize the 4 Cs into a financial model to determine the risk of doing business with you.

Two Ways to Obtain Business Financing

There are only two ways to obtain business financing. One is by using your social security number and your personal FICO score to personally secure every business loan.

The other is to use your business credit rating and get financing without having to personally guarantee every loan.

The biggest business financing mistake that almost every business owner makes is simply not knowing how to properly setup their business to have its own business credit rating. They never learn how to obtain a business credit score separate from their personal credit score. It is easy to do, so why do less than 5% of all business owners ever do it? Because, no one teaches you how. Business schools don't, trade associations don't, and banks certainly don't.

The next biggest mistake that business owners make is applying for business financing at multiple lenders at the same time without having a clue as to what it takes to get approved and without realizing what affect this has on your personal FICO score.

97% of all business loan applications are declined and since lenders sell your business information, approved or declined, explains why you can be seriously flooded with junk mail from every lender and credit card company all promising pre-approval and 0% on balance transfers!

Having an excellent business credit score is a key that will unlock a vast amount of business financing opportunities to you.

"I think if you've suffered, if you've experienced loss, you're probably more open to understanding it and more comfortable talking about it and experiencing it."
–Anderson Cooper

184

Most small businesses are initially financed by the personal savings or assets of the owners and can rapidly reach a state of growth where they are forced to seek credit or investment solutions to fund that growth. However, business owners quickly realize that applying for business credit is a much more complicated process than applying for personal credit because it requires careful preparation and demands that you understand the process and what it takes to qualify.

The single largest form of lending in the entire world is trade credit, which is even larger than the amount banks loan to businesses. Trade credit or business credit is a critical part to the success of a small business. Nothing is more important and vital to the health of a business than having the right amount of capital in place.

Building a Positive Business Credit Profile

In order to successfully obtain business credit, you must first build a favorable credit profile for your business. To accomplish this you must:

1. Have a business that can apply for its own tax identification number by forming a corporation or an LLC. As a business owner you need to separate your personal assets from your business assets and this includes separating your personal credit completely from the business credit.
2. Office Location. Your business must be real and not just an attempt to build personal credit by using a business. Your business must have a physical office space (even if it is a home address), a separate directory listed telephone line and fax.
3. You must obtain the required city/county/state business licenses and if applicable, a tax resale license.
4. Financial statements are critical the moment you start a business. Income Statement, Balance Sheet and Cash Flow Statement are the 3 essential scorecards you need to run a successful company. Accurate financials and professionally prepared tax returns are required.
5. Trade References. This can be one of the most difficult steps in the credit building process. What most business owners don't realize is that you could be spending thousands of dollars with a vendor thinking you are building business credit, but if they do not report your credit history to the credit reporting agencies you end up with no trade references at all.
6. Bank References. Your business must have a minimum of one bank reference. Select a bank you want to work with for the duration of your business because the longer the relationship the more willing they will be to extend credit.
7. There are three major business credit reporting agencies in the United States (Equifax, TransUnion, Experian) that most lenders look to for information about your company's credit profile. You will want to establish a presence with these companies. Once you have a number of businesses reporting your company's payment experiences, a credit score will be established.
8. Business Credit Cards and Lines of Credit. Once you have established a presence with the credit bureaus and have a score, your business will be eligible for various business retail credit cards, trade credit accounts and lines of credit without the need for a personal guarantee or personal credit check.

Why Develop Business Credit and Incorporate?
Let's take a look at the following chart.

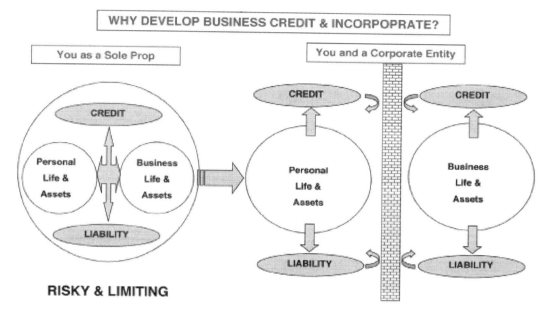

Building business credit is just that, a "building" process. This normally takes 3-4 years or longer but what if you could do the following in only 6 months?

1. Build a clean Credit Profile with several business credit reporting agencies which will separate you from your business;
2. Develop great business Credit Scores;
3. Build the Credit Profile of the company with 6-12 accounts that will show on the businesses credit report;
4. Eliminate the use of personal guarantees;
5. Stop using personal credit for business purposes;
6. Find it much easier to apply for a business loan or lease.

To learn more about the Sage Business Credit Builder Program call 1-800-254-5779, email: corpinfo@sageintl.com or visit www.sageintl.com

Shut The Door on Business Identity Theft

Case Study 13 (Sage International, Inc.)

Three years ago I got a call from the Reno Police Department asking me if I had ever heard of "this" person who was trying to cash a payroll check at the cashier's cage in the Alamo Truck Stop. I said no. He proceeded to tell me that the gal behind the counter noticed something strange about the check and asked the guy to show his Driver's

"Sometimes the situation is only a problem because it is looked at in a certain way. Looked at in another way, the right course of action may be so obvious that the problem no longer exists."
     –Edward de Bono

License and give her a fingerprint. He bolted. She immediately called the police, who called me, who immediately called the bank, and was told to get my behind down there right now to close the account!!!!

Apparently there was a fraudulent check cashing ring just starting to hit the city. This is when I knew I had good Kharma because this was the first check they tried to cash. Somehow they got a hold of one of my checks (I think it was through a service provider) and made their own version.

If that girl had not followed her instincts to detect when fraud is being committed, I would have lost within a matter of days at least $10,000 and would never have known what hit me. I know I certainly wouldn't have been able to recover from the thousands lost. And I know I was spared the agonizing times that were in store.

And to let you know, I sent her a nice reward and thanked her profusely!

Business Vulnerability

Many people worry about hackers stealing their passwords or Dumpster divers grabbing their financial documents. But a big chunk of identity theft is committed by the victim's nearest and dearest – or at least someone the victim knows.

Personal Identity Theft is all too common. But what do you do when your business information is stolen and someone charges purchases to your accounts and ruins your business credit history?

The major risks to businesses include:
- Victimization of owners, managers, employees, customers, clients, and vendors
- Fraudulent use of the business identity
- Public, legal, and financial consequences of privacy, security, and regulatory breaches

When any person with a relationship to a business becomes a victim of identity theft, the business is potentially at risk. Identity theft can have a significant impact on the management, operations, financial credit, public credibility, and income of a business.

The business, itself, can become a victim of financial and non-financial types of IDT. Privacy or security breaches will leave a business reeling to address the ensuing employee and client public relations crisis. The impact to the business will be multifaceted in terms of lost business, lost work time, regulatory issues, fines, legal expenses, and civil law suits.

Ten Things You Can Do
- Put your business records under lock and key. Use locking filing cabinets for your financial paperwork and throw all of your unsigned checks, bank information, and credit cards in their too. Keep the files locked any time you're not actually using them.

- Password protect your computer and any financial files contained inside. Change the passwords often. (And – just in case it's not the obvious already – don't put the password on a post-it note attached to the screen.)
- Don't give anyone else your credit or debit cards or PINs. If you already have, call the issuer and get new cards and change the PIN.
- Monitor your accounts online. Everybody should be checking their accounts daily and doing month end reconciliations for all bank accounts, petty cash, and credit card statements. And you should have more than one account (payroll, cash, savings) so if there is a problem with one, they don't get it all!
- Don't give every employee a key to your office. (Learned that lesson the hard way too when an employee – soon to be fired – came in over the weekend and stole a bunch of stuff!)
- Shred it. Be careful about the information you and your staff put in the trash about your company, you personally and most importantly, your clients. Pay special attention to the mail, a favorite source for identity theft. Anything that has your name and address on it should be shredded, and that includes most bills. I highly recommend you get cross-cut shredders or like me, we have a shredding service that comes in whenever we call. They provide the bins and it's super easy!
- Disconnect ex-employees immediately. When employees no longer work for your business, you need to be sure that their access to your computer network and company data is cut off immediately. I also make it a habit to change the locks on the doors.
- Secure your business premises with locks and alarms. Alarm systems are effective deterrents to criminals thinking of breaking into your business, including those intent on identity theft – especially alarm systems that are monitored by a security company. Make sure external doors have deadbolts and that exposed windows are secured with security film, bars, screens or shatter-proof glass.
- Avoid broadcasting information. The other day I made a purchase at a computer store. The clerk asked me for my phone number and guess what, all of my personal information popped up on a terminal in front of her – right in plain view of three other customers!

This sort of cavalier sharing of personal information, which makes identity theft so easy, has to stop. Train your employees to be sensitive to customer information issues, making sure they keep customer information private when they're dealing with individual customers. Turning computer screens so that they can't be viewed by anyone except the operator is a simple thing. So are practices such as not repeating customer information out loud or not leaving files with customer information lying open on desks or counters, especially when you leave at night!

- Be cautious on the phone. It's easy for someone to pretend to be someone they're not on the phone. Whether it's someone who wants personal information on a particular customer, or someone who claims they need to verify one of your personal accounts, don't give out information over the phone unless you can positively confirm the caller's identity.

"Information thieves and stalkers tell authorities over and over how easily they were able to obtain all sorts of valuable information simply by calling small business owners or personnel departments and asking. Posing as government agencies or credit grantors or health insurance providers, these thieves have found that a well-crafted, believable story can often get past the best locking file cabinets or password-protected computers," warns the Better Business Bureau.

If your information has been compromised, immediately report the fraud to police. For more tips, visit www.identitytheft.org or the Association of Certified Fraud Examiners at www.cfenet.com.

Conclusion

- The importance of shopping your insurance cannot be overstated – not just for price considerations, but also for the services you desire. Now is the time to take up your armor and defend your business from harm. You are now prepared to fight the insurance battle and win the right coverage at the right price.

- Build Business Credit; as a corporation or LLC you can build business credit separate from your personal credit and establish lines of credit from other companies under your business name. Start this right away. You don't want to wait until you need a $100,000 line of credit from a bank the 4th year in business and have them tell you they can't issue the credit because your business doesn't have a credit file.

- Identity crisis: make no mistake-business identity theft can happen to you if you're not careful!

"If nature has made any one thing less susceptible than all others of exclusive property, it is the action of the thinking power called an idea, which an individual may exclusively possess as long as he keeps it to himself; but the moment it is divulged, it forces itself into the possession of every one, and the receiver cannot dispossess himself of it."
– *Thomas Jefferson*

Chapter 6:
Protect Your Intellectual Property

- What is Intellectual Property?
- Copyrights
- Trademarks
- Trade Secrets
- Patents
- Legal Basis for Intellectual Property Laws
- Hold Your IP in an LLC

"A customer is the most important visitor on our premises, he is not dependent on us. We are dependent on him. He is not an interruption in our work. He is the purpose of it. He is not an outsider in our business. He is part of it. We are not doing him a favor by serving him. He is doing us a favor by giving us an opportunity to do so."
–Mahatma Gandhi

Case Study 14 (Sage International, Inc.)

I was at a very large event and picked up a business card and literature from someone I thought would make a good connection for Sage because they held financial education workshops in the Bay Area. Several weeks later, I finally got around to digging out the information because I wanted to call them and pursue my original thought. As I was flipping through their materials, I came to the last page and was absolutely stunned to see the details of an upcoming workshop titled, After the "Inc." Dries...® and the description of the event was word for word an exact replica of a piece I had created for our own website. I have owned that trademark for years so you can imagine how angry I felt. Who were these people? What right did they have to steal my stuff? How long have they been using it? Were they making a profit off my intellectual property?

What a bizarre stroke of luck that we both were in attendance at the same event in Los Angeles and what's even weirder, is that out of the hundreds of people in attendance, I actually picked up their marketing materials!

Long story short, I contacted my attorney which cost me $1,000 to get the issue resolved.

Key Points

- Intellectual Property Law consists of several discrete legal categories. Although these categories can overlap with respect to a particular intellectual property, they each have their own characteristics and terminology.

- Intellectual Property Law also governs a valuable asset that each of us (each individual) possesses - a right of publicity, to determine who profits, and how, from use of our name, image and/or likeness.

What is Intellectual Property?

Building a business starts with an idea. An idea by itself has little value. But an idea which has been sufficiently developed to merit intellectual property protection has value. Intellectual property is valuable to a business in part because the IP provides leverage in funds acquisition, licensing, and market-place competition. Angel investors, venture capital firms, banks and pension fund managers, all want to see that a funding proposal is backed by intellectual property. Potential licensees want to know that they are paying for IP protection from competitors who are not licensees. Intellectual property serves as the basis for litigation, the ultimate aggressive form of business protection.

The creation of acquisition of intellectual property is one way of increasing the value of a business. The various forms of intellectual property – patents, trademarks, copyrights, trade secrets, licenses and other contracts—are business assets.

The first step in building the IP assets of a business is recognizing where possible IP exists or may be generated.

In simple terms, intellectual property is a product of the human intellect that has commercial value. The commercial value comes from the ability of its owner to control its use. Intellectual property law is an umbrella term for all the statutes, government regulations and court decisions that together determine who owns intellectual property and what rights go along with that ownership. It specifies:

- the conditions under which intellectual property rights may be sold or loaned (licensed) to others for specific purposes
- how to settle contract disputes that arise from marketing intellectual property, and
- how to take advantage of government procedures and programs that establish or enhance protection of intellectual property rights.

The law primarily offers protection to the owner of intellectual property by giving the owner the right to file a lawsuit asking a court to enforce whatever rights are being transgressed. As a result, some experts describe IP laws as "affirmative rights" rather than as "protection." Noted patent attorney and author David Pressman suggests thinking of intellectual property laws as tools that can be used when needed, but not as any kind of defensive shield. In other words, the law doesn't prevent someone from stepping on the owner's rights. But the laws do give an owner the ammunition to take a trespasser to court.

Justice Department Focuses on Efforts to Protect Intellectual Property Rights

Attorney General Urges Congress to Enact Important New Legislation

WASHINGTON - (Former) Attorney General Alberto R. Gonzales today highlighted the Justice Departments ongoing efforts to protect intellectual property rights, and announced a comprehensive legislative proposal entitled the **Intellectual Property Protection Act of 2007**, before members of the U.S. Chamber of Commerce Coalition Against Counterfeiting and Piracy.

In addition to the proposed legislation, the Departments ongoing commitment to combating intellectual property includes measures for implementing valuable resources, and aggressively prosecuting counterfeiters, each elements of the government-wide Strategy Targeting Organized Piracy (STOP) Initiative.

Copyrights

Copyrights protect literary, artistic, musical, and other "creative" works, including architectural works and semi-conductor chips ("mask works"). The owner of a creation protected by copyright law has numerous rights once the creation is "fixed in a tangible medium of expression" (memorialized). The author or creator is most commonly the owner of the copyright. Copyright registration is not required for a creation to be "copyrighted," but it is required before you can sue for copyright infringement.

Work for Hire

You should be greatly concerned about who owns the work you specially commission. For example, unless there is a special kind of agreement in place before any work begins, someone who contributes material to your new book or web site can, in theory, sell that same material elsewhere without your permission. Worse still, if there is no written agreement, and you want to adapt that material, or publish it elsewhere, you will probably need that person's permission. Similarly, if you hire someone to illustrate one of your short stories, unless there is a written agreement that says otherwise, you may be surprised to learn that the illustrator has become your coauthor. These seemingly odd results follow from the fact that under copyright law, authors are presumed to own the copyright in the works they create. The best way to avoid these problems is by having a **written agreement** in place before any work begins.

With a work for hire, the author and copyright owner of a work is the person who pays for it, not the person who creates it. The premise of this principle is that a business that authorizes and pays for a work owns the rights to the work. There are two distinct ways that a work will be classified as "made for hire."

"Obviously everyone wants to be successful, but I want to be looked back on as being very innovative, very trusted and ethical and ultimately making a big difference in the world."

–Sergey Brin

- the work is created by an employee within the scope of employment; or
- the work is commissioned, is the subject of a written agreement, and falls within a special group of categories (a contribution to a collective work, a part of a motion picture or other audiovisual work, a translation, a supplementary work, a compilation, an atlas, an instructional text, a test, or as answer material for a test).

The work made for hire status of a work affects the length of copyright protection and termination rights.

Trademarks

What's in a name? To Shakespeare, "a rose by any other name would smell as sweet." But what is true in love can be the opposite in business. IBM would not smell half so sweet by another name, nor would Xerox, Apple Computer, McDonald's or Levi-Strauss. In the business world, the name of a successful product or service contributes greatly to its real worth. Every day, names such as French's Auto Parts or Stepping Stones Day Care Center identify these businesses for their customers, help customers find them and (assuming they provide a good product or service) keep the customers coming back, again and again and again.

Trademarks are words, names, symbols, or devices that a business uses to identify and distinguish its goods and services from those of others. Trademarks prevent consumer confusion regarding a source of goods and services and the affiliation of products. Trademarks enable a business to protect its reputation by allowing businesses to prevent others from using identical or confusingly similar trademarks for identical or similar goods and services. Registration is not required for trademark rights to exist, but grants the owner numerous additional rights and benefits.

Trade Secrets

Trade secrets consist of designs, devices, processes, compositions, techniques, formulas, information or recipes that are kept secret by their owner and which give their owner a competitive business advantage.

Ivan Hoffman, B.A. J.D. sums up the situation: an employee is leaving or has left his or her job (voluntarily or otherwise) and seeks to go to work for a competitor of the former employer. The employee has a great deal of knowledge about certain trade secrets and confidential information of the former employer **but there is no evidence establishing that the employee intends to use or has used those trade secrets in his or her new job.** The employee may or may not have previously signed an agreement promising not to compete with the previous employer for some period of time.

Question: can the former employer prevent the employee from taking the new job (or prevent the new employer from hiring the employee) merely because of that

"Intellectual property has the shelf life of a banana."
–Bill Gates

employee's knowledge about such trade secrets and confidential information if there is no evidence of actual or threatened use of those secrets?

Answer: like all good legal answers, it depends. It depends on which state in the United States has jurisdiction over the dispute and where the employment agreement, if there was one, containing the non-compete provision was entered into and under which law it is to be governed. The reader is strongly cautioned to consult an attorney experienced in these matters in the reader's state since the law varies from state to state.

Covenants Not To Compete

The law around the country varies as to the validity and enforceability of provisions in contracts that restrict the ability of an employee to compete with the former employer. Some states allow such restrictions provided they are reasonable in time and geography and other factors. Many states have adopted the Uniform Trade Secrets Act.

The rights of the parties are determined more on the basis of whether or not the past employer has protectable trade secrets and the issues surrounding the new employment. The issues in that regard are the possession of knowledge that, if used, would violate clearly established and protectable rights of the former employer in and to trade secrets.

Patents

U.S. patent system transformation long sought by high-tech industry players like Microsoft, Amazon.com and Cisco Systems may finally be gaining momentum in Congress.

The Senate Judiciary Committee approved by a 13-5 vote an amended version of the **Patent Reform Act of 2007.** Supporters say the proposal would go a long way toward staving off expensive court litigation, limiting what are perceived as excessive damage awards, and keeping questionable patents off the books in the first place.

"We have reaffirmed our commitment to ensuring that our nation's patent laws promote and protect the inventiveness of all of our industries," Chairman Patrick Leahy (D-Vt.), who co-sponsored the bill with Sen. Orrin Hatch (R-Utah), said in a statement after the vote.

Patents are a government-granted, limited monopoly (right to exclude others) for a new invention, design, or solution to a problem (process). Patents provide monetary incentive and reward for the creation of new inventions. An invention must be new, useful, novel (not known or used in the United States, nor patented or described in print outside the U.S., prior to the time at which the inventor claims to have invented it) and non-obvious (invention as a whole was not obvious to those skilled in the trade) in order to be patentable.

Legal Basis for Intellectual Property Laws

The sources of intellectual property laws vary according to the subject matter. Trade secret law derives both from federal and state legislation, and from court cases that have developed their own set of principles used to decide new trade secret cases that come before them (the term is "common law.") Trademark and unfair competition laws originate primarily in both federal and state statutes, but also, especially in the area of unfair competition, come from court decisions that apply principles developed by earlier courts. Copyright and patent laws originate in the U.S. Constitution and are specifically and exclusively implemented by federal statutes. In all these intellectual property areas, court decisions interpreting and enforcing applicable statutes also provide an important source of intellectual property law.

I strongly recommend you seek the advice of an **Intellectual Property Law Attorney** to protect your commercially valuable creations. I know you may be tempted to avoid investing precious start-up capital in IP-related expenses. Yet, it is dangerous to defer those costs.

Hold Your IP in an LLC

As this entire section relates to Asset Protection, we of course, would not hold our IP in our personal name. We would most likely hold it in an LLC (either owned by you or your company, if required). Most IP generates passive income (royalties) so it only makes sense. Also, if you have a company and you create a lot of Intellectual Property it's smart to hold the property in a separate entity so in case the main company gets attacked or goes bankrupt, the IP is separate and can continue to be licensed or sold to someone else.

Conclusion
- In simple terms, intellectual property is a product of the human intellect that has commercial value. The commercial value comes from the ability of its owner to control its use. If the owner could not legally require payment in exchange for use, ownership of the intellectual property would have intellectual worth but no commercial value.
- You must take the steps necessary to protect your Intellectual Property which means sorting through a myriad of government procedures and programs. Hire an Intellectual Property Law Attorney to help.
- Hold your IP in an LLC to create legal separation.

Chapter 7:

How Golden Will Your Golden Years Really Be?

- Retirement Planning
- Individual Retirement Accounts
- Self – Directed IRAs
- Real Estate Investing with your IRA
- Employer-Sponsored Retirement Plans

Key Points

- Your work life should be a journey up and down hills, rather than a climb up a sheer cliff that ends with a jump into the abyss.

Case Study 15 (Phil & Sarah)

Meet Phil and Sarah Blake, ages 35 and 32, respectively. Phil and Sarah represent the typical two-income American family, bringing in about $80,000 each year between the two of them.

Recently, they began contributing to their 401(k) plans. Each month, they diligently tuck away $200 of their monthly income into a 401(k) plan. So far, their combined plans have a value of about $8,000. By the time they are age 65, they hope to achieve their goal - earning 75% of their current after-tax income, or about $40,000 per year.

Can they achieve their retirement goals at this rate? Sadly, the answer is "No." Although Phil and Sarah believed they were ahead of the curve in retirement planning, they found they have a shortage of about $270,000. To meet their personal goals by age 65, they need to increase their monthly allocations.

Like most people, Phil and Sarah put off contributing to a tax-exempt retirement plan until they believed they had more disposable income at hand. As a result, time slipped away, leaving them vulnerable to income shortfalls as their retirement age crept near.

The table below illustrates the price of procrastination for Phil and Sarah Blake:

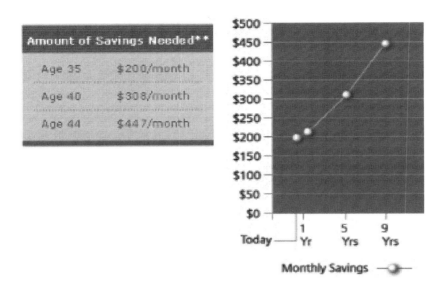

Amount of Savings Needed**	
Age 35	$200/month
Age 40	$308/month
Age 44	$447/month

Prior to the Civil War and the industrialization of America, there was no such thing as retirement. Older people remained a vital part of our society, offering insight and advice born of their experience.

Although many Americans now plan for a retirement of up to 20 years, there is evidence that the average retirement may last much longer. Half of those currently aged 65 will live to be older than 83 years, according to the National Center for Health Statistics. What's more, the latest U.S. Census found that the fastest-growing segment of the U.S. older population (those at least 65 years old) is the 85 years and older group.

In other words, living nearly a century may someday soon be almost commonplace. Starting to properly plan for retirement begins with asking the most basic of questions: What type of account do you want to open? Your answer is critical—so critical that it can affect your whole retirement picture in the future. Different types of retirement accounts provide you with different ways to deposit money, invest money, keep the money earned, and even to use the money you accumulate. So be sure to consider the differences among the types of accounts and choose the one(s) that work best for you.

Individual Retirement Accounts

Individual Retirement Accounts, or IRAs, are special accounts with tax advantages to help you save for retirement. And I want you to grasp this one simple, but powerful, premise: The longer your IRA is sheltered from taxes, the more it will grow in accumulated wealth. The key to sustaining that shelter and achieving such growth is to milk the tax laws for all they are worth!

"Human beings are the only creatures on earth that allow their children to come back home."
– Bill Cosby

There are two types of IRAs:

1. Traditional IRAs allow you to save money without paying taxes until you withdraw it. The money you put into the IRA can lower your taxable income and grows tax-free while it's in the IRA account.
2. Roth IRAs offer a slight twist on the traditional IRA. There are differences in the tax advantages and who can open a Roth IRA. The most attractive part of Roth IRAs is that your money is withdrawn without paying federal taxes.

Self– Directed IRAs

A self-directed IRA is no different than any other IRA. Having a self-directed IRA simply means you are allowed to direct the investments of the IRA and allows for complete diversification which includes traditional investments such as stocks, bonds, and mutual funds, as well as real estate, mortgages/deeds of trust, private placements, tax liens, and mobile homes.

Traditional IRAs, SEP IRAs, Roth IRAs, 401(k)s, 403(b)s, Coverdell Education Savings (ESA) a.k.a. Educational IRAs, Qualified Annuities, Profit Sharing Plans, Money Purchase Plans, Government Eligible Deferred Compensation Plans, Keoghs call all be moved into Self-Directed accounts.

A truly self-directed IRA allows Americans to use their knowledge and expertise to prepare not only for their future, but also their family's future. While some custodians claim to allow self direction, most only allow the proprietary investments such as CDs or an approved list of stocks, bonds and mutual funds. Truly passive custodians will allow you to make your own investment decisions within a wide range of acceptable investments.

A passive custodian is one that does not offer investment advice. When utilizing a passive custodian, you will never have to worry about conflicts of interest with regard to investments; nor will you have to worry about solicitations.

IRAs and Qualified Plans are the perfect tool for wealth accumulation

For most of us, our IRAs represent the bulk of our wealth, and yet we hardly know anything about the complete range of investments available to us:

- Mortgage Notes
- Stocks and Bonds
- Limited Partnerships
- Limited Liability Companies
- Private Placements
- Unsecured Loans
- Factoring
- Accounts Receivable Financing
- Building Bonds
- Tangible Asset Deeds
- Tax Lien Certificates

- Commercial Paper
- Leases and Lease Options
- Contracts of Sale
- Like and Unlike Exchanges
- Commodities and Futures Trading
- U.S. Treasury Gold and Silver Coins
- Gold Bullion
- Palladium (platinum used in electrical contacts)

**Tax Deferred is Great
Tax Free is Even Better!**

**People who understand Interest and Taxes,
Do not pay Taxes on their Interest - they Earn Interest on their Taxes!**

Prohibited Transactions and Self-Dealing

The most frequently asked questions about Self-Directed Retirement Plans are about which kinds of transactions are permitted and which are not. How much freedom do you have when it comes to investing with your tax-free or tax-deferred IRA?

The IRS tax code addresses this question by outlining and defining what is prohibited, or what you cannot do. Self-dealing transactions are prohibited. Under this context, the terms "self-dealing" and "prohibited transaction" may be used interchangeably.

A prohibited transaction is generally defined as the improper use of your IRA by you or any disqualified person.
For IRAs a disqualified person is:

- The IRA owner;
- The IRA owner's spouse;
- The IRA owner's ancestors (parents), lineal descendants and their spouses (children);
- Investment advisors and managers;
- Any corporation, partnership, trust or estate that at least 50% is owned (or at least 50% of the beneficial interests are held) by a combination of the above (e.g., if you and your spouse own 50% of an LLC, that LLC is a disqualified person with respect to your IRA);
- A 10% owner, officer, or director or highly compensated employee of such an entity;
- A fiduciary of the IRA or person providing services to the IRA (e.g., the trustee or custodian)

Your plan may not, directly or indirectly sell, exchange, or lease any property to or with you or a disqualified person.

"Why not invest your assets in the companies you really like? As Mae West said, 'Too much of a good thing can be wonderful'".
~ Warren Buffett

Some examples of prohibited transactions with your Plan or IRA are:

- Borrowing money from it
- Purchasing life insurance
- Receiving unreasonable compensation for managing it
- Using it as security for a loan
- Selling property you already own to it
- Buying property for personal use (present or future)
- The acquisition of collectibles (works of art, rugs, antiques, gems, stamps etc.)
- Owning shares of an S Corporation

Fundamentally, your retirement plan is intended to benefit you when you retire, and not before then. This simple concept is helpful in understanding the rules on permitted uses of your IRA. If you are planning any transaction that clearly appears to confer direct benefits to you prior to retirement, you should carefully examine the legality of such a transaction.

Do not think for one minute that this imposes unacceptable limitations. On the contrary, there are numerous methods, which do not violate the law that can be used to meet your long-term objectives, and allow you to get the most out of your plan.

Real Estate Investing With Your IRA

Investing in real estate through an IRA opens up a tremendous range of possible investment choices for individuals who are knowledgeable about real estate investing. This is a way to diversify your retirement portfolio to hedge against the cyclical changes in the economy, stock market, financial institutions, and government-based investments.

Real estate investments hold the potential to protect against the loss of principal while generating better than market rate returns through income production and capital gains. When real estate investments are not leveraged, both income and capital gains can flow back to the IRA tax-deferred (or tax-free if a Roth IRA).

Is investing in real estate with an IRA a new concept?

No, in fact, there are more than 7 TRILLION dollars held in retirement accounts, however, only about 3% of retirement accounts are self-directed and only about 2% are invested in real estate. You have been able to invest in real estate since the day IRAs were created in the 1970s!

For many years, financial institutions have effectively convinced us that IRA holdings can be invested only in stocks or bonds. **This misinformation is often perpetuated by the individuals who have the most to gain by your lack of knowledge: investment advisors.**

When it's time to retire, where do most people turn for investment advice? Usually it's an investment advisor, stockbroker, or financial planner. Of course they're more than happy to help secure your future by ensuring that you have enough money to retire. The only problem is that in most cases, these advisors will only offer investment opportunities that the advisor happens to make money on. Think about it. When was the last time your stockbroker called to tell you about a fantastic real estate deal you should jump on today? It just doesn't happen.

While they don't tell you that you can invest elsewhere, they sure don't make that fact well known. Were you even aware that your IRA could invest in real estate, trust deeds, joint ventures, and private stock offerings?

What your Plan or IRA can do:

- Purchase, sell or exchange any investment property as long as the property was never owned by you or any other disqualified person.
- Construct improvements on property owned by your Plan or IRA.
- You and your relatives, entities you own, and other individuals may own undivided interests along with your Plan or IRA. The purchase of this property in this scenario must be simultaneous to avoid a prohibited transaction.
- You may lease or rent the property to someone who is not a disqualified person.
- You can receive property from your IRA or Plan as a distribution.
- You may roll property over from one Plan to another.
- Property may be exchanged with non-disqualified persons or entities.

If your IRA invests in real estate through a down payment and debt financing, there are some significant issues that must be addressed.

1. You cannot personally guarantee a loan for your IRA;
2. Custodians often limit the amount of debt the IRA can carry;
3. Most banks do not allow an IRA to be the debtor without a personal guarantee;
4. Your IRA will pay Unrelated Business Income Tax (UBIT) each year, for any income received and/or capital gains attributable to the debt financed portion.

There are still many ways for your Plan or IRA to participate in a real estate investment without a full cash capital investment. For example, your IRA can co-invest with other parties. You could also have your IRA, and other parties as members of an LLC to buy and sell property.

Self-Directed Custodians

Knowing that you can make these transactions with your IRA is half the battle. The other half is placing your funds with a custodian who will allow you to make these transactions. The fact of the matter is that most IRA custodians are not aware of these exemptions either, so if you ask them to allow your IRA to purchase stocks from your personal account, they probably will not allow it. This is especially true with banks, insurance companies, and brokerage firms that may serve as the custodian of your IRA.

"The politicians say 'we' can't afford a tax cut. Maybe we can't afford the politicians."
–Steve Forbes

The better solution is to transfer all the assets of your IRA to a "true" self-directed custodian. This is usually a bank or trust company that serves as the custodian who will follow your instructions and invest your retirement funds in those investments you desire to make, not investments that are going to earn the custodian a commission.

This is how easy it is:

1. You establish an IRA account with a "true" self-directed IRA custodian.
2. You request the current IRA custodian to transfer the assets to the self-directed IRA custodian.
3. Now all of the assets are in the "true" self-directed IRA custodian's account and ready for you to invest them in the manner you want.
4. This is not a taxable event.

However, there are still some roadblocks to totally freeing up your money. Even though the money is inside the self-directed custodian, there could be some potential problems. In order for you to use your money with the self-directed custodian, you have to call them for every investment you want to make, and that's going to require a lot of paperwork which means additional time and administrative fees.

If you plan on making a lot of loans or investments with your IRA money, just having the money inside the self-directed IRA account may not be the most efficient way to hold your IRA assets.

Limited Liability Company - 100% owned by the IRA

For more flexibility, simplicity, and asset protection, the better solution is to have your self-directed IRA custodian create, and place all of the IRA assets into a limited liability company 100% owned by the IRA.

The end result is that all the assets of your IRA will be safely placed into an LLC account. Now instead of having to call up your IRA custodian and asking their permission to make an investment, you literally have checkbook control over your IRA money.

Can I add more money to the LLC?

So long as the LLC is 100% owned by the IRA you can make further contributions. However, if you personally, or anyone related to you has ownership in the LLC, you shouldn't make any further contributions to the LLC without consulting with your tax adviser.

What type of return does the LLC need to file?

Each year the IRS must receive an information return giving the value of the IRA. However, if the IRA is the sole owner of the LLC, then no partnership return needs to be filed, but if someone other than the IRA has ownership in the LLC, then a Form 1065 will need to be filed.

Because this is such a complex area of tax law and because one mistake could

"How about no income tax at all on people over 65? People would continue working, remain healthier, not be an economic and social drain on society. Then the elderly would also have more disposable income to help charitable activities."
–John Templeton

cost you everything, I strongly encourage you contact us to get the information and recommendations to do this properly; find the right custodians; learn about additional resources for continuing education, and so on.

Any strategy involving self-directed investing I cannot convey enough how important having the right experts around to help becomes. **<u>Do not attempt this on your own!</u>** Call Sage. We have an alliance partner that is an expert in self-directed IRA's.

Employer-Sponsored Retirement Plans

Employer-sponsored retirement plans come in the two types - defined benefit plans and defined contribution plans. This overview explains both types and outlines the specific kinds of defined contribution plans.

Defined Benefit Plans

A defined benefit plan is a retirement plan sponsored by the employer in which the employer's annual contributions to the plan are based on actuarial assumptions (mortality, investment return, employee turnover, retirement age, and salary scale). The benefits are usually a monthly retirement pension based on the employee's wage and the number of years with the employer.

Defined Contribution Plans

A defined contribution plan is a retirement plan sponsored by the employer in which a separate account must be set up for each employee covered by the plan. The benefits are based solely on contributions to the account, as well as its investment gains and earnings.

Types of Defined Contribution Plans

- Profit-Sharing Plan
- Money Purchase Plan
- Stock Bonus Plan
- SIMPLE IRA
- SIMPLE 401(k) Plan
- 401(k) Plan
- SEP-IRA
- 403(b) Plan

Profit-Sharing Plan - Contributions are generally computed by applying a contribution formula to employer profits. The level may be made variable and left to the annual discretion of the plan sponsor. Contributions need not be made every year but must be "recurring and substantial."

Money Purchase Plan - Employer contributions are fixed and not based on profits.

Stock Bonus Plan - This defined contribution plan must generally follow the same

"Everybody today seems to be in such a terrible rush, anxious for greater developments and greater riches and so on, so that children have very little time for their parents. Parents have very little time for each other, and in the home begins the disruption of peace in the world."
–Mother Teresa

rules as a profit-sharing plan except that distributed benefits usually are in the form of the employer's stock.

SIMPLE IRA - Savings Incentive Match Plan for Employees ("SIMPLE" plan) can only be established by employers that have 100 or fewer employees who receive at least $5,000 in compensation during the preceding year. Contributions to the plan are made up of: (1) the employee's elective contributions that are made under a salary reduction agreement, limited to 100% of pay or $11,500 plus catch-up contribution, and (2) the employer contribution that is made either as a "matching contribution" or a "nonelective contribution."

- Matching Contribution - Employer must match dollar-for-dollar the first 3% of compensation for each participating employee. Employer may reduce match to 1% in two years of any five-year period.
- Nonelective Contribution - Employer must contribute 2% of compensation for all eligible employees, regardless of whether or not they participate.
- Catch-up Contribution - Employees who will be at least age 50 by the end of the tax year can contribute an additional $2,500.

SIMPLE 401(k) - This plan involves the same contribution limits and qualifications as the SIMPLE IRA; however, the SIMPLE 401(k) plan does not have the same nondiscrimination and top-heavy testing requirements as a regular 401(k) plan.

401(k) Plan - Elective deferrals by employees are limited to $16,500 for 2009. Employees who will be at least age 50 by the end of the tax year can contribute an additional $5,000 to a 401(k) plan. Employer's matching contributions are not treated as part of the employee's elective contributions. Nondiscrimination and top-heavy testing are required.

SEP-IRA - Simplified Employee Pensions (SEP) are established for employers to make contributions to IRAs of the employee.

A SEP IRA owner may contribute up to 25% of an employee's compensation up to the annual compensation cap. And then subject to annual cost-of-living adjustments for later years.

It should also be noted that your spouse and children may also participate in the plan and open their own SEP IRAs - as long as they are employees of the company

403(b) Plan - Tax-Sheltered Annuity Plan (TSA) is a retirement plan for certain employees of public schools, employees of certain tax-exempt organizations, and certain ministers.

There are three benefits to contributing to a 403(b) plan.

- You do not pay tax on allowable contributions in the year they are made. You do not pay tax on allowable contributions until you begin making withdrawals from

"Life is full of uncertainties. Future investment earnings and interest and inflation rates are not known to anybody. However, I can guarantee you one thing.. those who put an investment program in place will have a lot more money when they come to retire than those who never get around to it."
– Noel Whittaker

the plan, usually after you retire. Allowable contributions to a 403(b) plan are either excluded or deducted from your income. However, if your contributions are made to a Roth contribution program, this benefit does not apply. Instead, you pay tax on the contributions to the plan but distributions from the plan (if certain requirements are met) are tax free.

- Earnings and gains on amounts in your 403(b) account are not taxed until you withdraw them. Earnings and gains on amounts in a Roth contribution program are not taxed if your withdrawals are qualified distributions. Otherwise, they are taxed when you withdraw them.
- You may be eligible to take a credit for elective deferrals contributed to your 403(b) account.

Excluded. If an amount is excluded from your income, it is not included in your total wages on your Form W-2. This means that you do not report the excluded amount on your tax return.

Deducted. If an amount is deducted from your income, it is included with your other wages on your Form W-2. You report this amount on your tax return, but you are allowed to subtract it when figuring the amount of income on which you must pay tax.

Health Savings Account

Health Savings Accounts (HSAs) were created in the Medicare legislation signed into law in December of 2003. The accounts provide an opportunity to reduce your costs for health insurance by as much as 70%.

For 2009, an individual may contribute $3,000, and a family may contribute up to $5,950.

In addition to the standard HSA contribution limits discussed above, if an individual is between 55 and 64 years old prior to the close of the calendar year, then the individual may also make a contribution known as a "catch-up" contribution. The limit for the catch-up contribution is $1,000. These limits are also pro-rated for the number of months the HDHP has been open.

Choosing a Financial Planner

No matter what they call themselves, whether it's account executive, investment advisor, financial consultant, or financial planner, their job is to help you analyze your finances and give you advice regarding investments, insurance, taxes, wills and trusts, and mortgages – in a way that helps you achieve your financial goals.

If you choose your planner well, your planner should become an important part of your life, and you should be working with them during your lifetime. A good planner can help make the financial planning process both fun and profitable for you.

You may come across planners with a variety of credentials, a regular alphabet soup (CFP; CFA; ChFC; CLU; CFS; CMFC; CRPC; RFC; PFS) All of these designations are awarded by private organizations. While they can suggest that a planner has a certain amount of experience or training, none is recognized by any federal or state government or regulatory agency. All of the planners I work with hold many of these designations, but in the eyes of the government, all of them are meaningless.

One word of advice, when selecting a planner: Make sure you ask people who have a lot more money than you who they recommend to use.

Conclusion

- There is, in fact, a specific cost to procrastination. If you are 20 years old and you want to raise $100,000 by age 65, you need to invest only $1,132 today. But a 50 year old would need to invest nearly $22,500 to obtain that same $100,000. This is the cost of procrastination. As you can see, it's not money that makes people financially successful, it's time.
- Match living arrangements to changing lifestyle needs and plan ahead for how you'll pay escalating health care expenses. Be prepared to make adjustments.
- Make sure that financial documents are true to your wishes and beneficiaries are consistent. In fact, a U.S. Supreme Court decision drives home the importance of keeping your beneficiary records current, otherwise the benefits could go to somebody you no longer want them to go to. The Supreme Court said that benefits will go to whomever you have designated on your employee records, even though a change in circumstances – death, divorce, etc. – may have made that designation out of date. **Please make sure you review and update all of your beneficiary designations!**
- The rich are taking their advice from professional financial advisors. The poor are getting their advice from Money magazine. Regularly consult with financial and tax professionals.

NOTES

Chapter 8:
Our Precious "Fur" Children

- Pet Trusts
- States that allow simple Pet Trusts

Key Points

- Every hour of every day 50 companion animals are euthanized in U.S. animal shelters simply because their human companions died and made no arrangements for their continuous care. This amounts to more than 500,000 orphaned pets killed every year.

The Lassie Dog
Author: Brian G. Jett

As Kevin sat intently in front of the old 19 inch Zenith television set with 'rabbit ears' and poor reception, his mother watched her little seven year old boy move almost theatrically as he cheered Lassie on. "Go get 'em girl, go get 'em!" He'd look forward to each episode as Lassie would save the day on each and every airing of this show. His mother had memorized Kevin's question as it was sure to follow at the end of every episode of "Lassie." Per usual, he quickly spun around while sitting 'Indian Style' on the floor and asked, "Mom?, Can I have a Lassie dog? Please mom!?"

As she gazed into his eager eyes she replied, "Honey, I'd love to give you a dog like Lassie, but I've said it before – dogs like Lassie like to be outside and run." Desperately trying to convince him she added, "Kevin, I have told you over and over again that our yard is too small for a Lassie dog!"

Kevin appeared pensive for a moment and then excitingly exclaimed, "I have an idea mom! I'll teach the Lassie dog to stay by me all of the time so she won't get lost or hurt!" His mother appeared surprised that Kevin could creatively think on his feet so quickly.

"That's a really neat idea sweetheart, but Lassie is what's known as a Collie and you can't teach a Collie to stay by your side all of the time because they're outside dogs and I'm afraid your Lassie dog would run away. Do you understand what I'm saying honey?"

Kevin looked down and was clearly disappointed by what he felt was his last ditch effort to gain his mother's favor as it would relate to his getting his youthful mind's hero – a dog and friend like Lassie.

Months passed and Kevin stopped asking his mother whether or not he could get a dog like Lassie. She noticed his increasing quietness and sadness with each passing episode and thought back to her childhood. Her parents surprised her one Christmas with a little scroungy mutt that she adored. She got this ugly little dog that Christmas when she was about her son's age and the guilt of not allowing Kevin to have a dog to be his best friend finally got to her. One afternoon after yet another episode of "Lassie", she decided, right or wrong, to give in to Kevin's earlier repeated desire to have a dog of his own. "Kevin?", she asked, "How about us going down to the dog pound today and getting you a dog? The dog won't be as pretty as Lassie, but I know we can find a dog that you'd love."

Kevin's eyes lit up like a 50 watt bulb with no lamp shade as he exclaimed, "Really mom?! Yes, I don't care anymore about getting a Lassie dog! Can we go now?", he enthusiastically asked. "We sure can honey! Put your shoes on and let's go on down to the dog pound and find you the perfect dog!" Kevin jumped up and hurriedly put his shoes on and headed directly to the car.

Upon arriving at the dog pound, she asked the old man who ran the shelter which dog out of all of the dogs there would be the most loyal and well trained dog for her eager little boy. Without a moment's pause, the man replied, "Oh, that's an easy question to answer. Follow me back and I'll show you the perfect dog for your son."

Kevin and his mother followed the old man back to the last cage on the right. "There she is ma'am. This would be the dog I'd choose and I'd already have her myself but we have half a dozen dogs at home and just don't have room for "Fire." She was taken back as she looked at this homely dog with little hair as the mutt looked like she had been badly burned. After she got over the initial shock of such a sight, she asked, "Has this dog been burned and are you sure this would be the right dog for Kevin?" The old man looked at Kevin and noticed his eyes were misting with tears. "Oh I'd bet my life on it ma'am!", he confidently replied.

"Ma'am?", he inquired, "Did you not hear about the dog that laid on top of the little girl during the forest fire up on Red Bird Mountain? This was the dog that they featured in the local paper. This rascal saved the little girl's life and just about lost her own by covering that little girl with her body!" She thought for a bit and answered, "Well of course I did! Are you telling me that this is that dog?" "Yes, it sure is. No one has taken her because of how she looks and I would have put her to sleep but it's hard to end a life that saved one!", he somberly replied.

"Do you want this dog Kevin? Sounds like you'd have yourself a hero like Lassie if we brought her home." Kevin's eyes had full-blown tears in them now. "I want her mom! Can we take her back with us?" She quickly glanced at the old man who was moved to tears himself at this point. "She's ours sweetheart."

They took "Fire" home and she never left Kevin's side and was his constant companion–never once even attempting to leave the yard or run out of the gate if mistakenly left open. Every night Kevin would say his prayers when his mother would tuck him in and he never failed to pray that "Fire" would be healed and get her hair back. After about five weeks, Kevin's constant prayers were obviously being answered as the once terribly disfigured mutt's hair rapidly began to grow back. Perhaps it was Kevin and his mother's imagination, but the more "Fire's" hair grew back, the more she resembled Lassie.

Kevin's mother opted to call the old man at the dog pound as her curiosity was overwhelmingly piqued. "Hello," the old man responded on the other end of the phone, "Corbin County dog pound. My name is Joe and how can we help you today?" "Hi Joe, I came in a month or so ago with my son and we got the dog you named "Fire." "Yes ma'am, he replied happily, "I'm glad you called... been wondering how old "Fire" has been doing. How can I help you?" She took a deep breath and asked, "Well Joe, I'm curious about just one thing and thought you might know the answer. What kind of mutt is 'Fire'?"

The old man softly chuckled before replying. "Ma'am", 'Fire' isn't a mutt." Confused she continued, "If she's not a mutt, what kind of dog is she?" He chuckled again and replied, "Fire's momma' and daddy are both show dogs. 'Fire' is a full-bred Collie."

Pet Trusts

Say this for Leona Helmsley: She loved her dog. Some of her grandchildren? Not so much.

The imperious hotel magnate, who died, left $12 million to her white Maltese, Trouble, ensuring that Trouble will continue to enjoy a lifestyle other dogs can only dream of.

Two of her grandchildren, meanwhile, got nothing. The two others got $10 million each, though their inheritance will be cut in half if they fail to visit their father's grave once a year.

If there's an upside to this dysfunctional saga, it's this: Helmsley's excessive bequest has focused attention on the importance of including your pets in your estate plans.

Thousands of pets end up in shelters every year because their owners died without making arrangements for their care, says Kim Bressant-Kibwe, trust and estates counsel for the American Society for the Prevention of Cruelty to Animals.

If you're worried about what might happen to your much-loved pet after your death, it's possible to create a pet trust to provide for the continuing care and well-being of a particular animal or animals.

You can choose for a pet trust to take effect upon your death or any disability that prevents you from caring properly for your pet.

As the "grantor" of the trust, you fund the trust with enough property or cash to

"And God took a handful of southernly wind, blew His breath over it and created the horse."
–Bedouin Legend

care for your pet for his or her expected lifetime. The "trustee" can make payments on a regular basis to your pet's caregiver, and pay for your pet's miscellaneous expenses as they come up.

If your pet is expected to live longer than 21 years, there may be a problem with what's called the "rule against perpetuities," which forbids trusts that last forever (or beyond the lifetime of a specifically-identified human being). The Uniform Trust Act, which has now been enacted in over a dozen states, allows for trusts for the care of an animal, regardless of how long the animal is expected to live.

The pet trust laws buck centuries of legal precedent frowning on the practice, in part because the trusts have no human beneficiary. But unlike other recent attempts to expand the legal standing of pets and other animals, the pet trust movement largely has been without controversy.

"This is clearly an idea whose time has come," says Gerry Beyer, an estate law professor at St. Mary's University in San Antonio who has written about pet trusts.

"The idea (of a trust fund for a pet) has gone from something that seems laughable to something that's very mainstream, almost overnight," Beyer says.

Pet trusts are not without drawbacks. Animals can't complain to a probate judge if their trustee is shortchanging them on food or accommodations. And a dishonest trustee could fraudulently extend the life of the trust to continue receiving a trustee stipend.

Beyer has written of a San Francisco maid who was appointed trustee for an ordinary looking black cat. When the cat died, the woman adopted a look-alike to keep the trust fees flowing. She was on her second replacement cat before she was detected.

But pet laws do take into account one key fact of modern life: Surviving adult children may be reluctant to carry out a parent's final wishes.

If it was just you and your pet, and you weren't so sure that your kids halfway across the country would take them, the only way you might get peace of mind is by setting up a pet trust.

"The greatness of a nation and its moral progress can be judged by the way its animals are treated."
– Mahatma Ghandi

Information You Need To Know About Trust Funds For Pets

Many people leave money in their wills to a person they've chosen who will care for their pet after they're gone. But, there's no guarantee the money will be used that way. Now, many animal lovers are setting up legal trust funds for their pets. They appoint a trustee who makes sure the caretaker is taking care of the pet properly.

A trustee is the best. Because he or she can make sure that the money is being spent properly, can make sure that your pets are getting the adequate standard of care that you expected. It's just another level of oversight. It's a watchdog. It's a legal watchdog to protect your animals.

David and Charlotte Congalton set up a trust fund for their pets…all 17 of them! "What you're looking for is a caretaker and the key issue is finding somebody who is going to share your compassion for animals," says David…adding, "These pets are our children." Congalton believes in the practice so much, he's written a book on the booming business of pet trusts

So how much will it cost to set up a pet trust?

"You're going to be paying an attorney to draft a document. That could be anywhere between $500 and $1,500 dollars. There will be annual administrative costs. You're effectively going to be choosing a caretaker and that person is going to be monitored most likely by a trustee. So, you're most likely going to have to pay an annual fee to the trustee to monitor the caretaker and that can get very expensive," says J.J. McNab, an estate planner.

Then you have to add in the costs for caring for the animal. "We use $500 per year as a base line," says Congalton. That's if you have a healthy pet. But you also need to think about other expenses. For instance, how old is the animal? How much longer will it realistically live? Are there any special needs, like daily insulin shots for diabetes? Answers to questions like those could result in extra costs.

Congalton says there's one more important thing that you should carry with you at all times… it's a pet emergency card that's about the size of a credit card and that you can make at home.

"It has the name of caretaker and her phone number. It also has our home address. On the backside, it has the name, phone number, and address of our veterinarian. So, if we're in an accident, they can go through my wallet and say 'oh, we got to get to this place because this guy has all these animals here. We better call the caretaker and make sure the animals are cared for.' That's absolutely important. We've also set up a photo identification system and a pet identification file for all of our animals. Pet identification system is paramount, because, if we were killed in that accident, people come in this house and see all these animals. But, they don't know what cat is which. They don't know which dog is which. So, we've set up this file system."

212

States That Allow Simple Pet Trusts
As of September 1, 2007

These states allow statutory pet trusts, which are less expensive than traditional trusts:

STATE	YEAR ENACTED
Alabama	2006
Alaska	1996
Arizona	1995
Arkansas	2005
California	1991
Colorado	1995
District of Columbia	2003
Florida	2002
Hawaii	2005
Idaho	2005
Illinois	2005
Indiana	2005
Iowa	2000
Kansas	2003
Maine	2006
Michigan	2000
Missouri	2004
Montana	1993
Nebraska	2005
Nevada	2001
New Hampshire	2004
New Jersey	2001
New Mexico	1995
New York	1996
North Carolina	2005

"A dog has lots of friends because he wags his tail and not his tongue."

North Dakota	2007
Ohio	2006
Oregon	2005
Pennsylvania	2006
Rhode Island	2005
South Carolina	2005
South Dakota	2006
Tennessee	2004
Texas	2005
Utah	1998
Virginia	2006
Washington	2001
Wisconsin	1969
Wyoming	2003

Source: American Society for the Prevention of Cruelty to Animals

If you plan to set up a pet trust, talk to an estate planning attorney. Ideally, look for one who has handled estate planning for pets. Some factors to consider:

- Who will manage the trust. Most pet trusts designate both a trustee to manage the money and a caretaker to handle the day-to-day care of the pet. You can name the same person as the caretaker and trustee, but that's usually not preferable, Bressant-Kibwe says. Naming two individuals, she says, creates a system of checks and balances. "The trustee can make sure the caregiver is doing what he's supposed to do."
  You should also name a backup caregiver in case the primary caregiver is unable to care for your pet.
- How you want the money to be spent. With a trust, you can specify your pet's favorite foods, how often the pet should be taken to the vet, even where your pet should be buried, says Lacie O'Daire, an attorney with Walter & Haverfield in Cleveland who has drawn up pet trusts.
- What to do with unused funds when the pet dies. Some trusts direct that leftover money goes to the caretaker, which is a nice way to reward the person who's cared for your pet. But it also gives the caregiver an incentive to skimp on your pet's care in the meantime. You can avoid conflicts by arranging for any unused money to go to charity, Bressant-Kibwe says.
- How to fund the trust. You can set aside money from your estate to cover the costs. Another alternative is to buy a life insurance policy and name the trustee as the beneficiary.

Other arrangements:

If you can't afford a trust, you can still take steps to make sure your pets are cared for if you die or become incapacitated.

If a friend or relative has agreed to care for your pet, you could set up a separate bank account to cover expenses and name the caretaker as the beneficiary.

Many pet owners assume that a family member will step in and adopt their pets if they're no longer around. But that's not always the case. Maggie, now one of O'Daire's cats, spent 10 months in a shelter after her owner went into a nursing home. The woman had children, but none of them wanted the cat.

When O'Daire first approached Maggie at the shelter, the cat didn't want to have anything to do with her.

"She was so devastated in the shelter," O'Daire says. "No one wanted to adopt her."

Within hours of leaving the shelter, though, "She was on my lap," O'Daire says. "She's a beautiful, wonderful cat."

Maggie's story ends happily, but her experience points out the importance of estate planning for pets.

"You always know someone will take care of your kids," O'Daire says, "but you don't know that someone will take care of your cats."

Conclusion
- If you find it hard to think about life without your pet, imagine your pet's life without you.
- If you plan to set up a Pet Trust, talk to an estate planning attorney. Ideally, look for one who has handled estate planning for pets.

"Until one has loved an animal, a part of one's soul remains unawakened."
~Anatole France

"I feel sorry for the person who can't get genuinely excited about his work. Not only will he never be satisfied, but he will never achieve anything worthwhile."
~Walter Chrysler

Chapter 9
The Exit Strategy

- Planning for Your Exit
- Potential Deal Forms to Consider
- Valuation Methods
- The Business Exit Planning Process
- Maximizing the Sale Value of Your Business

Case Study 16 (George & Anita)

George and Anita operate a very successful publishing company. One division publishes a local newspaper. A second division publishes a home and apartment guide. George and Anita have two daughters, both of whom are married with children. One daughter is actively involved in the business, the other is not. George and Anita have stated they want to provide equally for both daughters, and their grandchildren, however they do have one concern about the stability of one of their daughter's marriages.

Their Objectives:

- Treat both daughters fairly
- Reward daughter #1 for all of her hard work in the family business
- Retain some control over the business
- Ensure that the family business and wealth stays in the family and does not end up in their son-in-laws hands.

The Solution:

- George and Anita use a tax-free corporate reorganization to split-off the local newspaper and set up a family limited partnership to hold their interest in the newspaper. George and Anita are general and limited partners.
- George and Anita sell the home/apartment guide to an outsider. They set up a trust for daughter #2 with a portion of the proceeds from the sale. The trust purchases a second-to-die life insurance policy on their lives. The beneficiaries of the policy are their second daughter and their grandchildren.
- The family limited partnership and the trust prevent their daughters' husbands or third parties from obtaining an interest in the business or the proceeds.
- The value of the business is removed from their estate.

Key Points
- Exit plans are important to protect your family's financial future.
- Exit plans allow your business to continue with minimal disruption in the event of your death or disability.
- Exit plans allow you to plan for your financial security and retirement.
- Exit plans eliminate non-participating spouses and family members from the business.
- Exit plans prevent the shock of a capital gains or estate tax nightmare.

Don't skip this chapter just because you have "no intention of leaving your business." Exit strategies are an important part of the planning process, even if we don't think we'll make use of them because eventually every business owner leaves his or her business – either on his or her own accord or forced by certain circumstances. In fact, only one out of five small business owners have a plan in place and more than 40% of family owned businesses have a CEO 60 years of age or older. Out of those, only 42% have chosen a successor.

Some of the events that may trigger a business exit plan include:

- When the business owner or partner dies
- When the business owner or partner suffers from a disability
- When the business owner or partner goes through a divorce that affects business property ownership
- When the business owner or partner decides to retire or leave

All four events can potentially affect the survival of the business and the exit plan helps guarantee the owner receives the maximum amount of money to meet personal, financial, income and estate planning objectives.

Whatever the situation, it is imperative to begin considering the future of your business today. Many business owners are lulled into the belief that they can wait until much later to start preparing their business for sale. Unfortunately, as the years pass by, they miss out on opportunities to enhance their business value and position it for the maximum selling price. If you decide that selling your business is the best option, your next steps are:

Planning For Your Exit

Every business owner should have a personal exit strategy. Key issues to consider could include:
- Passing on your business to your children or other family members, or a family trust
- Selling your share in the business to your co-owners or partners

- Selling your business to some or all of the workforce
- Selling the business to a third party
- Public flotation or sale to a public company
- Winding up
- Minimizing your tax liability
- What you will do when you no longer own the business?

The right time to sell

You need to weigh up the factors which might influence the right time for you to sell your business such as:

Personal factors
- When do you want to retire?
- Has your health begun to deteriorate?
- Do you still relish the challenges of running your business?
- Does your business have an heir apparent?
- Will your income stream and wealth be adequate, post sale?

Business factors
- What are the current trends in the stock market?
- To what extent is your business 'trendy' or at the leading edge?
- Is your business forecasting increases to the top and bottom lines?
- Is your business doing better than other similar businesses?
- Is your business at, or near, its full potential?

Should you attempt to sell your business on your own?

Generating interest in your business is definitely something you can undertake on your own. You will want to list your business for sale in as many "confidential" media as possible. This will provide you with the greatest exposure possible while not alerting your competition, employees, and suppliers of your intentions to sell your business. Also, generating interest in your business on your own reduces your need to pay very high fees to brokers for this activity, which results in a significant savings to yourself.

Once you have identified one or more possible buyers for your business, in most cases you will need to consult one or more advisors to help you through the process of completing the sale. The type of advisors and the extent to which you will need them depends on your experience, your company's size, and the complexity of the transaction. Even small businesses can be confronted with complicated governmental regulations.

An accountant can advise you on the financial and tax aspects of the sale. In fact look for a CPA with a designation of ABV. These are the ones that perform valuation services for numerous purposes, including transactions, financings, taxation planning and compliance, intergenerational wealth transfer, ownership transition, financial accounting, bankruptcy, management information, and planning and litigation support.

An attorney can advise you on the legal aspects, ensure compliance with relevant state and federal requirements, and review the pertinent contracts. And business brokers and business consultants are experienced in the intricacies of the sale itself. They can provide a realistic value range for the business, help package the offering into the selling memorandum, negotiate the details of the sale, and manage the details.

In other words, no don't do this on your own!

Why is confidentiality important?

If it becomes known that a business is for sale it can be destructive to the relationships the business has in place among its employees, creditors, competitors, and customers. Weakened relationships can deteriorate the company's position and thereby make it less valuable.

How will the sale be kept confidential?

Most buyers will be required to sign a non-disclosure agreement (prepared by an attorney). Only a limited amount of information should be disclosed prior to determining if the potential buyer is either legitimate or capable of completing the transaction.

Potential Deal Forms to Consider

The various choices of deal structure each offer unique cost/benefit trade-offs. Here is an overview of the options:

Buy-Sell agreement – This arrangement is designed to permit business co-owners to terminate their business relationship by setting the parameters for some participants to buy out others. It enables one or more associates to maintain involvement in a business when others might wish to sever their ties to it. It can also provide funding for a buyout in the event of the disability or death of a co-owner. A buy-sell agreement requires careful design to ensure that its execution does not work at cross-purposes with other estate and succession planning tools.

Cash sale to a third party – A pure cash transaction may create the greatest immediate liquidity for the seller (and taxes), but other financing structures may have the potential to generate greater net yield over time. A cash sale may also be the simplest means to execute a complete and immediate separation from the business. However, keep in mind that one of the challenges of seeking a third-party buyer is that quite often there is no ready market to sell a small business. Simply put, it can take time and money to find the most profitable deal.

Buyout or recapitalization – In leveraged transactions partners, managers, or the business as a corporate entity borrow the funds to purchase the stock of the exiting entrepreneur. These deals may be especially useful for dissolving a multiple ownership arrangement while otherwise maintaining the business as a going concern. They are also often used for transferring business responsibility to children or other heirs while creating financial independence from them. Recapitalizations can also be used to finance an annuity for a business owner who might wish to combine financial independence with limited business involvement.

"People with clear, written goals, accomplish far more in a shorter period of time than people without them could ever imagine."
–Brian Tracy

Employee Stock Ownership Plan – An ESOP is a form of leveraged buyout designed specifically to give control of the business to a broad base of its current employees. ESOPs may have higher transaction costs than ordinary cash sales, but in many cases these costs are not out of line with the costs of other more complex deals. There are also specific tax benefits for ESOP transactions that may improve their net value significantly.

Valuation Methods

Adjusted Book Value

One of the least controversial valuation methods, it is based on the assets and liabilities of the business.

Asset Valuation

Often used for retail and manufacturing businesses because they have a lot of physical assets in inventory. Usually it is based on inventory and improvements that have been made to the physical space used by the business. Discretionary cash from the adjusted income statement can also be included in the valuation.

Capitalization of Income Valuation

Frequently used by service organizations because it places the greatest value on intangibles while giving no credit for physical assets. **Capitalization** is defined as the Return on Investment that is expected. In a nutshell, one ranks a list of variables with a score of 0-5 based on how strong the business is in each of those variables. The scores are averaged for a capitalization rate which is used as multiplication factor of the discretionary income to arrive at the business' value.

Capitalized Earning Approach

Based on the rate of return in earnings that the investor expects. For no risk investments, an investor would expect eight percent. Small businesses usually are expected to have a rate of return of 25 percent. Consequently, if your business has an expected earnings of $50,000, its value might be estimated at $200,000 (200,000 * 0.25 = 50,000).

Cash Flow Method

Based on how much of a loan one could get based on the cash flow of the business. The cash flow is adjusted for amortization, depreciation, and equipment replacement, then the loan amount calculated with traditional loan business calculations. The amount of the loan is the value of the business.

Cost to Create Approach (Leapfrog Start Up)

Used when the buyer wants to buy an already functioning business to save start up time and costs. The buyer estimates what it would have cost to do the startup less what is missing in this business plus a premium for the saved time.

"The three great essentials to achieve anything worth while are, first, hard work; second, stick-to-itiveness; third, common sense."
~ Thomas Edison

Debt Assumption Method

Usually gives the highest price. It is based on how much debt a business could have and still operate, using cash flow to pay the debt.

Discounted Cash Flow

Based on the assumption that a dollar received today is worth more than one received in the future, it discounts the business's projected earnings to adjust for real growth, inflation and risk.

Excess Earning Method

Similar to the Capitalized Earning Approach, but return on assets is separated from other earnings which are interpreted as the "excess" earnings you generate. Usually return on assets is estimated from an industry average.

Multiple of Earnings

One of the most common methods used for valuing a business. In this method a multiple of the cash flow of the business is used to calculate its value.

Multiplier or Market Valuation

Uses an industry average sales figure from recent business sales in comparable businesses as a multiplier. For instance, the industry multiplier for an ad agency might be .75 which is multiplied by annual gross sales to arrive at the value of the business.

Owner Benefit Valuation

Computed by multiplying 2.2727 times the owner benefit.

Rule of Thumb Methods

Quick and dirty methods based on industry averages that help give a starting point for the valuation. While not popular with financial analysts, this is an easy way to get a ballpark on what your business might be worth. Many industry organizations provide rule of thumb methods for businesses in their industry.

Tangible Assets (Balance Sheet) Method

Often used for businesses that are losing money. The value of the business is based essentially on what the current assets of the business are worth.

Value of Specific Intangible Assets

Useful when there are specific intangible assets that come with a business that are highly valuable to the buyer. For example, a customer base would be valuable to an insurance or advertising agency. The value of the business is based on how much it would have cost the buyer to generate this intangible asset themselves.

"When somebody buys a stock it's because they think it's going to go up and the person who sold it to them thinks it's going to go down. Somebody's wrong."
~George Ross

The Business Exit Planning Process

Establishing the Business Owner's Goals

Every business owner has three primary retirement goals that help move the business forward:

- The exact time the owner wants to sell, leave or retire from the business
- The annual post-tax income the owner wants after selling the business
- The people to whom the owner wants to transfer the business (e.g., business partners, members of the family, key employees, or outsiders)

In addition to these, the owner may have secondary goals such as transferring wealth to heirs or funding charitable institutions.

The planners' role in this part of the business exit planning is to create a financial retirement model for the owner based on the following:

- The business owner's retirement income needs based on current lifestyle expenses
- Projected inflation rate
- Size of current investments
- Current and future investments earning assumptions
- Number of years before the target retirement date
- Life expectancies of the business owners and his or her spouse

Establishing the Value and Cash Flow of the Business

Typically the business makes up between 65% and 90% the owner's assets. To determine if the owner's financial goals can be reached at present through a conversion of the assets to cash, it is important to accurately establish the current value of the business.

If the current assets of the business owner are insufficient, this step will determine how much growth the business value should achieve in order to reach the owner's retirement objectives.

Needless to say, a precise and complete valuation is vital. The valuation should also be conducted early in the business planning process because it serves as a basis for all succeeding planning.

For business owners who want to give ownership to children or sell stock to employees, valuation should represent the lowest defensible value for tax purposes. If the business is to be sold to a third party some valuation method includes:

- Preliminary (or "ballpark") estimate to know if the business can be sold for sufficient cash to satisfy the exit plan conditions.

> "Business is not financial science, it's about trading, buying and selling. It's about creating a product or service so good that people will pay for it."
> –Anita Roddick

- In-depth formal valuation to confirm the preliminary estimate usually performed by the business broker, investment banker, and other professionals.
- Marketability and pricing analysis is performed during the preliminary and formal valuations to gauge existing market conditions, evaluate potential market price for the business and determine the best time to sell the business.

The cash flow forecast is required for tax projection purposes, and maximizing leverage of the future cash flow. The cash flow forecast also is instrumental in projecting how much cash flow must increase in order to meet the owner's financial objectives.

Growing the Value of the Business

If the owner's objectives involve selling the business for cash to a third party, an audited financial review is suggested to document the company's earnings track record for the previous two to three years. Additionally, the value of the business can be enhanced by:

- An efficient business operating system
- A good management team
- A well-established and diverse client foundation
- A practical strategy for growth
- A good appearance of facility
- A tax efficient company structure
- Sound financial controls
- Stable and increasing cash flow

Audited financial statements are not necessary if the business owner plans to transfer the business to family or employees. In a non-cash sale the owners must minimize their exposure to business risk after leaving the business while maximizing the ability of the business to pay off the owner.

Selling the Business to a Third Party For Maximum Profits

This business exit strategy is recommended when the business is so valuable that only those with considerable amount of funds should be regarded as potential buyers. A third-party sale also generates a more substantial amount of cash than if the owner sells to a partner, an employee or a family member.

The most effective method in marketing a business involves creating a competitive or controlled auction to bring together several qualified buyers to make an offer for the company at the same time. The controlled auction includes pre-sale planning, marketing, negotiating, documentation and closing.

The auction allows the business owner to easily pick the most attractive sale price and deal structure while maintaining control of the sale process.

Most substantial third party sales involve investment bankers and transaction lawyers. Smaller businesses worth less than $5 million often use the services of a business broker in lieu of the investment banker.

After the sale, the IRS takes its share from the proceeds. In the absence of a good plan, the tax cut may exceed 50% of the sale price. Conversely a good tax plan can reduce IRS's take by half.

Transferring The Business To Partners Or Family Members

If this is the case, the exit plan must minimize the income tax due from the transfer for both the seller and the buyer while ensuring the purchase price provides the owner maximum financial security.

Often the buyer (owner's children or key employees) has no funds and they can only pay the selling owner's purchase price through installment from future cash flow of the business. One way of keeping most of the company's cash flow for the departing owner is to minimize the company's income tax consequences. Because it will take the owner an extended period of time to receive the full purchase price, the transaction should be designed to maximize the owner's retirement.

Exit planners also recommend a mechanism to sell to outside buyers in the event the owner's children or key employees fail to meet their business transaction obligations.

Put In Place A Contingency Plan For The Business

A contingency plan ensuring the continuation of the business in the event the owner dies is crucial. The consequences of having no such plan when a business owner dies or is incapacitated can kill the business as well. In the case of sole owners, the contingency plan should establish the following:

- Should the business be continued or liquidated?
- Who assumes responsibility to continue and supervise the business operations, financial decisions and administration?
- How will these people be compensated for their time and commitment to continue working until the company is transferred or liquidated?
- Should the business be sold to a third-party or employees?
- Should the business be transferred to family members?

To make certain the company maintains its liquidity, the contingency plan should include a buy-sell agreement or stay bonus program (paid to employees who opt to stay until the completion of the transition) funded by a key person insurance policy on the owner's life.

Put In Place A Contingency Plan For The Business Owner's Family

The final step in the business exit planning process is providing an estate plan for the owner's family in the event of his or her death or disability. This issue is often addressed by a life insurance and disability insurance policy.

"If you think of life as like a big pie, you can try to hold the whole pie and kill yourself trying to keep it, or you can slice it up and give some to the people around you, and you still have plenty left for yourself."

–Jay Leno

Maximizing The Sale Value of Your Business

Whoever buys your business will want to be clear about the underlying profitability trends – are the profits on the increase or decrease? Up-to-date management accounts and forecasts for the next 12 months and beyond will be close to the top of the list of the information which you will need to make available to prospective purchasers.

The value attributable to many businesses is driven by their historical profits, and therefore a rising trend in profitability should result in an increase in the business's value.

Profitability planning is always important, but is particularly so in the years leading up to the sale. So, what is the range of values for your business? Although you may think you can make an educated guess, a professional valuation gives you more solid ground.

Issues that may affect the value of your business include:

- Are sales flat, growing only at the rate of inflation, or exceeding it?
- Is yours a service business with limited fixed assets, or are stock and equipment a large part of your company's value?
- To what extent does your business depend on the health of other industries or of the economy?
- What is the outlook for your line of business as a whole?
- Will your company's products and processes be outmoded in the near future?
- Are your company's products and services diversified?
- Does your company use up-to-date technology and have an effective research and development program?
- How competitive is the market for your company's goods or services?
- Does your company have to contend with extensive regulation?
- What are your competitors doing that you should be doing, or could do better?
- How strong is the company's staff that would remain after your sale?

Taxes

The sale of your company brings you income, and, as a result, taxes. All things in life are not taxed alike, making it advantageous for you to consider certain conditions before you sell your company. How the government taxes income, the structure of your company, and the terms of the sale are the most important issues you need to review. Because of the intricacies of the tax codes, hiring a knowledgeable tax advisor can be invaluable in this process.

Conclusion

- Exit strategies are your way of planning and controlling your eventual departure from the business. You WILL exit your business. Start figuring out now what that will look like and what you need to do today to reduce the tax consequences and maximize the profits from it.

NOTES

Section Six:
The Buck Stops Here!

Chapter 1:
Whom Can You Turn to for Help? A Profile of a Great CPA
- Eleven Solid Tips for Selecting a Great CPA
- Who should prepare my taxes? The differences between CPAs, enrolled agents, tax attorneys, and bookkeepers.
- Bookkeepers love to keep your books!

Chapter 2:
Every Business Needs an Information System
- When does recordkeeping begin?
- "Ordinary and Necessary" Business Expenses
- Your Responsibilities to the IRS
- Tax Reporting Schedule
- How to Pick Accounting Software that's Right for You

Chapter 3:
That Sounds Like a "Capital" Idea!
- The Business Plan
- Sources of Capital
- Initial Public Offerings (IPOs)

Chapter 1:
Whom Can You Turn to for Help?
A Profile of a Great CPA

- A profile of a great CPA
- Eleven Solid Tips for Selecting a Great CPA
- Who should prepare my taxes? The differences between CPAs, enrolled agents, tax attorneys, and bookkeepers.
- Bookkeepers love to keep your books!

Case Study 17 (Lisa) —
A Profile of a Great CPA

On rare occasion there's a professional that decides to take the initiative to step out of the box to investigate their profession to no end and determine how to turn that around for people and change their lives. The person I'm about to introduce has done that. She's painstakingly reviewed the tax code and has determined the various areas for people to maximize that code, in essence, the strategies that the major corporations of the world use to bring them down to the level where you and I can use them in our small business.

This profile is given as an example of how you should regard your CPA.

Lisa Tom is one of the greatest friends a business can have. I say this because I have seen her work wonders with clients of ours. I have seen her pull out tax codes, apply them to tax returns and reduce client taxes legally and simply up to 70 percent. I have seen her move a client from the red into the black just by restructuring the accounting system. And more important, she is excellent at simple explanations.

These seem to be miracles to the people she is serving, but they are not miracles to her. They are standard operating procedures.

Because she is my personal as well as my business CPA, I have set the bar high for others within the industry.

A great CPA can be your best business partner. They can provide you, objectively with information to help you make crucial business decisions. A CPA can play a vital role in the day-to-day operations, investment strategies and, of course, tax planning for your business.

Key Points
- Within your industry, ask successful business owners for recommendations before you select a CPA.
- You're building a relationship. Like and trust the CPA you choose.
- Do your due-diligence so you find the best to prepare your taxes.

If you really want to save taxes, you must find a specialist who can…
- ❏ Help you rethink your tax situation in light of any new laws or regulations.
- ❏ Guide you through financial transactions.
- ❏ Tell you which tried-and-true tax-saving strategies are still good, and which aren't.
- ❏ Inform you of new tax-saving opportunities.
- ❏ Alert you to dangerous tax traps.
- ❏ Represent you before the IRS. Unless you're extremely lucky, you'll have at least one confrontation with the IRS during your taxpaying lifetime.

Eleven Solid Tips for Selecting a Great CPA

Hiring your accountant is like hiring any other employee: You wouldn't do it without a thorough interview or checking their references. I suggest that you even contact the state board of accountancy to see if there have been any disciplinary actions. Once you have narrowed your choices down to at least a minimum of three, schedule a face-to-face meeting with the most promising candidates to find out the following:

1. **<u>You need to evaluate their styles and the chemistry you sense between you.</u>** What characteristics and qualities do you think your CPA should have? Good communication skills, ability to apply knowledge and creativity, someone you could ask "stupid" questions, and just how comfortable you feel with this person when sharing the most intimate details of your financial life.

2. **<u>Is the accountant willing to explain what he or she is doing and why?</u>** You need a CPA that will explain things to you. Not someone who hands you doubletalk, or says a proposed strategy is too complicated to explain. This usually means they don't understand it and certainly doesn't want you to understand either.

3. **<u>Does your accountant present you with Advanced Tax Planning by Choice or merely Tax Compliance?</u>** There is a difference! You need to understand that <u>Your accountant does NOT take care of your taxes</u>. All of the numbers included in your tax return are your responsibility. You create the numbers not your accountant. In fact, your accountant depends on you for the numbers and information. And if you're like most people you take your information to your accountant during the busiest time of year. Consequently, your accountant does not have time to think through every business deduction that may be coming to you. *So the question is, what system does this CPA have in place to make sure they are communicating with you throughout the tax year vs. sending you once a year reminder that it's time to file your tax return?*

A side note: One of the biggest issues that accountants face is that the client does not inform them about every possible deductible expense. What I mean is that so many people decide for themselves what they think may not be deductible so they never talk

"Man's mind, once stretched by a new idea, never regains its original dimensions."
– *Oliver Wendell Holmes*

to their CPA before they make a major financial decision. By talking to them before entering into a transaction your accountant can inform you the best tax advantaged way to handle it. This is worth repeating. You have to talk to your tax advisor **before** you make major financial decisions or it will potentially cost you thousands in lost tax benefits.

4. **Is he or she asking lots of questions, too?** Not every approach will work for every person. No two individuals share identical financial situations so a good accountant will customize their advice for each client. The only way they can do that is to ask lots of questions to get to know you and your business. You need someone that listens to what you have to say and not someone who assumes he or she already knows everything there is to know about you.

5. **Do they offer a free initial consultation to see if the match is good for both of you?** If they do make sure you come prepared. Bring your last 3 years' tax returns, a projection of income and expenses for the current year and your specific questions to give them a quick glance of your personal circumstances. Also, this is the time to establish a good understanding of the level of service you want and are willing to pay for. Do you want them to contact you every quarter, twice a year, or be available every month to review your financials?

6. **Ask about their fee structure.** Remember that CPAs sell time, which is their only product. While the fees are a consideration they should not be the only influence on your decision. Often times, many offices have staff accountants that do a lot of the preliminary work at a lower rate. Also, I recommend that you find a CPA that specializes in your type of business. If they are familiar with the particulars of your industry, the CPA doesn't have to do a lot of research at your expense. Ask successful friends, relatives and business colleagues for references.

7. **How do they handle deadlines?** You don't need the extra stress of an accountant who's cavalier about deadlines or returning your calls. If they are too busy to meet a deadline they may be short-changing you. A tax return that is filed late or full of errors means penalties and interest for you. Also, what's their back-up plan when they are out of town? Who is available to answer your questions?

8. **Look for someone whose tax philosophy mirrors your own.** Even with thousands of regulations and millions of pages of discussion, opinion and court decisions, interpreting tax law is as much an art as a science. There's no one-way to handle many tax questions. The range stretches from very conservative ("Let's avoid an audit at any cost") to very aggressive ("Nothing ventured, nothing gained!") You need someone who is going to discuss the pros, cons and consequences of each approach. If you're very aggressive, they should explain the possible costs you may suffer with regards to penalties, time, loss of privacy and certainly personal anxiety!

9. **<u>Do not hire friends or relatives as your financial advisers.</u>** It can be dangerous to entangle your interpersonal relationships with your business dealings, particularly your personal finances. Even though Sister-in-Law Jane may be a perfectly competent CPA, family strains can be amplified if something goes wrong. You have plenty of qualified non-relatives to choose from so don't get caught in this trap!

10. **<u>Do they believe in filing extensions?</u>** Filing an extension is a cardinal rule of tax-reduction planning. If the CPA does not like to file extensions because they just want to get your return done and out of the way, you get them out of the way and find someone else!

11. **<u>Networking.</u>** Can your accountant refer you to others when you need specific help? A person who has strong networking skills knows many people and every small business can gain from this.

Who Should Prepare Your Taxes?

What is the difference between a CPA, an enrolled agent, a tax attorney and a bookkeeper? Have you asked these questions before? The difference between them is in education and licensing requirements.

The Certified Public Accountant (CPA):

A person who has met state requirements for education and work experience, passed a national exam, and met other licensing requirements. Certified public accountants (in public accounting practice) prepare tax returns, perform audits, do accounting and give advice to their clients on financial matters. Their activities are monitored by a state board to ensure quality and integrity within the profession is maintained.

The Enrolled Agent:

A tax law specialist who passes a Treasury Department tax exam in order to become certified in advising and representing individuals when interacting with the IRS. Enrolled agents can make claims against the government on behalf of taxpayers. They can also prepare tax returns. However, they cannot perform audits. To better ensure quality within the profession, enrolled agents frequently belong (voluntarily) to organizations that require continuing education.

The Tax Attorney:

Tax attorneys must have a Juris Doctor (J.D.) degree and must be admitted to the state bar. Those are the minimum requirements for practicing law. Additionally, tax attorneys should have advanced training in tax law. Most will have a master of laws (LL.M.) degree in taxation.

Some tax attorneys also have a background in accounting. If you are facing a complex accounting as well as legal matter, you might want to look for an attorney who is also a Certified Public Accountant.

You definitely need a tax attorney if:

- You have a taxable estate, need to make complex estate planning strategies, or need to file an estate tax return.
- You are engaging in international business and need help with contracts, tax treatment, and other legal matters.
- You plan to bring a suit against the IRS.
- You plan to seek independent review of your case before the US Tax Court.
- You are under criminal investigation by the IRS.
- You have committed tax fraud (such as claiming false deductions and credits) and need the protection of privilege.

Commercial Tax Preparation Services:

H&R Block, Jackson Hewitt and others are certainly available. I have never personally used a commercial service so I have no experience to relate to you. However, I will state that they will most likely take a conservative stance because obviously, they are not going to risk having to pay penalties by taking a position that the IRS may question. Remember, we're all about Advanced Tax Planning, so ask yourself if it makes sense to use their services?

The Professional Bookkeeper:

Part accountant, part tax whiz, part financial analyst. Bookkeepers perform general accounting duties. They maintain complete sets of financial records, keep track of accounts and verify the accuracy of procedures used for recording financial transactions. They are employed by private businesses, governments and virtually every other type of institution.

Bookkeepers keep financial records that track a company's expenditures, profit and loss, cash flow, and other financial activities. In addition to keeping records, bookkeepers may prepare payrolls, tax reports, and customers' monthly invoice statements.

There are no licensing requirements, nor a monitoring board. We recommend that you hire one that belongs to The American Institute of Professional Bookkeepers (AIPB. org).

Bookkeepers love to keep the books!

When it comes to keeping records, you can either do it yourself, or hire someone. But don't make the mistake of doing this job badly or hiring the wrong person to do it.

Also, you need to consider the value of your time. Do you want to spend your days banging around in a computer program trying to figure out double entry accounting? Do you feel confident you can correctly post all of your income and expenses to the proper accounts? Do you have the knowledge to understand the myriad of reports and financial statements that ultimately serve as the critical points of analysis to ascertain the true health of your company? Please ask yourself this question: "Does handling the bookkeeping and the workload it requires maximize the absolute best use of my time, talents and skills?" If the answer is No….

Hire a competent bookkeeper to handle this aspect of your business. According to Pam Newman, Certified Management Accountant, Author, and Certified QuickBooks® ProAdvisor, they should be:

1. KNOWLEDGEABLE. Make sure they have a basic understanding of accounting and how the "big" picture all fits together. The difference between an accountant and a bookkeeper is that an accountant will do more analysis and usually has additional training. So, while you may not need an accountant on staff, you do want someone who has a basic understanding of the difference between assets, liabilities, equity, income, cost of goods sold, and expense accounts.

2. AVAILABLE. Ensure that they will be available and dependable to keep your bookkeeping up to date. Your information should be input on a consistent basis so you can get reports in a timely manner. If they are trying to "squeeze" this function into their other responsibilities, they may not give it the focus they should.

3. ACCOUNTABLE. You want a bookkeeper that will keep you accountable. If they have checks or deposits that they are unsure of, you want them to be willing to hold you accountable and get good information for record keeping. You don't want someone who is going to code everything to "miscellaneous."

4. TECHNOLOGY KNOW-HOW. You want to keep your books on a computer, not by hand. So ensure that your bookkeeper is competent in using a computerized bookkeeping program, like QuickBooks®. You want a full-service package that incorporates your budgeting, estimating, invoicing, job costing, bookkeeping, and reporting aspects all in one. Though it is key that they are competent enough to be able to input good information into the computer system, bottom line they should be able to use the available technology to provide information and strategic intelligence to the business owner.

5. FAMILIAR. Having a bookkeeper that is familiar with your industry will shorten the learning curve and provide better details. While the basic bookkeeping fundamentals are applicable to all industries, there are very different specifics needed for different industries. Construction companies rely on job costing to understand their profitability. While, retailers are focused on inventory aspects. Restaurant, non-profit, and service-based industries require different insights too. It's important to have some basic accounting knowledge, but ideally you want someone with industry familiarity.

And I am going to add ORGANIZED. You never want to walk into your bookkeepers office and see piles of paper all over her desk or stacks of papers and documents on top of the filing cabinet (instead of in the filing cabinet), or boxes full of last years stuff sitting around on the floor. Professional bookkeepers are neat, tidy, hate disorganization, and are very aware of the confidential nature of every piece of paper, document, or file they are requested to handle or store for safe-keeping.

Conclusion

- Get recommendations from friends, neighbors, members of clubs or trade associations you belong to, your banker, and business colleagues. Word of mouth is by far the best way to find the right tax advisor.
- The ideal tax advisor should be familiar with your line of work especially if you run your own business.
- Select the person whom you are comfortable with personally and professionally.
- Make sure they will meet with you at least quarterly during the year. Saving taxes is an ongoing process-one meeting a year at tax time isn't enough.
- Use your time wisely (like generating income) instead of trying to figure out how to do double entry accounting! Bookkeepers love to keep the books!

"A head for business - that's not something inherited, or something shared by only the talented few, it's something you can acquire, and it's essential."
    – Colette Wolff, author

Chapter 2:
Every Business Needs an Information System

Our tax system is based on individual self-assessment and voluntary compliance. The vitality of this system hinges on the good faith or the American people and their willingness to report their income accurately. This good faith is largely dependent upon the public's general confidence that our tax laws are fair, and that they are impartially and uniformly administered and enforced so that everyone is paying his just share.

Our primary objective and task is sustaining and strengthening this public confidence. To do this we must focus our efforts on a vigorous, reasonable and well-directed enforcement program. It is clear to me that all agents must perform quality audits to insure that we obtain maximum benefit from our enforcement efforts.

It should be emphasized that the Guidelines clearly allow you to exercise your judgment on scope and depth of the audit. At the same time, they will allow you to proceed on each examination with a clear understanding of how to conduct your audit to best carry out the mission of the Service.

The material contained in this Handbook is confidential in character. It must not, under any circumstances, be made available to persons outside of the Service. It is issued for your use as a revenue agent and must be returned upon transfer or separation.

Mortimer M. Caplin, Commissioner

This was part of the forward as written by former IRS Commissioner, Mortimer Caplin for the ***Confidential Official IRS Tax Audit Guide***.

Key Points
- When does recordkeeping begin?
- The Chart of Accounts
- What are "ordinary and necessary" business expenses?
- What are your responsibilities to the IRS?
- How to pick accounting software that's right for you

The IRS hasn't changed much. Their goal is to keep you, the taxpayer, uninformed and ignorant. You may think this is strong language in this land of the free and home of the brave, but how many people do you know who are not afraid of the IRS?

From its inception the rules for income taxes have grown from a relatively simple system to a morass of rules involving regular tax, alternative minimum tax, and many other taxes, often with requirements that two or more sets of records be maintained for the same transactions. Most tax professionals admit that the income tax area has become too big and complicated for one individual to understand completely.

236

The actions you take now...in this critical stage of starting your business, will make or break your finances for the next several years and beyond.

When does recordkeeping begin?

Recordkeeping should begin the minute you start down the path to creating your business, especially if you are going to incorporate. As you begin this process you will immediately start to have expenses. In fact, you will do yourself a great disservice if you are not keeping records at this very moment (the purchase of this book is a business expense!)

You will also have to invest some personal funds into the business for working capital. All of these transactions need to be recorded as your journey progresses.

Many of your initial expenses will be amortized over a period of years however; Congress has seen fit to allow you to deduct $5,000 as a direct write-off in the first year if you have begun to actively pursue your business. These may include:

- Expenses incurred while investigating the business opportunity, be it creation of, purchase or acquisition of a trade or business.
- Survey and analysis of potential markets, products, labor supply and transportation facilities. Pre-opening advertising costs, salaries and wages paid to employees being trained and to their trainers, travel and other expenses while engaging prospective distributors, suppliers or customers.
- Professional services (consultants, legal, tax, or others)
- Machinery and Equipment
- Office furniture, equipment and supplies
- Intangibles such as patents, copyrights or trademarks, domain names etc.
- Organizational costs to form a corporation or LLC
- Research and development costs

"Ordinary and Necessary" Business Expenses

To be deductible, a business expense must be both "ordinary and necessary" – one that is common and accepted in your field of business, trade or profession. A necessary expense is one that is *helpful and appropriate for your trade, business or profession.* The key here is that it is best not to get too creative or imaginative in your interpretation of ordinary and necessary. A good rule of thumb is to do what others in similar business do. (I call it being reasonable.) Precedence is after all, the rule most often applied by the IRS in their determination of ordinary and necessary.

For instance, say you own a micro brewery and love Formula One airplane racing. You decide your hobby could afford you a high level of exposure by painting a cool logo of your business on the plane. At that point, your hobby becomes a part of your marketing strategy. If the IRS were ever to question, you can always point to the racing car industry as a sterling example. However, if you own the only hardware store in Hillsboro, New Mexico, you are going to have trouble writing off a Formula One airplane called Miss Frank's Hardware.

Is it common and accepted? Is it helpful and appropriate for your business? It's your word against theirs, and their word is "disallowed" unless you can prove the IRS has allowed it for other businesses similar to yours.

Be very clear and specific. Do not expense an item under office expenses when it should be designated as advertising or marketing. Do not say cleaning when you mean office janitorial service. Always label your expenses appropriately.

And remember, you are allowed to enjoy operating your business. You need not intend to maximize profits. You may choose expenses that give you personal satisfaction and recreational opportunities without the legitimacy of your business necessarily being called into question.

The Chart of Accounts

Setting up a chart of accounts is **the first** task you perform when setting up an accounting system, which in a sense is like a table of contents for your finances.

A business needs to know where the money is coming from and where it is going to. Your chart of accounts is the tool you use to gather and organize all of this information. And depending on how well you design it determines how well the use of this information will show up on your financial reports.

The chart of accounts is the **FOUNDATION** that your financial record keeping system is built upon.

Typically the accounts are listed in the following order:

Balance sheet accounts	• 1000-1999 Assets • 2000-2999 Liabilities • 3000-3999 Owner's Equity
Income statement accounts	• 4000-4999 Operating Revenues • 5000-5999 Cost of Goods Sold • 6000-6999 Expenses • 7000-7999 Operating Revenues and Gains • 8000-8999 Non-operating Expenses and Losses

Within the categories of operating revenues and operating expenses, accounts might be further organized by business function (such as producing, selling, administrative, financing) and/or by company divisions, product lines, etc.

A chart of accounts will likely be as large and as complex as the company itself. An international corporation with several divisions may need thousands of accounts, whereas a small local retailer may need as few as fifty or one hundred accounts. Many industry associations publish recommended charts of accounts for their respective industries in order to establish a consistent standard of comparison among firms in their industry.

The IRS generally requires you to break out certain income and expense and balance sheet items. There are slight variations in the rules depending on the way you do business (e.g., corporation, partnership, etc.). Talk with your bookkeeper or tax advisor to get your Chart of Accounts set up properly right from the start of your business, **before** it becomes a costly nightmare to fix!

Your Responsibilities to the IRS

Our tax system is a self-reporting system. One of your obligations as a citizen of the United States of America or as a legal alien working in the U.S. is to report your income and expense.

First, you are responsible for timely tax filings and the timely payment of tax liabilities. This includes income tax and employment taxes.

Second, you are required to file returns and for maintaining your tax records. You have the burden to keep records showing why your taxes should not be higher than you have reported. You also have the burden to show why bank deposits are not income instead of loans or transfers from other bank accounts. To claim ignorance or even incorrect IRS verbal advice does not cut it. Your records must be permanent, accurate, complete and must clearly establish your income deductions and credits.

Your failure to keep proper books and records of your income producing activities, and of all allowable expenses, gives the IRS a distinct advantage. The IRS has the right to use the best evidence available in order to determine taxable income.

And remember, the IRS gets information from third parties and matches this information to you through its computers. Stay one step ahead by being extra careful to report on your tax returns what the IRS already knows about you.

Documentation System

It's not unusual for business owners to have their financial records in disarray. Don't. Being organized is essential and setting up manila folders to separate all of your paperwork is quick and easy.

"Even if you're on the right track, you'll get run over if you just sit there."
– Will Rogers

You will need three separate and distinct tax records:

- Permanent Files are documents that include prior year's tax returns, stock purchases and sales, real property purchases and sales, equipment purchases and sales. Generally, any record that relates to more than one tax year should be kept in your permanent files.

- Regular Files are the yearly accumulation of receipts, invoices, credit card statements, canceled checks, bank statements, time sheets etc.

- Personal Organizer. This is a critical piece of your documentation system especially if you operate a personal service business. This should record all of your appointments, where and when you traveled, your vehicle mileage and when, where and whom was entertained as a business contact.

Retaining Records

Keep all records for a minimum of three years. However I recommend seven years for substantiation in the event the IRS (or others) requests to review them. Store them in file boxes properly labeled (A/R 2009, A/P 2009, Payroll 2009, General Ledger 2009 etc.) Keep them offsite in a locked storage facility to avoid clutter and to keep all information secure and confidential. You should also have separate computer back-ups for each year stored in a different location as well.

As important as the records of your business is the way in which you protect them once they're established. I've heard many sad stories about loss of irreplaceable records and other papers-everything from fire, flood, tornados and earthquakes. But closer to home, damage caused by pipes that burst in the winter flooding the basement where everything was stored. Be aware of the risks and take the necessary precautions to protect your important business records.

Tax Reporting Schedule

This is only a general guide and not meant for use as a final authority. Depending on your state, city or county, you may be responsible for additional reports and returns that are not listed below.

Monthly:
1. Payroll tax liability. Make a deposit on the 15th of each month for the taxes of the previous month.
2. Sales tax reports. You may be required to file monthly, quarterly, or annually, according to your sales tax volume. You also may be required to put up a bond or prepay sales taxes based on an estimate of sales volume.

Quarterly:

1. **Estimated taxes.**

   ❑ For corporations you file the 15th day of the 4th, 6th, 9th, and 12th months of the tax year. For most businesses this will be April 15, June 15, September 15, and December 15. If the due date falls on a weekend day, the due date will be the following Monday.

   ❑ S Corporations the due dates tend to be April 15, June 15, September 15, and January 15.

2. **FICA and withholding returns (Form 941).** File Employer's Quarterly Federal Tax Returns reporting Social Security (FICA) tax and the withholding of income tax. Check early to see if you are required to make deposits.

3. **FUTA deposits (Form 8109).** Make Federal Unemployment tax deposits on April 30th, July 31st, October 31st, and January 31st.

Annually:

1. **FICA and withholding information returns**. Provide information on Social Security tax and the withholding of income tax. (Check for any state requirements).

   ❑ W-2 to employees no later than January 31st.
   ❑ W-2 and W-3 reports to the Social Security Administration by the last day of February.

2. **1099 information returns**. Send information for payments to nonemployees. (If you paid a corporation directly for its services, you do not send it a 1099.)

   ❑ Forms 1099 due to recipient by January 31st.
   ❑ Forms 1099 and transmittals 1096 due to IRS on the last day of February.

3. **FUTA tax returns**. File federal unemployment (FUTA) tax returns with the IRS. Due date is January 31st.

4. **Income tax returns.** File with IRS and your state, if applicable.

   • Form 1040: Sole proprietor, individual who is a partner (member of an LLC), or S corporation shareholder file on the 15th day of the 4th month after end of tax year (generally April 15th, Schedule C, Form 1040).

   • Form 1065: Partnership returns (LLCs taxed as a partnership included) on the 15th day of the 4th month after the end of tax year (generally, April 15th).

   • Form 1120: A corporation files on the 15th day of the 3rd month after end of the tax year. (If fiscal year ends December 31, return due by March15; If fiscal year end is June 30, return due by September 15th.)

- Form 1120S: An "S" corporation files on the 15th day of the 3rd month after end of the tax year (generally March 15th).

How to Pick Accounting Software that's Right for You

Starting and running a small business is full of challenges, and one of the biggest challenges is dealing with the finances of the business. No doubt people have recommended to you a variety of different types of software to help you with your bookkeeping, but you want to be sure that you pick the software that will be the most beneficial to you.

Use the following four steps to help you select the accounting software you need to manage your business.

Step 1: Decide what type of records you plan to keep.

There are two accounting methods for recording income and expenses – cash and accrual.

Cash accounting. Records the income or expense on the date it occurs A company that uses the cash accounting method is considered to have made a transaction when the cash is physically received or paid out for services or products. Most businesses that sell services use the cash method of accounting because you simply report the income in the year you receive it and an expense the year you pay it.

The Accrual Method (aka Managerial Accounting) allows you to record the expense when it's earned or incurred, regardless of when the cash for the transaction is received or paid out. Many C corporations, manufacturers and businesses with inventories of goods must use the accrual method of accounting. In other words, income is treated as received when it is earned-regardless of when it is actually received. On the flip side, an expense is recorded at the time the obligation arose-which is not necessarily when it is paid.

When selecting a managerial accounting program, you first should decide what you want to measure. Knowing what end-results you want to achieve, or reports you want to run, will help you select the best software.

Step 2: Select software that's compatible with your advisers.

Once you've decided what type of accounting software to buy, you'll want to make sure it is compatible with the system your tax adviser or financial consultant uses.

Compatibility of systems means that your tax adviser can take all of the information you have entered into your computer and dump it into his system to figure your taxes. Software compatibility eliminates the headache of having to re-enter the data.

So, before you buy, ask your advisers what software they use, if they have recommendations for your use, and then make sure that what you buy will allow you to share information with them.

"It's a funny thing about life: If you refuse to accept anything but the best, you very often get it."
~ W. Somerset Maugham

Step 3: Look at the software's requirements.

Next, consider if the software will run on your computer. That's right, not all software will work on all computers.

- What are the hardware requirements?
- Does this company have support personnel to help me if I have problems?
- How user-friendly is the system?
- What types of training are available?
- What happens if my needs expand? Can I add additional modules?
- Does the system produce the types of reports and documents I want?

Once you've determined what the software requires, confirm that your computer has enough memory and hard drive to accommodate it. The commands to check these on your computer differ based on the operating system you're using, so if you're not sure how to do it, instructions should be listed in your manual.

Step 4: Ask for an evaluation copy.

Before you purchase the software, ask for a free evaluation copy so that you can use the software before buying it. Or, check to see if the software comes with a money-back guarantee. Some programs, such as QuickBooks®, come with a 30 or 60-day money-back guarantee. Either way, both options allow you to load the software onto your computer, go through the setup and actually use the software to see if you like how it works.

Review Your Books Regularly

When you're running your business, you may not take the time to sit down and look at your financials. In order to effectively manage your money, you have to have the facts! Every day you need to know what's going on with cash flow. At least every week you should be reviewing accounts payable, receivables and inventory. And certainly every month, review your profit and loss statement and your balance sheet.

The only way you can manage growth, save money and prepare for the future is to know what's going on in your business "financially" each day.

Conclusion

- The more "professional" your records look to an auditor, the more likely he will conclude that you are running your business in a businesslike manner, and that you pay attention to details. Those two perceptions will help you greatly in the event of an audit.
- Documentation is key to sustaining your tax position and any failure to meet the adequate documentation standards required by the IRS could result in disallowance of your valid deductions.
- Every business is unique. The accounting system you use must be tailored to your individual needs.
- Simplicity is the key. Your records must be complete, but no so complicated that they cannot be read and understood.

Chapter 3:
That Sounds like a "Capital" Idea!

- The Business Plan
- Sources of Capital
- Initial Public Offerings (IPOs)

Case Study 18 (Felix)

Friends and family thought Felix had lost his mind when he sold his house and left a successful 27-year career with Proctor & Gamble to launch his own business. But after three years of hard work and research, he achieved his dream in August 2006, by opening TastTea. The business is a gourmet teahouse that also specializes in serving a delicious array of raw foods (and I'm not just talking about carrots and celery sticks!). His fabulous restaurant provides a relaxing environment, offers a variety of raw food classes to educate consumers, offers specialty catering services, and provides a full-menu of healthy alternatives as compared to regular restaurant fair.

As an exhibit manager for P&G, Felix spent a lot of time traveling for business, and finding a good restaurant that offers any type of raw food or totally vegan was nearly impossible. This gave him the idea. He visited natural food stores, specialty delis and multi-cultural restaurants all over the country, but never found one that had all the components as he imagined his business could. His first step was to create a business plan. He spent the next year researching the feasibility of a raw food enterprise. With a complete description of the business, bundled with the financial and marketing plan, he was ready to quit his job and pursue his passion.

Key Points

- A Business Plan is a guide for your company. It's how you answer the questions; "Where do you want the company to go?" and "What are you going to do to get there?"
- Every idea has value potential. Capital develops ideas.
- Anyone has the legal opportunity and RIGHT to raise capital in a free capital society.

The Business Plan

Whether you're starting a new business or expanding an existing one, a business plan is an indispensable tool.

Lenders, investors, employees and partners are all looking for the same information in a business plan. And while there is a standard format used in a written business plan, I learned from my friend and business mentor, Keith Cunningham who wrote the book, Keys to the Vault that really what everyone is looking for is the answer to the following questions:

1. Who are you? What skills, knowledge, expertise and track record are you and your management team bringing to the table? Who do you have for your advisors and what are their credentials?
2. What is it? You need to be able to define your product or service in easy to understand terms.
3. Where are you in this process? Have you hit any benchmarks, do you have working prototypes, anyone beta testing for you?
4. Where are you going? What's your goal? Are there certain milestones you will hit along the way?
5. Who wants it? Clearly define who your target market is and what pain or problem is your product/service going to solve?
6. How many people will want it? How large is the market share you are going after?
7. How do you know they want it? What's your proof of concept? Have you done any testing/research/studies to confirm if you build it, they will come?
8. How much do they want it? What's the true value you are bringing to the customer? Are they looking for the best price, or the best quality? And based on what you find out, can you sell your product and make a profit?
9. How will you tell them about it? How do you intend to differentiate yourself and position yourself in the market? What's the marketing plan?
10. How will you deliver it to them? What are your distribution channels? What costs are involved every step of the way?
11. Who else has it? Who's your competition within the industry? Who's your competition outside of the industry? (People only have so much discretionary income and yet, they have unlimited choice as to how they are going to spend it.) Everyone has competition!
12. What are the risks? These are the what if's, the unknowns, what could go wrong?
13. What are the rewards? What are the projected financial results and the potential returns?
14. What do you want? How much money do you need and why is that enough? What deal are you proposing between you and the investor?
15. What's the exit? How does the investor ultimately cash out of this deal?

To answer all of these questions will take a lot of your time and effort. But it's worth it. To be able to know if your business idea is viable long before you or anyone invests one dime is critical. The magic is in the process. This is how you fine-tune your business concept, making it all the more likely that your venture will succeed and grow. And as happens most often, you will also find out that it is going to cost more money than you thought it would and that it will take longer to get up and running than you thought it would.

Always plan to operate six months into the future from your start date. When raising capital you want to make sure you can cover operational costs for 180 days. That includes salaries for you and your team.

"People seldom improve when they have no other model to copy after."
– Oliver Goldsmith

Check out BPlans.com for an easy to use Business Plan program.

And now with plan in hand, next it's time to identity sources of capital.

Sources of Capital

Capital is any asset that a business uses to create value and generate profits, including financial resources, equipment, and even employees.

Working capital is cash and is of course, necessary to pay for all those people, equipment, supplies, inventory, and other expenses required to operate a business.

So how can you raise capital for your business?

Personal funds - Using personal finances or "bootstrapping" is one of the first sources that an entrepreneur may consider using when they decide to raise capital for their new business. This includes:

- Personal checking and savings accounts
- Credit cards (dangerous!)
- Retirement accounts
- Sale of real estate, vehicles, recreational equipment, jewelry, and even your stamp and coin collection
- Life Insurance
- Second mortgage
- Family and friends: Many of these loans can be made available rather quickly because your family and friends know you personally and are caught up in the excitement of the new business venture. Borrowing money from those closest to you can work both for and against the new business owner. Family members and friends may feel that they should have a say in every company decision or may desire a large stake in the new business since they had lent money to the entrepreneur. This can lead to resentment and relationship strains among all parties involved. New business owners need to evaluate the different possibilities that may occur when they decide to use their friends and family members to raise capital since it can result in complicated matters.

After "seed" capital is provided by "founders" of the business, the most common method of raising Balance Sheet Capital is through a Private Placement of Securities.

The two general categories of financing available for businesses are debt and equity.

Debt financing - Debt is a direct obligation to pay an asset (usually money) to a creditor who supplied your business with an asset. This means you will have payments based on the amount borrowed, the interest rate and the length of the loan.

An advantage of debt financing as a way to raise capital is that the entrepreneur is able to retain maximum control over their new business. In addition, interest on debt financing is often tax deductible. However, one disadvantage of debt financing is that the high debt may look unattractive to other investors who are also involved in the project. This money owed may discourage other financiers from lending further funding and can often disqualify a new business owner from the opportunity to raise capital in the future.

Sources of debt financing include Banks, Credit Unions, Consumer Finance Companies, Commercial Finance Companies, Community Development Loan Funds (CDLFs), and leasing companies which usually offer long-term rental agreements that allow funds to be available for other needs.

What Resources Are Available Through the U.S. Small Business Administration?

When assessing your capital needs, you should consider programs offered through the U.S. Small Business Administration (SBA). Congress established the SBA in 1953 to aid, counsel, and protect the interests of the Nation's small business community. The SBA accomplishes this in part by working with intermediaries, banks, and other lending institutions to provide loans and venture capital financing to small businesses unable to secure financing through normal lending channels. The SBA offers financing through the programs listed below.

- 7(a) Loan Guaranty Program: This is the SBA's primary lending program and was designed to meet the majority of the small business lending community's financing needs. In addition to general financing, the 7(a) program also encompasses a number of specialized loan programs. The following are a few of the many specialized loan programs:

- Low Doc: This program is designed to increase the availability of funds under $100,000 and streamline or expedite the loan review process.

- CAPLines: An umbrella program to help small businesses meet their short-term and cyclical working-capital needs with five separate programs.

- International Trade: If your business is preparing to engage in or is already engaged in international trade, or is adversely affected by competition from imports, the International Trade Loan Program is for you; and

- DELTA: Defense Loan and Technical Assistance is a joint SBA and Department of Defense effort to provide financial and technical assistance to defense-dependent small firms adversely affected by cutbacks in defense.

- Microloan Program: This program works through intermediaries to provide small loans from as little as $100 up to $25,000.

"Never mistake motion for action."
– Ernest Hemingway

- Certified Development Company (504 Loan) Program: This program, commonly referred to as the 504 program, makes long term loans available for purchasing land, buildings, machinery and equipment, and for building, modernizing or renovating existing facilities and sites.

Small Business Investment Companies (SBICs), which the SBA licenses and regulates, are privately-owned and managed investment firms that provide venture capital and start-up financing to small businesses. To find additional information on these and other financial programs please contact your local SBA District Office (call 1-800-8-ASK-SBA for the nearest office) or look on SBA's Web site (http://www.sba.gov).

Types of Loans

- **Secured loans**. You will need to find collateral in order to raise capital for the new business. Personal, commercial or residential properties, invoices, or even recreational equipment can be considered deposits to secure the loan. Secured loans are a popular alternative for entrepreneurs to raise capital for their new businesses.

- **Unsecured loans.** If the new business owner does not want to use collateral as a form of security to raise capital for their new business, they have the option to apply for an unsecured loan. Even though unsecured loans are not as large in amount as secured loans, this may be more compatible with the new business owner's needs. An unsecured loan is also a popular option to raise capital for a new business.

In both types of business loans, entrepreneurs are able to raise capital for their new business based on their credit rating.

Equity financing - This is a type of financing which is essentially an exchange of money for a piece of ownership in a new business.

An advantage of using equity financing as a way to raise capital is that the new business owner can pay back the loaned amount throughout a fixed duration of time. In addition, the new business owner can focus on making their product(s) profitable rather than worrying about paying back the investors immediately.

The disadvantage is that investors often want the ability to exercise some control over business operations. This loss of control is permanent, unless you have negotiated a **buy-out clause** that allows you to buy the shares back from the investor at an agreed-upon price. A good scenario would be that the right investor may be able to provide the business with additional management expertise.

In a corporation, the investor becomes a holder of either common or preferred stock in the business, and can exercise the powers of a stockholder as defined in the bylaws. Preferred stockholders receive any dividends (a percentage of profits) paid by the business before any common stockholders.

Initial Public Offerings (IPOs)

In the chaotic securities markets of the 1920s, companies often sold stocks and bonds on the basis of glittering promises of fantastic profits - without disclosing any meaningful information to investors. These conditions contributed to the disastrous Stock Market Crash of 1929. In response, the U.S. Congress enacted the federal securities laws and created the Securities and Exchange Commission (SEC) to administer them.

The Securities Act of 1933 fulfills two objectives:
1) To provide prospective investors with full and fair disclosure of the character of new securities.
2) To prevent fraud and misrepresentation in the sale of securities.

Are There Legal Ways To Offer and Sell Securities Without Registering With the SEC?

Yes! Your company's securities offering may qualify for one of several exemptions from the registration requirements. I'll explain the most common ones below. You must remember, however, that all securities transactions, even exempt transactions, are subject to the antifraud provisions of the federal securities laws. This means that you and your company will be responsible for false or misleading statements, whether oral or written. The government enforces the federal securities laws through criminal, civil and administrative proceedings. Some enforcement proceedings are brought through private law suits. Also, if all conditions of the exemptions are not met, purchasers may be able to obtain refunds of their purchase price. In addition, offerings that are exempt from provisions of the federal securities laws may still be subject to the notice and filing obligations of various state laws. Make sure you check with the appropriate state securities administrator before proceeding with your offering.

A. Intrastate Offering Exemption

Section 3(a)(11) of the Securities Act is generally known as the "intrastate offering exemption."

This exemption facilitates the financing of local business operations. To qualify for the intrastate offering exemption, your company must:

- Be incorporated in the state where it is offering the securities;
- Carry out a significant amount of its business in that state; and
- Make offers and sales only to residents of that state.

There is no fixed limit on the size of the offering or the number of purchasers. Your company must determine the residence of each purchaser. If any of the securities are offered or sold to even one out-of-state person, the exemption may be lost. Without the exemption, the company could be in violation of the Securities Act registration requirements.

If a purchaser resells any of the securities to a person who resides outside the state within a short period of time after the company's offering is complete (the usual test is nine months), the entire transaction, including the original sales, might violate the Securities Act.

It will be difficult for your company to rely on the intrastate exemption unless you know the purchasers and the sale is directly negotiated with them. If your company holds some of its assets outside the state, or derives a substantial portion of its revenues outside the state where it proposes to offer its securities, it will probably have a difficult time qualifying for the exemption.

You may follow Rule 147, a "safe harbor" rule, to ensure that you meet the requirements for this exemption. It is possible, however, that transactions not meeting all requirements of Rule 147 may still qualify for the exemption.

B. Private Offering Exemption

Section 4(2) of the Securities Act exempts from registration "transactions by an issuer not involving any public offering." To qualify for this exemption, the purchasers of the securities must:

- Have enough knowledge and experience in finance and business matters to evaluate the risks and merits of the investment (the "sophisticated investor"), or be able to bear the investment's economic risk;
- Have access to the type of information normally provided in a prospectus; and agree not to resell or distribute the securities to the public.

In addition, you may not use any form of public solicitation or general advertising in connection with the offering.

The precise limits of this private offering exemption are uncertain. As the number of purchaser's increases and their relationship to the company and its management becomes more remote, it is more difficult to show that the transaction qualifies for the exemption. You should know that if you offer securities to even one person who does not meet the necessary conditions, the entire offering may be in violation of the Securities Act. Visit www.sec.gov for legal compliance information.

Are There State Law Requirements in Addition to Federal Ones?

The federal government and state governments each have their own securities laws and regulations. If your company is selling securities, it must comply with federal and state securities laws. If a particular offering is exempt under the federal securities laws, that does not necessarily mean that it is exempt from any of the state laws.

Legal Compliance Issues

Legal compliance is complex. Hire the right attorney and let them do the work for you. Hire the experts that know what has to be done. A Securities attorney will know what filings and what registrations are mandated for the various forms of capital fund-raising. They will know how much information you must disclose and what rules and guidelines you must follow for state and federal compliance.

Conclusion

- Taking the time (that means soul-searching and hard work) to do all of the research necessary to determine if your idea will convert to a viable and profitable business venture can mean the difference between failure and success.
- Capital is the fuel that powers ideas. Capital requires a legal structure to attract sources of capital. Capital sources are interested in safety first and profit second.
- By recognizing that there are many creative options available to capitalize your business, you need to make sure you have enough working capital to keep the doors open today and tomorrow!
- All of your stock, membership interest, and limited partnership interest's are considered securities. Make sure you understand the law with regards to the SEC and your state. Any questions should be directed to a Securities attorney in your home state.
- As you can see there is a new language you have to learn. It's called the language of Raising Capital.

Section Seven:
Building Your Wealth
Securing Financial Freedom the Easy and Simple Way by Letting Your Corporate Tax Savings Work for You — Automatically

Chapter 1:
Grow Rich — One, Two, Three
- Learn the Rule of 72
- Apply the Rule of 72
- Watch your wealth grow

Chapter 2:
Figure Your Fortune by Using Your Tax Savings and the Rule of 72!
- Your seven-step plan

Chapter 1:
Get Rich — One, Two, Three

- Learn the Rule of 72
- Apply the Rule of 72
- Watch your wealth grow

Case Study 19 (Erik, Sunshine, Holly and Sam)

Erik retired a millionaire at the age of 60. He incorporated his struggling little business when he was just 23. He learned all he could about money management and investments. No matter how tight money was, he invested $2,000 a year from the money he was saving on paying taxes in business as a corporation rather than as a sole proprietorship. His plan was to do this for seven years, let the money accumulate and at age 60 retire a millionaire. He carried out his plan of investing $2,000 for each year from age 23 to 30. His investment totaled $14,000. He never touched his savings until retirement. By age 60 his $14,000 had turned into $1 million. Was he exceptionally smart? No. He found out about the Rule of 72 and applied it to his savings. At retirement he enjoyed a life of affluence.

Everyone who starts saving at a young age should be able to do the same.

Sunshine heard about Erik's retirement plan. She wanted to do the same. The only difference was that she was 30. She invested $2,000 a year for the next 30 years. That's a total of $60,000 invested. A very substantial investment. She, too, retired at 60, with a million dollars. Why did it take her 30 years and $60,000 to end up with the same amount of money? You'll see as we progress.

Holly was a financial genius. When she turned 21, she took her first $1,000 tax savings from her incorporated business and put it to work for her during the next 40 years. Guess what her retirement was from that investment, which she kept at the highest rate (about 18%) she could find? She turned $1,000 into $16 million. Not bad, right?

How could this be? You'll see when we review the Rule of 72.

People always said that everything she touched turned to gold. Her friends saw her in one new Porsche after another. A couple of trips around the world. Skiing in the Alps. Deep-sea diving off the coast of Australia at least once a year. And on and on. But she had money smarts, and she was not going to waste it all, even though she had her $1,000 active investment.

She structured her business wisely. Yes, she had a corporation, and she saved a lot on taxes. All her dollars from tax savings she committed to good sound investments. She had six million dollars from investing her tax savings over the years and was going strong. No financial worries for her. Holly enjoyed life. What a way to live!

Sam never did start investing. He was a brilliant entrepreneur. He made lots of money, spent lots, lost lots and ended up, at 60, broke. You've got it right. He never did incorporate his business. He never kept good records. He never developed an accounting system that worked. He was always in trouble with the IRS. And he never protected his assets. You've got it right. He never saved a dime even though he had heard about the

Rule of 72. No, at 60, Sam was not affluent, just sad, working hard at odd jobs just to survive while trying desperately to start another business without any money.

Key Points

- Incorporate so you can take advantage of the lower corporate tax and spend money before taxes.
- Invest your tax savings at a good rate from 10 percent to 15 percent consistently.
- Invest with the Rule of 72 in mind and in practice.

How Can You Get Rich On Your Tax Savings-

What do the above stories have to do with you? They simply exemplify how you can use the tax savings you get by running your business as a corporation rather than as a sole proprietorship or general partnership and investing some of your tax savings the smart way. And in the case of Sam? Obviously an example of what not to do.

This section will show you only one way to wealth. It is simply taking some of your tax savings, investing it wisely and over time watching the Rule of 72 work for you. This is by no means the only way to secure financial freedom. There are many. This section is not intended to give you a course in investment and savings. A good accountant and financial planner can help you do that.

There is no one way to riches. Each person's fortune must be planned individually for that person. But a quick look at one simple strategy — one financial rule (the Rule of 72) — will do a lot to open your mind to the possibilities. Granted most of you are not 21 and do not have 40 years to let money ride and roll over and over and over. But sooner is always better than later.

Letting your money work for you rather than you working for money is the rich person's way to more riches. Let it be yours, too, and your children's way. Just think of it, your children have time in their favor; so consider applying the Rule of 72 to their lives and see what a gift you can leave them.

Okay, you ask, "What is the Rule of 72, and what can it do for me?"

How to Get Rich to Gain the Freedom that You Need/Want/ Deserve!

Once you apply the Golden Tax Secrets and other tax codes you have reviewed earlier, you need to consider how you can gain financial freedom by investing some of your tax savings each year. The process is very simple. You will understand the rewards when you understand the Rule of 72.

The Rule of 72 "Eighth Wonder of the World"

- Take the interest rate you are getting on your investment
- Divide it into the Number 72

254

The answer = the number of years it takes for your money to double. Let's use 6 percent, 12 percent and 18 percent interest rates.

How to Apply the Rule of 72
- Determine the amount of money you wish to invest each year.
- Determine the rate of interest you wish to receive.
- Determine the number of years you intend to let your investment grow.

If you invest just $2,000 for seven years from age 23 to age 30, your $14,000 investment at 15 percent will turn into more than a million dollars by the time you reach 65. Consider the possibilities if the investment was made at birth.

Two thousand dollars a year is $5.48 per day. Think of it this way. That's free money from tax savings. But even if it were not, that $5.48 a day is one Coke, one cup of coffee, one candy bar and one ice cream or frozen yogurt a day or playing five video games. Incredible, isn't it.

How much money do we waste all the time?
How much do we spend wisely?
How much do we contribute to a good cause?
How much do we save?

Rule of 72 (Interest Over Time) Work Sheet

Let's take a moment and do some figuring. Record different interest rates (five percent, 10 percent, 12 percent, 15 percent, 18 percent). Record the sum of money you wish to invest ($1,000, $10,000). Record the number of years (10, 20, 30, 40) you wish to invest. See the vast difference time and interest rate make.

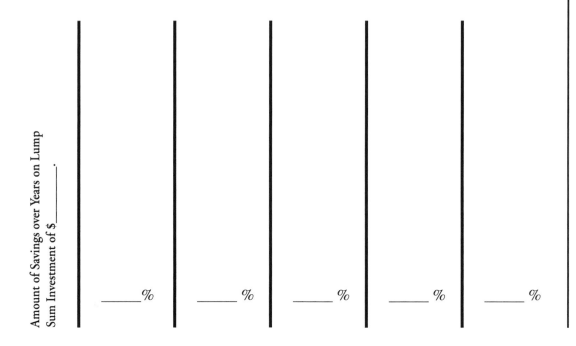

Amount of Savings over Years on Lump Sum Investment of $ _____ .

_____%   _____%   _____%   _____%   _____%

Rule of 72 —
Compare Investment Over Time at Various Interest Rates

Do you think rich people know about the Rule of 72?

Do you think banks know about the Rule of 72?

Do you think credit card firms know about the Rule of 72?

Do you think insurance firms know about the Rule of 72?

Do you think they all apply the Rule of 72?

Yes, of course they do.

Why shouldn't you apply the rule of 72? You can and will prosper! If you are not in the habit of saving, it is hard to start. But if you incorporate your business, instead of running it as a sole proprietorship, then you are giving yourself a gift of 15.3 percent in tax savings from the self-employment tax alone. Or if you have a hobby, turn it into a side business. You don't have to quit your regular job. Incorporate the business. Follow the guidelines in this book, and you will save on taxes. Then take the tax savings, invest and apply the Rule of 72 to them.

By using this simple principle, you are merely doing what the rich are doing and have been doing all along. This is the basis of wealth building. There are only four principles that the rich use to get rich and richer. You can use them, too.

Four Founding Principles of Getting Rich and Staying Rich

1. Go into business for yourself and incorporate your business!
2. Spend first — tax later (by operating as a corporation).
3. Own nothing — control everything (all your assests protected).
4. Use the magic of compound interest (apply the Rule of 72).

Applying the Four Founding Principles of the Rich to Get Rich and Grow Richer Year After Year

Follow these steps:

1. Go into business for yourself and incorporate your business to take advantage of lower corporate taxes, and you will get by with a lower personal income, yet have more money in your pocket and more money for savings.
2. You can spend first by taking benefits that are deductions to your corporation and paid with pre-tax dollars.
3. Your corporation(s) owns everything and yet you actually control everything. Your assets are protected and you can pass them on to those you choose without costs.
4. You invest your tax savings at a good rate of interest over time.

It's great to know what to do. Now how do you do it?

> **The best service in the world won't do you much good...**
> **unless it comes from people who are willing to do whatever it takes**
> **to make sure every detail is covered for you.**

If you have a profitable home state enterprise, you may want to consider multiple corporate strategies as indicated in the Special Supplement of this book.

When you use the tax code to maximize your profits and apply the Rule of 72 to your tax savings, then you can experience the freedom you need, want and deserve.

As visionary of your enterprise, you have chosen well to gain the understanding this book has to offer. I trust at this stage of your reading that your mind has been opened and your wealth-building horizons have expanded. As you are moving closer to the last few pages of reading, I want to remind you that corporations and the concepts presented throughout these chapters are merely tools. You, as the visionary, are now equipped with the knowledge of using these tools. It is up to you to act now while the tools are sharp and ready to craft a splendid masterpiece.

Let me encourage you to press on as you now have a very special opportunity to create a new exciting and extraordinary experience in your life...an experience in which rivers of enriching abundance can flow if you, and only you, act on your vision.

Conclusion

- Incorporate so you can take advantage of the lower corporate tax rates and spend before taxes.
- Invest your tax savings at a good rate of return from 10 percent to 15 percent consistently.
- Invest with the Rule of 72 in mind and in practice.
- Explore other ways to make your money work for you.
- Use expert help when structuring your business entities with thoughts of now and the future.

Gettting the Individual Help You Need

So often, we speak with individuals such as yourself, who hesitate on moving forward because of the concern of what happens after you set up a business structure. There can be a lot of new information, things to do and perhaps you feel like your loading yourself up with a lot of extra paperwork in your already busy and complex life. Who is going to help you run it, answer your questions that right now you're not even sure what questions to ask, and still show you how to maximize the benefits of the entity far into the future.

Do this for me. I would like for you right now to clear your mind and together let's think about the process of building a house. First, we have picked out a beautiful piece of land with a gorgeous view that holds so much promise and potential you can't wait to begin the process of creating your ideal home. This piece represents your ideas, your dreams and your goals. Next we lay the foundation. It must be strong and made of mortar and stone. With careful planning we have designed this foundation to support everything else that must follow. Visualize that this foundation represents the business structure we need to form. The same foundation any successful business will need to start or perhaps merely to secure the progress of a going concern. The third step is the construction of the wood frame, the very infrastructure that supports the walls and roof. Think of this phase as the creation of the articles, the bylaws, or operational agreements that define the very essence of the entity you need to create. Now we'll add the windows and doors to represent your outlook, your direction, a magnificent golden horizon. And finally, we add you and your family. You represent the players: the shareholders, officers, directors, members or partners sitting in this beautiful and comfortable home crafted and designed to your exact specifications. It has been built to provide the mental and financial security that represents the essence, the very heart of the entire project. Of course, it took time to put all of this together and yet the end result is exactly what you envisioned. You did it. You built it. Now go forward and do what you do best, realize the dream!

Now let me ask you this. When you visualized the construction of this home, did you see yourself building it alone? Without any help or guidance? I want you to know the relationship you develop with Sage is an opportunity to work with very talented and knowledgeable individuals who will literally hold your hand through the entire process before, during and after the entity is formed.

And we work very hard to provide you with continuing information and educational opportunities. In fact, that's exactly the reason why we have an 800# so that we're always available to answer your questions, send you additional information when you need it, or simply to let you know what's new. I am proud to be part of a team that takes the time to listen, makes every effort to define your exact needs, and then follows through every step of the way to make sure the entire process is easy and simple to understand.

We enjoy being a part of your growth and prosperity. Hearing the success stories associated with so many of our clients and knowing that we were able to offer a helping hand along the way.

Cheri S. Hill, President/CEO

Chapter 2:
Figure Your Fortune by Using Your Tax Savings and the Rule of 72!

Dream it

Detail it

Do it

Protect it

Invest it

Share it

Enjoy it

Case Study 20 (You)

A successful entrepreneur's profit portfolio.

This section is yours to write. It is included here for you to outline your "Incorporate & Get Rich!" story even before it happens.

Your Name

_____

_____

_____

_____

_____

_____

Key Points

Dream it

Detail it

Do it

Protect it

Invest it

Share it

Enjoy it

A Journey Down Your Profit Potential

- **Dream it** — Take the time to list all you want your profit potential to be.
- **Detail it** — Tell how you can accomplish each item in the above list. Give the names, phone numbers and addresses of the people and firms that can help you.
- **Do it** — Create a calendar of events. Make it realistic so you will be able to achieve your profit potential. Give the date you will start and conclude each activity and who will help you.
- **Protect it** — Decide upon the business structure(s) you should have to operate your business most efficiently and profitably and that will help you protect your assets. List the names, phone numbers and addresses of the people and firms that can help you.
- **Invest it** — Create your investment plan to achieve your profit potential. List the names, addresses and phone numbers of those who can help you.
- **Share it** — List the ways you would like to share your wealth. Include how you will share it, now and after you are gone. Be specific. Set up a system for sharing it. List the names, addresses and phone numbers of those you wish to help and who can assist you.
- **Enjoy it** — List all the ways you want to enjoy your life when you achieve your profit potential. List who will help you. Be specific. Give the names, addresses and phone numbers of those who will help you in this process.

It may seem unrealistic to make a comprehensive get rich and stay rich plan. Most people do not. In fact, we have been taught to believe that wealth is akin to wickedness. Well, it is not. Money for money's sake, as Ebenezer Scrooge learned, has little value. But when it is shared, it is highly rewarding.

If you spend money the instant you get it or even before you get it, then money will always be a problem to you. Most people have the tendency to enjoy first and plan later. When you plan first you have a better opportunity to accomplish what you want to accomplish and to acquire the wealth you want.

Look back over your life. What did you do with a dime when you were a kid? Did you spend it on something expendable such as candy? You might have been told to save some of it, share it with someone and not spend it all at once. This was all good advice, but you were probably not told to plan what you would do with it before you received it.

In life it is the rare person who shares first, saves next and then spends what's left on his or her own pleasure. People would say, "I would have nothing left to enjoy." But this has been proven to be untrue when you plan. In fact, when you plan, you will get a lot more out of your money in the long run. Also, your joy is much greater, longer lasting and more abundant.

Without planning (in other words, putting things in their proper perspective), things don't usually go well. Everyone enjoys dreaming about being wealthy, but few turn those dreams into plans. You have that opportunity right now.

This book has given you the basic information you need to create your financial plan for the rest of your life. Enjoy it, now and for the rest of your life.

Conclusion

- Dream it.
- Detail it.
- Do it.
- Protect it.
- Invest it.
- Share it.
- Enjoy it.

Special Supplement
Multiple Corporate Strategies

- Use more than one corporation to upstream your money to tax-free Nevada (no corporate taxes in Nevada).
- Use more than one corporation to protect your assets — forever (no disclosure of stockholders in Nevada).
- Use more than one corporation to keep your taxes at the lowest possible tax rate (the lowest corporate federal tax rate is 15 percent).

Multiple Corporate Strategies

- How to eliminate state corporate taxes
- How to keep federal corporate taxes at the lowest tax rate
- How to protect your assets against attack

What Do Most People Do?

When most people go into business and decide to incorporate, they simply incorporate in the state in which they are doing business. That is not always the smartest thing to do, as you know. They usually form only one corporation and assume that they now have protected their assets with a corporation. That is not all they can do to fully protect their assets, as you will discover. They also usually do not take full advantage of the tax codes and rarely consider the tax advantages of operating with more than one corporation. You will discover in these next few pages the secrets that the rich use to get richer and richer.

What Do People Need to Know?

As astonishing as it may seem, the federal and state tax codes are written to help the entrepreneur make money and pay as little tax as possible. The trouble is that most people do not know how to do this.

All of these benefits can be achieved by using what is known as "dual and/or multiple corporate strategies." You will be shown how corporations can work together (independently from one another) to obtain tax and asset protection benefits.

However, this section is not meant to be a definitive instructional text on dual and multiple corporate strategies. Instead, this is only to introduce you to some of the possibilities that might be open and advantageous to you. Each situation is different: therefore, you are not given a blueprint to follow. If you decide to use the dual or multiple corporate strategies, it is imperative that you seek professional advice from an attorney specializing in corporate tax law and an accountant specializing in corporate tax accounting. You need to structure your businesses correctly, so as not to form a control group, and operate each corporation completely independent of one another.

You also cannot use dual and multiple corporate strategies as an individual, all by yourself. You need to involve other people.

Who Can Benefit from More than One Corporation?

The first consideration is determining who needs more than one corporation.

- If you have a corporation that has a net profit of $50,000 or more, you should consider forming a second corporation.
- If you are incorporated in a state that has a state income tax on corporations, then you should consider incorporating in Nevada to upstream your profits to tax-free Nevada.

- If your corporation has assets, then you should consider forming a Nevada corporation to secure those assets that are exposed to lawsuits and other attacks. This can be done either through a note or by owning them outright and leasing them to your corporation.

If you meet any of the above three conditions then you should explore the benefits you might receive from forming additional corporations. You also need to explore how this can be done and who can help you most effectively.

What's It All About?

The chart on the following page gives you a cursory glimpse of how two corporations can work together. We have called one Nevada, Inc. and the other Home State, Inc. Study the chart so you see how the money flows from Home State, Inc. to your corporation in tax-free Nevada. It also illustrates how your assets can be protected when your home state corporation borrows money from your Nevada corporation and the Nevada corporation secures the loan with all the assets of Home State, Inc.

By applying these two simple processes, you have impoverished your home state corporation. Home State, Inc. has no net profit, therefore no state taxes to pay. Home State, Inc. has no assets, therefore it is highly unlikely that anyone would sue Home State, Inc. Nevada not only has no corporate or inheritance taxes, it has tremendous privacy laws. The stockholders of a Nevada corporation are not recorded on any public record. Explore the possibilities of upstreaming income to tax-free and non-disclosing Nevada.

"Whatever you steadfastly direct your attention to, will come into your life and dominate it."

~ Emmet Fox

Upstreaming Income and Asset

Nevada, Inc.	**Products/Services** 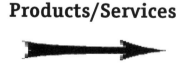 $$$$$$$$$$$$$$$ **Contract/Security Agreement/UCC-1 Filings**	Home State, Inc.

Nevada, Inc. can provide the following services and many others for Home State, Inc.

- Purchasing
- Independent Contractors
- Sales Agents
- Equipment Leasing
- Lending Money

- Research/Development
- Factoring Receivables
- Consulting Services
- Advertising
- Marketing

Protection Strategies

When you legitimately upstream money by providing products and services to Home State, Inc. from Nevada, Inc., the profits of Home State, Inc. are upstreamed from the home state (in a state that taxes corporate income) and flow into Nevada. The state of Nevada does not impose any taxes on a corporation, and the annual filing fees are minimal.

Another benefit of upstreaming income into other corporations is that you divide the net profits between the corporations and place each company in a lower federal income tax bracket. (Care must be taken to do this correctly.)

Using more than one corporation, particularly one or more Nevada corporations, provides tremendous asset protection. When the exposed Home State, Inc. owns nothing and is in debt to a Nevada corporation totally separate from it, neither becomes a likely target for lawsuits. Home State, Inc. has nothing to take.

Nevada, Inc. is non-exposed to public activity and is totally separate from Home State, Inc. Corporate laws in Nevada, regarding security and privacy, are the most stringent in the country. A Nevada corporation will protect the assets it holds. There is no disclosure of stockholders in Nevada, and Nevada offers nine different types of stock including the permitted use of bearer shares. Bearer stock is initially issued. Then, after the initial issue, whoever holds the stock is now the shareholder.

Because a corporation does not die when the directors, officers and stockholders do, (the use of buy-sell agreements are absolutely essential and a fundamental business-planning tool), the assets can be protected virtually forever.

If You Can Benefit, Seek Professional Assistance

Dual and multiple corporate strategies offer many benefits. However, as with any legal and tax matter, you should have legal counsel with a tax attorney or an accountant that specializes in corporate taxes. As explained later, the process of dual or multiple corporations is very simple, but the rules have to be strictly followed.

How Does Upstreaming Work?

You form two corporations. One is the exposed corporation and the other is a non-exposed corporation.

Exposed Corporation:

Your corporation is exposed to lawsuits if you conduct business, have employees and own property/assets in your home state. Even though your business is incorporated, any assets owned by the business may be subject to lawsuits, creditors and the IRS. In fact, the more you have, the more you will be targeted.

Non-Exposed Corporation:

A corporation that serves as a vendor to your other corporation is not exposed to the public and probably does not have employees except for you and your family. When this second corporation is a Nevada corporation, it is your non-exposed, non-disclosed, non-liable corporation because it has the protection of the Nevada corporate statutes. No one can cross the Nevada state line and ignore Nevada state law.

How Two Corporations Work Together:

How can both corporations work together to protect the assets of the exposed corporation? There are many ways. Let's use Home State, Inc., your home state corporation and Nevada, Inc., your Nevada corporation.

1. Home State, Inc. can borrow money from Nevada, Inc. and thereby become indebted to Nevada, Inc. The money Home State, Inc. owes Nevada, Inc. is evidenced by a security agreement and a promissory note — due on demand when Nevada, Inc. calls it due.

2. Nevada, Inc. and Home State, Inc. have agreed that the assets of Home State, Inc. will be the collateral and security for the note by executing a security agreement (a document that sets out the terms of the security interest, lists and describes the property involved and tells when the lender can take the property and what can be done with it).

3. As notice to the world and evidence that these assets are collateral for the loan, a UCC-1 (a standardized form that is filed with the secretary of state's office or county recorder's office in some states, to record the existence of a security agreement, also known as a financing statement), is filed in Nevada and in your home state. For additional collateral, Nevada, Inc. may require that a trust deed be filed on any real property that the owners of Home State, Inc. own.

4. Nevada, Inc. is in first position on the assets of Home State, Inc. and no one suing Home State, Inc. can touch those assets until the debt to Nevada, Inc. is paid. (If Home State, Inc. already has a first position lien holder on some of its assets, then Nevada, Inc. will hold second position.) This still means, however, that your Nevada corporation gets paid before anyone suing you (some tax claims are the exception).

This is known as "priority" and is very important to a creditor because it determines the position occupied by a creditor's claim or lien on a debtor's property or collateral.

"Computers are magnificent tools for the realization of our dreams, but no machine can replace the human spark of spirit, compassion, love and understanding.
~ Louis Gerstner

In the case of Hilst v. Bennett, 485 P2d 880 (Colorado 1971), the holder of a perfected security interest (filed UCC-1s) on equipment and fixtures of a tavern could not be placed behind a judgment creditor. The priorities of the parties are set by their time of perfection. The appellate court found for Hilst and, quoting from the Colorado version of the Uniform Commercial Code, said:

"When a person in the ordinary course of his business furnishes services or materials with respect to goods subject to a security interest, a lien upon goods in the possession of such person given by statute or rule of law for such materials or services does not take priority over a perfected security interest unless a statute expressly provides otherwise."

5. You are conducting business with protected assets. Even if there is a judgment entered against Home State, Inc., there is nothing to get. You can actually give your home state corporation to the person suing. This will not hurt you at all. After all, Home State, Inc. has no assets, only debt. This debt can exist even after Nevada, Inc. has taken possession of all the assets of Home State, Inc. If the person suing wants Home State, Inc. then they receive the corporation and all of its debt as well. No one wants a corporation without a single asset and loaded with debt payable on demand.

The proper handling of paperwork and the importance of timing bring up another critical issue, transferring property. When you pledge property as collateral, you actually transfer the right and future rights of possession to the creditor until the debt is paid. What you need to be aware of and avoid at all times is the act of fraudulent conveyance. What this term means is that there was an improper transfer that removed the property from the reach of a creditor. A typical situation occurs when a person transfers property out of his or her name (to a wife, child, best friend) in order to put it out of reach of his or her creditors. Under certain circumstances, a court has the authority to undo or reverse a transfer of property. The courts look to the following "badges of fraud:"

- A relationship between the grantor and the grantee
- The grantee's knowledge of litigation against the grantor
- The insolvency of the grantor
- A belief of the grantee that the asset transferred was the grantor's last assets subject to execution
- Inadequacy of consideration
- Consummation of the transaction contracts outside of normal business procedures

To minimize risks, the issue of transfers between related parties is eliminated by doing business with corporations. Even though you may control them, they are separate legal persons. Proper documentation and valid consideration (anything of value that is received in exchange for the property, and the value should be close to the fair market value of the property conveyed) is critical.

Nevada business presence makes it work for you. In order for this dual corporate strategy to work, a legitimate Nevada business presence for Nevada, Inc. is essential.

"The common denominator of success and happiness is other people."
– The Mastermind

To really see how this all works, let's walk through some actual situations.

Case SS-1 — Seeing Double
D&D

Dan and Debbie had a retail store in California. They had heard from Debbie's friend Ann that a Nevada corporation could save them taxes.

Case SS-2 — Ann's Company
Ann

Ann had been running her multilevel marketing company through a Nevada address. She knew that, because fulfillment of products in her company occurred somewhere other than in California (products were shipped to places all over the country), this was not a California-source company.

- Ann did not have to pay California corporate income tax on the income earned from the company.
- She drew a small salary from her Nevada corporation, which would be income for her personal income tax return, and which would be subject to California personal income tax.
- Her corporation paid for the bulk of the expenses, tax-free to her (meaning tax-free for federal and state). Because she was an employee of the Nevada corporation, she drew all of the employee benefits available to her — including a pension plan.
- The pension plan grew — in Nevada — and was waiting for her the day she retired.
- Additionally, the corporation purchased a split-dollar life insurance plan for her. This unique insurance policy was growing in value in Nevada, so that she could borrow against it (tax-free) in the future.
- Ann was doing a great job at providing for her future financed entirely by her tax savings.

Could this same plan work for her friends Dan and Debbie?

Case SS-1 Continued — Retail Outlet

The important point to remember with a retail outlet is that the income earned is subject to source tax. Actually, there isn't a separate tax called "source tax." This term is used here as a way of referring to the state of location where the income was earned. In Ann's case, she earned income in Nevada, because fulfillment occurred there. But in the case of a retail outlet, fulfillment occurs where the sale is made — at the store. If the store is in California, you have to pay California income tax. If the store is in Arizona, you have to pay Arizona income tax. But all is not lost …

1. Dan and Debbie formed a Nevada corporation,

D&D
California, Inc.
Authorized to do business in California.

(The Nevada corporation is filed as a foreign corporation in California. Though the Nevada corporation costs less than a California corporation — filing as a foreign corporation brings the cost back up to the cost of a California corporation. So the costs are the same, but the benefits are greater with a Nevada corporation.)

Dan and Debbie could have formed a California corporation instead. However, they chose a Nevada corporation because of the better asset protections available. Income in this company will be subject to California tax. Read that again. Income is subject to California tax. The key is not to have income. Let's call this company D&D California, Inc. and follow how this works.

D&D
Nevada, Inc.

2. Dan and Debbie now form a second Nevada corporation that will do business in Nevada. This company will be set up as a marketing company, D&D Nevada, Inc. It will charge D&D California, Inc. a fee each month for its services. Dan and Debbie are aware that they must run the Nevada corporation in a legitimate fashion. The Nevada corporation places ads for the California corporation. It is responsible for research and development of new products. Most important, the Nevada corporation must have a Nevada business presence.

3. If profits increase in California, the fees to Nevada increase. At the end of the year, D&D California, Inc. has no net profit! That means there is no California corporate state income tax. Yes, you read that right — no tax! It is only logical. If a company has no profits, it will have no taxes to pay. Zero profits means zero taxes. D&D California, Inc. would pay no California state taxes or corporate federal income taxes.

Now, isn't this strategy beginning to look interesting and profitable to you?

D&D Nevada, Inc. had a great year. And since it is domiciled in Nevada, California taxes do not apply.

Now, let's consider another fact. Let's assume that D&D California, Inc. made zero income. And let's assume that D&D Nevada, Inc. made a net profit of $100,000. The combined profit would be $100,000. The state taxes are zero.

If the companies had been California-based companies doing business in California, the net profit (taxable income) would be $100,000, and the California state corporate income tax would be (under the current tax rate of 9.3 percent) $9,300.

Is it worth investigating the possibilities of dual/multiple corporate strategies?

The federal taxes would be 15 percent on the first $50,000 ($7,500) plus 25 percent on the next $25,000 ($6,250) plus 34 percent on the next $25,000 ($8,500). The federal corporate taxes on the $100,000 net profits would be $7,500 plus $6,250 plus $8,500 equals $22,250 or an average of 22.25 percent.

If an additional Nevada corporation was formed, the income could be spread between the two Nevada corporations and show a legitimate income for each at $49,999 each. This means that each corporation would be taxed at 15 percent of $7,500 each to total $15,000. This is a savings of $7,250 on federal corporate taxes and $9,300 on California state corporate taxes. You would pay only $15,000 instead of $37,800. This yields a total savings of $16,550.

Now you can easily see how advantageous this is and how the costs of the added corporations are insignificant in comparison to the savings.

By investing some of the tax savings — over time — you can also see how people who use sound tax and investment strategies become millionaires. It's not a mystery; it's just know-how.

D&D California, Inc. and D&D Nevada, Inc. together form what is called a "dual corporate strategy" or in the case of three or more — a "multiple corporate strategy." This simply means that two or more corporations work together to provide you with the best possible protection and the lowest possible taxes.

Dan and Debbie knew that it was important that the transactions between their two companies be conducted at arm's length. Each company had its own checking account. Each company had its own address. Additionally, they made sure that their Nevada corporation had a true Nevada presence, which includes:

- A telephone listing in a Nevada telephone directory
- Corporate headquarters in Nevada with a legitimate street address in Nevada (not a P.O. Box, unless it is in rural Nevada where postal delivery requires a P.O. Box. In this case, you still need a physical address.)
- Nevada state business license (and local business license, when applicable)
- Corporate bank account in Nevada
- Paper trail showing real transactions occurring between Nevada, Inc. and Home State, Inc.

"Love your client."
~ C.W. "Al" Allen

The Possibilities Go On and On...

There are many variations possible regarding dual/multiple corporate plans.

- You can stagger year-ends to defer taxes.
- You can utilize insurance products to pull tax-free money out of Nevada.

All of these great benefits can be yours by utilizing dual and multiple corporations. However, they must be structured properly and run according to the law or they cannot work for you.

Caution:

- It is important that you have expert advisors who are experienced in these strategies and will set up your plan properly.
- •• All transactions must be conducted at arm's length and properly documented.
- ••• Avoid badges of fraud when conveying property to remove property from the reach of creditors.

You also want to avoid being considered a control group. If this should happen, you would lose your dual and multiple corporation benefits.

If you can avoid the dreaded controlled group status, there are even more benefits available through the use of these strategies. Primarily, there are some significant tax advantages, above and beyond what we have already discussed. Remember the corporate tax rate tables:

Taxable Income Over	But Less Than	Tax Rate
$ 0	$ 50,000	15%
50,000	75,000	25%
75,000	100,000	34%
100,000	335,000	39%
335,000	10,000,000	34%

Multiple corporations that are not controlled corporations can take the lowest rate for each corporation. For example, a successful corporation that, despite every deduction you could possibly take, made $200,000 taxable income would face a federal income tax of $61,250. But if you could split this company's income (using the dual corporate strategy) into four $50,000 companies, your federal tax would only be $30,000. That's a savings of $31,250! In addition, there would be no state income tax if these corporations were set up as Nevada corporations.

Even better, each company can take their own Section 179 limit for depreciation. Each is subject to its own calculation for accumulated earnings tax. Each corporation can have its own year-end allowing for incredible flexibility in tax planning and the ability to "push" income off into the distant future.

What Is a Controlled Group?

The concept of controlled groups is complicated, so, as with any idea from "Incorporate & Get Rich!," make sure you have a good advisor helping you with the proper structure. Basically, if ownership exists with one person, a controlled group exists. That is, if Dan and Debbie each own 50 percent of both the California and Nevada corporations, the tax benefits are not allowed.

A parent-subsidiary controlled group exists if a corporation owns at least 80 percent of the stock and value of another corporation.

A brother-sister controlled group exists if five or fewer people (including partnerships, individuals, trusts and the like) own at least 80 percent of the voting stock or value of shares of each corporation and these five or fewer people own more than 50 percent of the voting stock or value of shares of each corporation, considering a particular person's stock only to the extent that it is owned with regard to each corporation.

The main thing to remember is that if you have ownership, whether through a trust or some other entity, of more than one corporation, you run the risk of being called a controlled group.

What Is Not A Controlled Group...
Here Are Some Examples:

- You own less than 50 percent of one corporation and your child (over 21 years of age) owns the rest. You also own 100 percent of another corporation.
- You own less than 80 percent of one corporation and a totally unrelated person owns the rest. Plus, you own 100 percent of another corporation. You could even control both corporations.
- You own 100 percent of one corporation, and your spouse owns 100 percent of another corporation. You and your spouse manage the corporations separately and maintain complete separation of the assets.

Warning: As with all tax strategies, it is important that you avoid an IRS determination that you have created a sham transaction. My analogy is that if it walks like a duck and talks like a duck — it is likely a duck. This also applies to multiple corporations hoping to avoid being called a controlled group. It is very important that owners of multiple corporations doing business with each other transact all business at arm's length.

Don't take shortcuts! Treat the business conducted between the two corporations just as you would in any other business transaction with any other unrelated third party. Keep all documentation and make sure you leave an excellent paper trail.

If your corporations act as if they are in a controlled group, they are in a controlled group. The IRS can invoke Section 482 if:

- there is a significant element of tax avoidance or evasion, or
- when there is a sharp separation of the expenses of producing gain from the gain itself

The more corporations interact like unrelated third parties, the less likely they are to be called controlled corporations.

As you can see by these two examples, you can reduce your corporate state income tax and reduce your federal corporate income tax using dual corporations that are structured properly and run separately.

There is even a greater benefit for most entrepreneurs who personally own assets as well as having a business with assets. With 90 million lawsuits annually in the United States and more than 20 million civil lawsuits, people who have anything anyone would want had better protect their assets and may want to consider implementing a dual or multiple corporate strategy. The following story reveals why.

J&B

James and Barbara owned a tire store in Midland, Iowa. They never considered themselves high risk. They had a modest home in which they had about $50,000 in equity.

They had some bonds and stocks they had inherited. The cash value was about $40,000. They had a doll collection worth about $10,000 and antique jewelry and furniture approximating $35,000. Their personal assets then totaled $135,000. It had taken their family three generations to accumulate these assets.

Their business assets were a little more — about $180,000 including inventory and accounts receivables. So if something happened — real or trumped up — someone could get $135,000 from this couple. Their children's education would be jeopardized, their retirement gone and their income source stripped from them.

Who would want to sue?

James and Barbara were very nice people, and they treated everyone who came through their door as their best friend.

Then the unexpected happened. Someone bumped into a tire stand. It fell on a customer's child. The child was taken to the emergency room with a broken leg and trauma. Who was at fault?

The person who bumped into the stand didn't have a dime to his name. Though he was named in the suit, it didn't matter. He had nothing with which to pay.

He counter-sued the store because he had not seen the stand, which he claimed was hidden behind a large poster. His suit named the storeowner, claiming insomnia for causing injury to a small, fragile child. He needed psychological help to get over the trauma.

The tire manufacturer was named in the suit because it had provided the tires and the tire stand. Well, everyone knows the tire manufacturer would have to pay big bucks for this unfortunate accident and would probably settle before trial.

During the course of discovery, it was determined that the store owner had not put the stand at least 20 feet from anything else in the store as the instructions had called for. Therefore, the storeowner, who displayed the stand and had not read the fine print, became totally liable.

JaBar Tires, Inc.

James and Barbara ran their store through an Iowa corporation, JaBar Tires, Inc. The corporate assets would be attacked but not their personal assets.

Of course the attorney would try to pierce the corporate veil by claiming the owners were only an alter ego of their corporation and not operating properly as a corporation to go after their personal assets. If proven, James and Barbara could lose everything. At 45, with three children in college, they could be wiped out. Disaster.

Let's look at another possibility.

James Tires, Inc.
+
Bar Marketing, Inc.

- James owns James Tires, Inc., an Iowa corporation.
- Barbara owns Bar Marketing, Inc., a Nevada corporation.
- Bar Marketing, Inc. contracts with James Tires, Inc. to do its advertising, marketing, sales and promotions.
- James Tires, Inc. borrows money from Bar Marketing, Inc.
- Bar Marketing, Inc. holds a first position note on the assets of James Tires, Inc. Even the accounts receivables go to Bar Marketing, Inc. in case of a lawsuit. What do the investigating attorneys find out?
- James Tires, Inc. owns nothing and is very much in debt. There is nothing to get.
- The personal assets of James and Barbara have been protected with family trusts and family limited partnerships.
- Bar Marketing, Inc. has nothing whatsoever to do with the case. It is just a vendor that is doing business with James Tires, Inc.
- Because Bar Marketing, Inc. is a Nevada corporation, the shareholders are not of public record, unless expensive court discovery is pursued.
- The case goes away because James Tires, Inc. has no assets and no ability to pay. Or it may be settled for pennies on the dollar.

While in most every jurisdiction it is considered unlawful to fraudulently transfer assets simply to avoid paying a known creditor, you do have the right to structure your affairs to protect your assets against unforeseen events.

Wantulok et al., 214 P2d 477 (1950) states: "Where there is no creditor, there is no fraud... The motive with which such a conveyance is made and the fears by which it is prompted, are of no import unless there are creditors to be protected by the statutes."

Just think about it. How often do corporations conduct business with one another? All the time.

Do stockholders own stock in different corporations? Yes, of course, throughout the United States and internationally. It is very common for corporations large and small that want to grow big profits to exercise these strategies. The federal government has enacted The Interstate Income Law (P.L. 86-272, 73 Stat. 555, 15 U.S. Code 381-384) and individual state governments have adopted laws, rules and regulations for interstate business.

What Legal Position Are You In?

The law specifically states how to operate your business from an out-of-state corporation and not have to file as a foreign corporation in your home state. The following information taken from case law and regulations regarding interstate business practices and taxation clearly states the conditions under which you can operate your out-of-state corporate business and not be accountable to the state of domicile or residence.

Interstate Income Law (P.L. 86-272, 73 Stat. 555, 15 U.S. Code 381-384)

Title I — Imposition of Minimum Standard

Sec. 101.(a) No state, or political subdivision thereof, shall have power to impose, for any taxable year ending after the date of the enactment of this act, a net income tax on the income derived within such state by any person from interstate commerce if the only business activities within such State by or on behalf of such person during such taxable year are either, or both, of the following:

1. the solicitation of orders by such person, or his representative, in such state for sales of tangible personal property, which orders are sent outside the state for approval or rejection, and if approved, are filled by shipment or delivery from a point outside the state; and
2. the solicitation of orders by such person, or his representative, in such state in the name of or for the benefit of a prospective customer of such person, if orders by such customer to such person to enable such customer to fill orders resulting from such solicitation are orders described in paragraph(1).

(b) The provisions of subsection (a) shall not apply to the imposition of a net income tax by any state, or political subdivision thereof, with respect to:

1. any corporation that is incorporated under the laws of such state; or
2. any individual who, under the laws of such state, is domiciled in, or a resident of, such state.

(c) For purposes of subsection (a), a person shall not be considered to have engaged in business activities within a state during any taxable year merely by reason of the maintenance of an office in such state by one or more independent contractors whose activities on behalf of such person in such state consist solely of making sales, or soliciting orders for sales, of tangible personal property.

(d) For purposes of this section:
1. the term "independent contractor" means a commissioned agent, broker or other independent contractor who is engaged in selling, or soliciting orders for the sales of, tangible personal property for more than one principle and who holds himself out as such in the regular course of his business activities; and
2. the term "representative" does not include an independent contractor.

Sec. 102. (a) No state, or political subdivision thereof, shall have power to assess, after the date of the enactment of this act, any net income tax, which was imposed by such state or political subdivision, as the case may be, for any taxable year ending on or before such date, on the income derived within such state by any person from interstate commerce, if the imposition of such tax for a taxable year ending after such date is prohibited by Section 101.

(b) The provision of subsection (a) shall not be construed:
1. to invalidate the collection, on or before the date of enactment of this act, of any net income tax imposed for a taxable year ending on or before such date, or
2. to prohibit the collection, after the date of the enactment of this act, of any net income tax that was assessed on or before such date for a taxable year ending on or before such date.

Sec. 103. For purposes of this title, the term "net income tax" means any tax imposed on, or measured by, net income.

Sec. 104. If any provision of this title or the application of such provision to any person or circumstance is held invalid, the remainder of this title or the application of such provision to persons or circumstances other than those to which it is held invalid, shall not be affected thereby.

Quill v. North Dakota, 504 U.S. 278 (1992). The ruling of the Supreme Court was in favor of Quill, the taxpayer. The ruling was based on the fact that there is no sales/use tax responsibility when a seller's only activity within a state is through the mail, telephone or by common carrier. The only activity Quill had in North Dakota was in soliciting orders by the use of flyers, catalogs and phone calls.

How Do These Corporations Work Together?

Figure 1

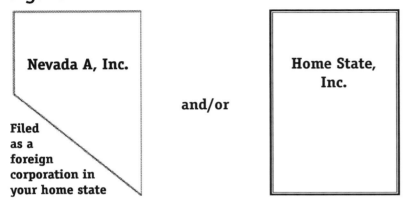

Nevada A, Inc.

Filed as a foreign corporation in your home state

and/or

Home State, Inc.

Figure 2

Nevada B, Inc.

+

Nevada C, Inc.

+

Nevada D, Inc.

With dual or multiple Nevada corporations you can:
1. Reduce or eliminate state corporate taxes
2. Reduce federal corporate income taxes
3. Protect your assets so that they are very secure
4. Pass your assets to those you wish without taxation

"The world is before you, and you need not take it or leave it as it was when you came in."
– James Baldwin

Conclusion

Dual and Multiple Corporate Strategies …

- Dual and multiple corporate strategies are tested and proven to be legal when they are set up and used properly.
- You can greatly reduce state income tax, reduce federal income tax, limit liability and better protect your assets.
- You can defer taxes to a distant future and use the government's money (via savings in taxes) to provide for a comfortable retirement.
- The tax code is the key to wealth. Instead of approaching it as a liability, learn how to take advantage of all the things you can do to enhance your ability to create wealth.

NOTES

GLOSSARY OF TERMS

A

Acquisition: Obtaining control of another corporation by purchasing all or a majority of its outstanding shares, or by purchasing its assets.

Administrative dissolution: An involuntary dissolution of a corporation by an act of the Secretary of State or similar state authority, caused by the corporation's failure to comply with certain statutory requirements; especially the failure to file an annual report, to pay franchise taxes or maintain a valid Registered Agent.

Advisory board of directors: Advisory boards of directors are individuals appointed to advise an elected board of directors. This board is not bound by the duties imposed upon elected board members, and the corporation is not required to follow their recommendations.

Agent: Anyone who is authorized to act on the behalf of another. A corporation acts only through its agents; therefore, it is important to define what actions an agent is authorized to perform.

Agent for service of process: An agent, required to be appointed by a corporation, whose authority is limited to receiving process issued against the corporation. Also known as a Registered Agent.

Amended certificate of authority: A document issued by a state to a foreign corporation evidencing that the corporation has amended its original certificate of authority.

Amendment: An addition to, deletion from, or a change of existing provisions of the articles of incorporation or articles of organization.

Annual meeting (aka Regular Meeting): A yearly meeting of shareholders at which directors are elected and other general business of the corporation is conducted.

Annual report: A required annual filing in a state, usually listing directors, officers and financial information. Also, an annual statement of business and affairs furnished by a corporation to its shareholders.

Application for certificate of authority: The form filed in many states to qualify a corporation to transact business as a foreign corporation.

Articles of incorporation: The title of the document filed in many states to create a corporation. Also known as the certificate of incorporation or corporate charter.

Articles of organization: The title of the document filed in many stated to register a limited liability company (LLC) with the state. Also known as articles of formation.

Assets: Property of all kinds, real and personal, tangible and intangible.

Assumed name: A name other than the true name, under which a corporation or other business organization conducts business. Also, referred to as a fictitious name, a trade name or "doing business as "(d/b/a).

Authorized shares: The maximum number of shares that a corporation may issue pursuant to it articles of incorporation.

B

Beneficiary: One who benefits from acts of another such as a transfer of property or other arrangement.

Blue-sky laws: A term used to describe state laws and regulations governing the issuance and sale of securities to residents of a state and the licensing and regulation of securities brokers and dealers.

Board of directors: The governing body of a corporation who is elected by shareholders. The directors are responsible for selecting the officers and the supervision and general control of the corporation.

Bond: A long-term debt secured by a mortgage on real property or a lien on other fixed assets.

Brother-sister corporation: More than one corporation owned by the same shareholders.

Business corporation act: A business corporation act is the collection of laws in each state that governs corporations.

Buy/Sell Agreement: An agreement between or among part-owners of a business that under stated conditions (usually severance of employment, disability or death), the person withdrawing or his heirs are legally obligated to sell their interest to the remaining part-owners.

Bylaws: The regulations of a corporation that, subject to statutory law and the articles of incorporation, provide the basic rules for the conduct of the corporation's business and affairs.

C

Capital: Accumulated goods, possessions, and assets, used for the production of profits and wealth.

Certificate of authority: Formal evidence of qualification issued by a state to a foreign corporation.

Certificate of good standing: A certificate issued by a state official as conclusive evidence that a corporation is in existence or authorized to transact business in the state. The certification generally sets forth the corporation's name, that it is duly incorporated or authorized to transact business, that all fees, taxes and penalties owed the state have been paid, that its most recent annual report has been filed, and, that articles of dissolution have not been filed. Also known as a certificate of existence or certificate of authorization.

Convertible security: A security that may be exchanged by the holder for another type of security.

Corporate indicator: A word or an abbreviation of a word that must be included in a corporation's name to indicate that the named entity is a corporation. Valid corporate indicators include incorporated, corporation, limited, company, inc., corp., ltd. and co. The list of acceptable corporate indicators will vary depending upon the jurisdiction in which the corporation is registered.

Corporate Seal: A corporate seal is a device made to either emboss or imprint certain company information onto documents. This information usually includes the company's name and date and state of formation. Corporate seals are often required when opening corporate or LLC bank accounts, distributing stock or membership certificates or conducting other corporate business.

Corporation: An artificial entity created under and governed by the laws of the state of incorporation.

Corporation law: The statutory provisions of a state relating to domestic and foreign corporations.

Cumulative voting: A procedure used for electing directors in which shareholders are entitled to multiply the number of votes they are entitled to cast by the number of directors for whom they are entitled to vote and cast the product for a single candidate or distribute the product among two or more candidates.

D

Debenture: A long-term debt issued mainly to evidence an unsecured corporate debt.

282

Debt financing: A method of raising capital in which a corporation borrows money.

Deferral of taxes: Postponement of taxes from one year to a later year. For example, individuals can defer axes by contributing money to an individual retirement account (where contributions, as well as any earnings on the contributions, are taxes only when actually withdrawn from the IRA).

Deferred compensation: Compensation that will be taxed when received and not when earned. An example is contributions by an employer to a qualified pension or profit-sharing plan on behalf of an employee. The employee will be taxed when the funds are made available or distributed to the employee at retirement.

Derivative suit: A lawsuit brought by a shareholder on behalf of a corporation to protect the corporation from wrongs committed against it.

Directors: The individuals who, acting as a group known as the board of directors, manage the business and affairs of a corporation.

Dissenter's right: A right granted to shareholders that entitles them to have their shares appraised and purchased by the corporation if the corporation enters into certain transactions that the shareholders do not approve of.

Dissolution: The statutory procedure that terminates the existence of a domestic corporation.

Distribution: A transfer of money or other property made by a corporation to a shareholder in respect of the corporation's shares.

Dividend: A distribution of a corporation's earnings to its shareholders.

Double taxation: The structure of taxation under the Internal Revenue Code which subjects income earned by a corporation to an income tax at the corporate level and a second tax at the shareholder level if the same income is distributed to shareholders in the form of dividends.

Durable Power of Attorney: Exists when a person executes a power of attorney which will become or remain effective in the event he or she should later become disabled.

E

Earned income: Income from services (e.g., salaries, wages, or fees); distinguished from passive, portfolio, and other unearned income.

Entity: A real being; existence. An organization or being that possesses separate existence for tax purposes. Examples would be corporations, partnerships, estates and trusts.

Entrepreneur: One who, on his own, initiates and assumes the financial risks of a new enterprise and who undertakes its management.

Equity financing: A method of raising capital in which a corporation sells shares of stock. This is contrasted with "debt financing" which is the raising of capital by issuing bonds or borrowing money.

Equity interest: An ownership interest; the interest of a shareholder as distinguished from that of a creditor.

E.R.I.S.A.: Employee Retirement Income Security Act. Federal Act governing the funding, vesting, administration, and termination of private pension plans.

Estate: The degree, quantity, nature, and extent of interest which a person has in real and personal property.

Estate planning: That branch of the law which, in arranging a person's property and estate, takes into account the laws of wills, taxes, insurance, property, and trusts so as to gain maximum benefit of all laws while carrying out the person's own wishes for the disposition of his property upon his death.

Estate tax: A tax imposed on the right to transfer property by death. Thus, an estate tax is levied on the decedent's estate and not on the heir receiving the property.

Exempt securities: Securities exempt from registration requirements of federal state securities laws.

F

Fair market value: The price property would command in the open market.

Fictitious name: A name other than the true name, under which a corporation or other business organization conducts business. Also referred to as an assumed name, a trade name or "doing business as" (d/b/a).

Fiduciary duty: A duty to act for someone else's benefit, (trustee, guardian) while subordinating one's personal interests to that of the other person. It is the highest standard of duty implied by law.

Financial statement: Any report summarizing the financial condition or financial results of a person or organization on any date or for any period. These include the balance sheet and the income statement (P&L).

Fiscal year: A period of twelve consecutive months chosen by a business as the accounting period for annual reports. A corporation's accounting year. Due to the nature of a particular business, come companies do not use the calendar year for their bookkeeping.

Foreign corporation: A term applied to a corporation doing business in a state other than its state of incorporation.

Fractional share: Ownership in a corporation in an amount less than a full share.

Franchise tax: A tax or fee usually levied annually upon a corporation, limited liability company or similar business entity for the right to exist or do business in a particular state. Failure to pay the franchise tax or similar fees may result in the administration dissolution of the company and forfeiture of the charter.

Fraudulent conveyance: The transfer of property (for little or no consideration), the object of which is to defraud a creditor, or hinder or delay him, or to put such property beyond his reach.

G

General partner: One of two or more persons who associate to carry on business as co-owners for profit and who are personally liable for all debts of the partnership.

Gift tax: A tax imposed on the transfer of property by gift. Such tax is imposed upon the donor of a gift and is based on the fair market value of the property on the date of the gift.

Going Public: The process by which a corporation first sells its shares to the public.

H

Holding company: A company that usually confines its activities to owning stock in (controlling interest), and supervising management of, other companies.

Homestead exemption laws: Laws passed in most states allowing a head of family to designate a house and land as his homestead, and exempting the same homestead from execution by creditors for his general debts.

Hostile takeover: A takeover that occurs without the approval of the target corporation's board of directors.

I

Income tax: A tax on the annual profits arising from property, business pursuits, professions, trades, or offices. A tax on a person's income, wages, salary, commissions, emoluments, profits, and the like.

Incorporation: The act of creating or organizing a corporation under the laws of a specific jurisdiction.

Incorporate & Get Rich! C.W. "Al" Allen & Cheri S. Hill

Incorporator: The person(s) who perform the act of incorporation and who sign the articles of incorporation and delivers them for filling.

Indemnification: Financial protection provided by a corporation to its directors, officers, and employees against expenses and liabilities incurred by them in lawsuits alleging that they breached some duty in their service to or on behalf of the corporation.

Inheritance tax: Tax imposed in some states upon the privilege of receiving property from a decedent at death.

Insurance: A contract whereby, for a stipulated consideration, one party undertakes to compensate the other for loss on a specified subject by specified perils.

Internal Revenue Code (I.R.C.): That body of law which codifies all federal tax laws including income, estate, fit, excise, etc. taxes. Such laws comprise Title 26 of the U.S. Code, and are implemented by the Internal Revenue Service and through it by Treasury Regulations; Revenue Rulings, etc.

Intestate: To die without a will. Under such circumstances, state law prescribes who will receive the decedent's property. The laws of intestate succession generally favor the surviving spouse, children, and grandchildren and then move to parents and grandparents and to brothers and sisters.

Involuntary dissolution: The termination of a corporation's legal existence pursuant to an administrative or judicial proceeding: dissolution forced upon a corporation other than decided upon by the corporation.

Involuntary lien: A lien, such as a tax lien, judgment lien, etc., which attaches to property without the consent of the owner, rather than a mortgage lien, to which the owner agrees.

J

Joint and several liability: A liability is said to be joint and several when the creditor may demand payment or sue one or more of the parties to such liability separately, or all of them together at his option. A husband and wife that file a joint income tax return usually are collectively or individually liable for the full amount of the tax liability. I.R.C. § 6013.

Joint tenants: Two or more persons who own lands by a joint title created expressly by one and the same deed or will.

Judicial dissolution: Involuntary dissolution of a corporation by a court at the request of the state attorney general, a shareholder or a creditor.

Judgment creditor: A person in whose favor a money judgment has been entered by a court of law and who has not yet been paid.

K

K-1: Partner's Share of Income, Credits, Deductions, etc. The form that's used to show partners distributive shares of reportable partnership items.

Key man insurance: Type of insurance coverage purchased by companies to protect them on the death or disability of a valued employee or by partnership to provide for funds with which to buy out the interest of such partner on his death or disability.

Kiddie tax: A tax imposed on unearned income (in excess of a minimal amount) of a child under the age of 14. Such income is taxed at the parent's highest rate. The Tax Reform Act of 1986 instituted the "kiddie tax" in an effort to stop the shifting of income producing assets within families (i.e., from parents to minor children) which, prior to the TRA, resulted in substantial tax savings to upper bracket parents. I.R.C. § 1(i).

L

Land trust: A property ownership arrangement whereby, a trustee holds legal and equitable title to trust, and the beneficiary, who has personal property interest, retains power of direction over the trustee and power to manage and receive income from trust property.

Leverage: The ability to finance an investment with a small amount of one's own funds, such as a down payment, with the balance consisting of borrowed funds. The use of a smaller investment to generate a larger rate of return through borrowing.

Liability: All character of debts and obligations one is bound in law or justice to perform.

Limited Liability Company (LLC): An artificial entity created under and governed by the laws of the jurisdiction in which it was formed. Limited liability companies are generally able to provide the limited personal liability of corporations and the pass-through taxation of partnerships or S corporations.

Limited partnership: A statutory form of partnership consisting of one or more general partners who manage the business and are liable for its debts, and one or more limited partners who invest in the business and have limited personal liability.

Limited personal liability: The protection generally afforded a corporate shareholder, limited partner or a member of a limited liability company from the debts of and claims against the company.

M

Majority: More than 50 percent, commonly used as the percentage of votes required to approve certain corporate actions.

Malfeasance: The commission of some act which is positively unlawful.

Management: The board of directors and executive officers of a corporation, limited liability company or similar business entity.

Managers: The individuals who are responsible for the maintenance, administration and management of the affairs of a limited liability company (LLC). In most states, the managers serve a particular term and report to and serve at the discretion of the members. Specific duties of the managers may be detailed in the articles of organization or the operating agreement of the LLC. In some states, the members of an LLC may also serve as the managers.

Mechanic's lien: A claim created by state statutes for the purpose of securing priority of payment of the price or value of work performed and materials furnished in erecting, improving, or repairing a building or other structure, and as such attaches to the land as well as buildings and improvements erected thereon.

Medicaid: A form of public assistance sponsored jointly by the federal and state governments providing medical aid for people whose income falls below a certain level.

"The man who moved a mountain was the one who began carrying away small stones."
~ Chinese Proverb

Members: The owner(s) of a limited liability company (LLC). Unless the articles of organization or operating agreement provide otherwise, management of an LLC is vested in the members in proportion to this ownership interest in the company.

Membership certificates: Evidence of ownership of and membership in a limited liability company.

Merger: The statutory combination of two or more corporations in which one of the corporations survives and the other corporation ceases to exist.

Minority stockholder: Those stockholders of a corporation who hold so few shares in relation to the total outstanding that they are unable to control the management of the corporation or to elect directors.

Minutes: The corporate minutes are the written record of transactions taken or authorized by the board of directors or shareholders. These are usually kept in the corporate minute book in diary fashion.

Multistate corporation: A corporation that has operations in more than one state; from which issues commonly arise relative to the assignment of appropriate amounts of the entity's taxable income to the states in which it has a presence.

Mutual fund: A fund managed by an investment company in which money is raised through the sale of stock and subsequently invested in publicly traded securities. The investment performance of the mutual fund depends on the performance of the underlying investments.

N

Name registration: The filing of a document in a foreign state to protect the corporate name, often in anticipation of qualification in the state.

Name reservation: A procedure that allows a corporation to obtain exclusive use of a corporate name for a specified period of time.

Negligence: The failure to use such care as a reasonably prudent and careful person would use under similar circumstances.

Net assets: A term used in accounting which is arrived at by subtracting a company's total liabilities from total assets.

Net income: Income subject to taxation after allowable deductions and exemptions have been subtracted from gross income.

Net profits: Profits after deduction of all expenses.

No par value shares: Shares for which the articles of incorporation do not fix a par value and that may be issued for any consideration determined by the board of directors.

Nonprofit corporation: A corporation no part of the income of which is distributable to its members, directors or officers. Corporation organized for other than profit-making purposes. For federal income taxation, an organization may be exempt as an "exempt organization" if it is organized and operated exclusively for one or more of the following purposes: (a) religious, (b) charitable, (c) scientific, (d) testing for public safety, (e) literary, (f) educational, (g) prevention of cruelty to children or animals, or (h) to foster national or international sports.

O

Officers: Individuals appointed by the board of directors who are responsible for carrying out the board's policies and for making day-to-day decisions.

Operating Agreement: A contract among the members of a limited liability company governing the membership, management, operation and distribution of income of the company.

Organizational meetings: Meetings of incorporators or initial directors that are held after the filing of the articles of incorporation to complete the organization of the corporation.

Organizer: The person(s) who perform the act of forming a limited liability company.

P

Parent corporation: A corporation that owns a controlling interest in another corporation.

Partnership: A business organization in which two or more persons agree to do business together.

Partnership agreement: The document embodying the terms and conditions of a partnership.

Par value: A minimum price of a share below which the share cannot be issued, as designated in the articles of incorporation.

Passive income: Income earned in an activity in which an individual does not materially participate. (e.g., investment in a limited partnership, rental income).

Passive loss: Any loss from (1) activities in which the taxpayer does not materially participate, (2) rental activities (with certain exceptions for individuals who actively participate), (3) tax shelter activities. The deductibility of passive losses are limited based upon when the activity was acquired, as well as the type of activity involved.

Payroll tax: A tax on an employees' salary or on the income of a self-employed individual.

Pension plan: A plan established and maintained by an employer primarily to provide systematically for the payment of preset benefits to his employees, or their beneficiaries, over a period of years after retirement.

Perpetual existence: Unlimited term of existence, characteristics of most business corporations.

Personal holding company: A closely held corporation which receives personal holding company income (dividends, interest, rents, royalties, etc.)

Preemptive right: The privilege of a stockholder to maintain a proportionate share of ownership by purchasing a proportionate share of any new stock issues.

Preferred stock: A class of shares that entitles the holders to preferences over the holders of common shares, usually with regard to dividends and distributions of assets upon dissolution or liquidation.

Private foundations: An organization which is operated privately for the advancement of charitable or education projects. An organization generally exempt from taxation that is subject to additional statutory restrictions on its activities and on contributions thereto.

Probate: Court procedure by which a will is proved to be valid or invalid. Generally, the probate process involves collecting a decedent's assets, liquidating liabilities, paying necessary taxes, and distributing property to heirs. These activities are carried out by the executor or administrator of the estate, usually under the supervision of the probate court.

Product liability: Refers to the legal liability of manufacturers and sellers to compensate buyers, users, and even bystanders, for damages or injuries suffered, because of defects in goods purchased.

Professional corporation: A corporation whose purposes are limited to professional services, such as those performed by doctors, dentists and attorneys. A professional corporation is formed under special state laws that stipulate exactly which professionals are required to incorporate under this status.

Profit: The gross proceeds of a business transaction less the costs of the transaction.

Profit-sharing plan: A plan established and maintained by an employer to provide for the participation in the profits of the company by the employees or their beneficiaries.

Proxy: A written authorization given by a person to another party directing the party to vote on behalf of him/her.

Q

Qualification: The filing of required documents by a foreign corporation to secure a certificate of authority to conduct its business in a state other than the one in which it was incorporated. Limited liability companies or similar business entities may also conduct this process.

Quorum: The percentage of proportion of voting shares required to be represented in person or by proxy to constitute a valid shareholders meeting, or the number of directors required to be present for a valid meeting of the board.

R

Record date: The date for determining the shareholders entitled to vote at a meeting, receive dividends, or participate in any corporate action.

Redeemable shares: Shares are subject to purchase by the corporation on terms set forth in the articles of incorporation.

Registered Agent: A person or entity designated to receive important tax and legal documents on behalf of the corporation. The Registered Agent must be located and available at a legal address within the specified jurisdiction at all times. Failure to maintain a Registered Agent in the jurisdiction in which the corporation is registered, may result in the forfeiture of the corporate status.

Registered Office: The statutory address of a corporation. In states requiring the appointment of a Registered Agent. It is usually the address of the Registered Agent.

Reinstatement: Returning a corporation that has been administratively dissolved or had its certificate of authority revoked, to good standing on a state's records.

Resolution: A formal statement of any item of business that has been voted upon.

Restated articles of incorporation: A document that combines all currently operative provisions of a corporation's articles of incorporation and amendments thereto.

Revised Model Business Corporation Act: A model corporation statute compiled by the American Bar Association that has been adopted in whole or in part by, or has influenced the statues of many states.

Revocable Trust: A trust in which the settler reserves the right to revoke.

S

S Corporation: A corporation granted a special tax status as specified under the Internal Revenue Code. The code is very explicit on how and when this election is made and the number of shareholders this type of corporation can have. Since this type of corporation pays no income tax, all gains and losses of the corporation pass through to the individual shareholders in proportion to their holdings.

Scrip: A form used to represent ownership of fractional shares in lieu of issuing share certificates.

Security: A contract between a business and an investor whereby the investor supplies money and expects to profit from his or her investment.

Securities laws: State and federal laws that govern the issuance, sale and transfer of stocks and bonds.

Series LLC: A Series LLC is a single LLC that provides for the separation of assets and liabilities among separate cells or "series" and each cell is permitted to have separate ownership and economic relationships among members.

Share: The unit into which the ownership interest in a corporation is divided.

Share exchange: A statutory form of business combination in which some or all of the shares of one corporation are exchanged for some or all of the shares of another corporation and neither corporation cease to exist.

292

Shareholders: Shareholders are the owners of a corporation based on their holdings. They own an interest in the corporation rather than specific corporate property. Also known as stockholders.

Short-form merger: The statutory merger of a subsidiary into its parent corporation in which shareholder approval is not required.

Sole proprietorship: An unincorporated business with a sole owner in which the owner may be personally liable for business debts and claims against the business.

Special meeting: A shareholder meeting called so that the shareholders may act on the specific matters stated in the notice of the meeting.

Stock: Stock represents ownership in a corporation. It may be represented by a certificate and can be common or preferred, voting or non-voting, redeemable, convertible, etc. The classifications and special designations, if any, of the stock are set forth in the articles of incorporation.

Stock certificate: Evidence of ownership of shares in a corporation. May also be referred to as a share certificate.

Stockholders: Stockholders are the owners of a corporation based on their holdings. They own an interest in the corporation rather than specific corporate property. Also known as shareholders.

Subscribers: Persons who agree under specific conditions to purchase shares in a corporation.

Subscription: The agreement executed by a subscriber.

Subsidiary: A corporation that is either wholly owned or controlled through ownership of a majority of its voting shares, by another corporation or business entity.

T

Takeover: A merger, acquisition or other change in the controlling interest of a corporation.

Target: A corporation that is the focus of a takeover attempt.

Tax avoidance: The minimization of one's tax liability by taking advantage of legally available tax planning opportunities. Tax avoidance may be contrasted with tax evasion which entails the reduction of tax liability by using illegal means.

Tax-exempt organization: Any organization that is determined by the Internal

Revenue Service to be exempt from federal taxation of income. A tax-exempt may be required to operate exclusively for chartable, religious, literary, education or similar types of purposes.

Tax Return: The form on which an individual, corporation or other entity reports income, deductions, and exemptions and calculates their tax liability. A federal tax return is filed with the Internal Revenue Service, and a state return is filed with the revenue department of the state.

Tax "situs": A state or jurisdiction which has a substantial relationship to assets subject to taxation.

Trademark: A word or mark that distinctly indicates the ownership of a product or service, and that is legally reserved for the exclusive use of the owner.

Treasury shares: Shares of a corporation reacquired by a corporation.

Trust: A legal entity created by a grantor for the benefit of designated beneficiaries under the laws of the state and the valid trust instrument.

Trustee: The individual that holds a fiduciary responsibility to manage the trust's corpus assets and income for the economic benefit of all of the beneficiaries.

U

Underwriter: A company that purchases shares of a corporation and arranges for their sale to the general public.

V

Venture Capital: Funding for new companies or others embarking on new or turnaround ventures that entails some investment risk but offers the potential for above average future profits. Venture capital is often provided by firms that specialize in financing new ventures with capital supplied by investors interested in speculative or high risk investments.

Voluntary dissolution: Action by shareholders, incorporators or initial directors to dissolve a corporation.

Voting stock rights: The stockholder's right to vote his stock in the affairs of his company. Most common shares have one vote each. Preferred stock usually has the right to vote when preferred dividends are in default for a specified period.

W

Watered Shares: Shares that have been issued for a consideration less than the par of stated value of the shares.

Will: An instrument by which a person makes a disposition of his real and personal property, to take effect after his death.

Winding up: The discharging of a corporation's liabilities and the distributing of its remaining assets to its shareholders in connection with its dissolution.

Withdrawal: The statutory procedure whereby a foreign corporation obtains the consent of a state to terminate its authority to transact business there.

**Turn the page to learn
HOW YOU can take your first
powerful step towards creating your
own Foundation for Freedom!**

*"Destiny is not a matter of chance.
It is a matter of choice:
It is not a thing to be waited for,
it is a thing to be achieved."*
— William Jennings Bryan

Essentials For Improving Your Financial Intelligence

1. You Were Born Rich - Bob Proctor
2. The World is Flat - Thomas L. Friedman
3. Getting Everything You Can Out of All You've Got - Jay Abraham
4. Think and Grow Rich - Napoleon Hill
5. The Science of Getting Rich – Wallace D. Wattles
6. Good to Great & Built to Last - Jim Collins/Jerry Porras
7. Lower Your Taxes Big Time - Sandy Botkin
8. Scientific Advertising - Claude C. Hopkins
9. Influence - Robert Cialdini
10. The E-Myth - Michael E. Gerber
11. Rich Dad/Poor Dad - Robert Kiyosaki
12. The Richest Man in Babylon - George S. Clason
13. The Living Trust - Henry W. Abts III
14. Keys to the Vault - Keith Cunningham
15. The Fred Factor – Mark Sanborn
16. Get Noticed…Get Referrals – Jill Lublin
17. The Language of Parenting - David M. Frees III
18. The Tipping Point – Malcolm Gladwell
19. You're Not the Person I Hired – Janet Boydell
20. Blue Ocean Strategy – W. Chan Kim
21. The Game of Work – Charles Coonradt
22. The Success Principles – Jack Canfield
23. Beyond the Grave – Gerald M. Condon, Esq.
24. Secrets of the Millionaire Mind – T. Harv Eker
25. Selling the Invisible – Harry Beckwith
26. From Wall Street to Main Street – Daniel Cordoba
27. Content Rich. Writing Your Way to Wealth on the Web – Jon Wuebben
28. It's How Much You Keep That Counts! Not How Much You Make – Ronald R. Mueller

FOR A COMPLETE SELECTION OF SAGE PRODUCTS
AND ADDITIONAL RECOMMENDATIONS
PLEASE VISIT WWW.SAGEINTL.COM

"Enjoy and Prosper!"

Financial Simplicity…Service…Empowerment!

In talking with so many of our clients, we have identified several ways we can contribute to your ongoing growth and prosperity. Just like you, Sage International, Inc. faces many challenges and triumphs in building and running a company. Where do we go for information? What resources do we use? Who are the mentors that help us understand the complexities of growing and protecting our business?

Over the last two decades, we have personally researched and fielded thousands of questions, asked many of the same questions that you ask everyday, and continually search for new products, services, information and untapped resources across the nation. We are very excited about furthering our commitment to nurture and champion the well being of our clients across America. We hope you join us…

▶ *SageAdvisers® Teleseminar Series*
Join Cheri S. Hill, CEO (that's Chief Empowerment Officer!) on the 3rd Wednesday of each month from 12:00-1:00 PM (PST). Each month features a new topic and industry expert Special Guest speaker.

▶ *SagePro™ Advisors Educational Series*
If you are an attorney, CPA, financial planner, estate planner, insurance agent, bookkeeper or other professional service provider, our goal with this series is to provide a dynamic, educational program which will facilitate change, growth and advancement within your industry. This program is designed to hone your professional skills and provide you with the resources that will enable you to become full service to your clients, thereby giving you the competitive edge.

"There is only one corner of the universe you can be certain of improving, and that's your own self."
– Aldus Huxley

▶ *Wealth Protection Workshops*
These one, two or three day ccompression-trainings will teach you how to Grow, Protect & Leverage your hard-earned wealth from The Three Flaming Arrows of Challenge: Income Taxes, Liability Exposure & Death Taxes. Every event features the latest in legal Wealth Protection Strategies.

To learn more visit www.sageintl.com; call 800-254-5779 email: corpinfo@sageintl.com

6286132R0

Made in the USA
Charleston, SC
06 October 2010